Practically Joking

Practically Joking

Moira Marsh

Utah State University Press
Logan

© 2015 by the University Press of Colorado

Published by Utah State University Press
An imprint of University Press of Colorado
5589 Arapahoe Avenue, Suite 206C
Boulder, Colorado 80303

 The University Press of Colorado is a proud member of
The Association of American University Presses.

The University Press of Colorado is a cooperative publishing enterprise supported, in part,
by Adams State University, Colorado State University, Fort Lewis College, Metropolitan
State University of Denver, Regis University, University of Colorado, University of Northern
Colorado, Utah State University, and Western State Colorado University.

∞ The paper used in this publication meets the minimum requirements of the American
National Standard for Information Sciences—Permanence of Paper for Printed Library
Materials. ANSI Z39.48-1992

ISBN: 978-0-87421-983-8 (pbk)
ISBN: 978-0-87421-984-5 (ebook)

Library of Congress Cataloging-in-Publication Data

Marsh, Moira, 1958-
  Practically joking / Moira Marsh.
    pages cm
  ISBN 978-0-87421-983-8 (paperback) — ISBN 978-0-87421-984-5 (ebook)
1. Practical jokes. 2. Wit and humor—History and criticism. 3. Wit and humor—Social
aspects. I. Title.
  PN6147.M175 2015
  809.7—dc23
                          2014024123

24   23   22   21   20   19   18   17   16   15   10   9   8   7   6   5   4   3   2   1

Cover photograph © ajt/Shutterstock.

In memory of Bob Smith—
father, role model, and humorist.

Contents

Figures

Acknowledgments

THE IDEA FOR THIS BOOK CAME TO ME on the plane as I was flying back from the American Folklore Society meeting in Anchorage. It was fall 2001, just weeks after the dreadful attacks of 9/11. Since it was a long trip—from Anchorage to Indianapolis via Dallas—I had plenty of time to reconsider. Evidently reason did not prevail, and so here we are.

A skilled analyst might see some significance in conceiving of a book on practical jokes at such a time, but it will be clear to everyone that it has been a long time in the making. Along the way I have accrued many debts of thanks. I will mention as many of these as I can remember, but I am acutely aware that some people may get left out. If this is you, please accept my silence as thanks.

I have been blessed with academic mentors who have served as role models and sources of support, encouragement, and criticism, especially Peter Russell, the late Alex Scobie, the late Linda Dégh, Greg Schrempp, Beverly Stoeltje, and Dick Bauman. John McDowell was a persistent voice of cheer and practical advice. Elliott Oring was an unstinting critic who pushed me to "carry these lines of research a lot further." He also encouraged me to go to my first meeting of the International Society for Humor Studies (ISHS), and in the years since I have found there an unfailing source of stimulation, good ideas, and serious thinking about humor.

I am grateful to Indiana University, the Indiana University Bloomington Libraries, and the Indiana University Librarians' Association for numerous small but essential grants in support of my research. I owe a special debt of thanks to former dean of the IUB Libraries Suzanne Thorin, who generously funded travel during my sabbatical year in 2005–2006 for research at several folklore archives and fieldwork in New Zealand. From August 2005 through April 2006 and again in December 2007 I was a resident scholar at the Stout Research Centre at the Victoria University of Wellington. I am very grateful to the Stout staff and other residents and fellows for providing a friendly, supportive environment and countless cups of tea during those months of interviewing and writing: Lydia Wevers, Richard Hill, Brad Patterson, and Francine Tolron.

Pastor Mark Whitfield and the members of St Paul's Lutheran Church in Wellington provided a warm home away from home as well as regular spiritual food. Rolf Brednich and Brigitte Bönisch-Brednich offered friendship and hospitality to a folklorist far from home. Michael Brown and Diane McAllen supplied enjoyable meals and long conversations about researching folklore in New Zealand. Bill Sheat and the late Les Cleveland offered practical help and support for the notion that New Zealand folklore was a research field ripe for harvest. Mike Lloyd was a regular coffee and conversation partner on all aspects of humor theory, and he also read drafts and gently prodded me toward more theoretical rigor.

Friends and colleagues in both folklore and humor studies have helped in many ways. Colleagues at ISHS meetings and at American Folklore Society meetings have given me constructive feedback and countless suggestions. Paul Jackson, the Sinn family, Sabina Magliocco, Diane Goldstein, Christie Davies, Jessica Milner-Davis, Anne K. Pyburn, Lynne Hamer, Mabel Agozzino, and Eduardo Jáuregui, among others, have helped by sharing their work, sending me references and practical joke stories that they came across, and repeatedly asking, "Is it done yet?" Early on, Alan Mays helped by posting a query about the "digging up the road" stunt to the alt. folklore.urban newsgroup and collating the replies for me. Along the way, Sharon Lockyer, Tom Sinn, and John Wolford read and commented on early drafts and laughed, but not too loudly and only in the right places. Riki Saltzman not only commented on various drafts but added her keen editorial eye as well. Nancy Michael was a constant discussion partner, writing coach, and editor on many early drafts.

Several folklore archivists were invaluable: Pauline Cox at the Berkeley Folklore Archive, Patricia Fulton and Kelly Revak at the Memorial University of Newfoundland Folklore and Language Archive, and the staff at the William A. Wilson Folklore Archives. I also thank the librarians at the National Library of New Zealand (Te Puna Matauranga o Aotearoa) for tracking down some elusive citations. I also extend my gratitude to several student interns and assistants, especially Wujung Choo, Sarah Marion, Jir-Shin Boey, and Nora Wood, who found obscure citations, downloaded articles, and digitized others.

I am very grateful to the many people who agreed to be interviewed by me about, of all things, practical jokes. From Wellington: Spiro Anastasiou, Tim Beaglehole, Gyles Beckford, Tack Daniel, Matt Elliott, Bronwyn Hayward, Ron Hill, Rudolph and Pauline Kotze, Gerard O'Neill, Pat Pilcher, Arthur Pomeroy, Hugh Price, Craig Rattray, Gordon Stewart, and Gordon Tait. From Bloomington: Ruth Aten, Mark Bevis, Peggy Brooks, Nancy Cassell, the Cobra Patrol, John and Susie Duenez, Sam Frushour, Bruce Harrah-Conforth, John Johnson, Steve Millen, Rob Mills, Amy

Quinton, Tony Rimmer, Jack Savage, Ken Shafer, Harvey Starr, Kurt Van der Dussen, and Brian Werth.

The anonymous reviewers of this manuscript made substantive comments and suggestions that have improved the final product considerably. My first editor, John Alley, encouraged the project in the early stages and gave me much-needed suggestions on how to write. My current editor, Michael Spooner, has been patience personified.

Finally—saving the best until last—my husband and friend, Gilbert Marsh, has been an unfailing source of love, support, proofreading, and hours of free psychotherapy. He provided the final push to get this thing out of the door, but even without that he would still be the greatest happiness in my life.

Practically Joking

Introduction

A TRANSGRESSIVE VERNACULAR ART

AMONG THE ROYAL TREASURES IN ROSENBORG CASTLE in Copenhagen is a carefully preserved seventeenth-century armchair that once belonged to Christian IV. A hidden mechanism in the arms would pin the king's guests in the seat, where they would be soaked with water from a container on the back. When they were released, a small trumpet tooted the news to all who cared to hear, thus proving that fart jokes have an ancient and royal lineage. Centuries later, the FartDroid app has been downloaded more than 2 million times, despite a "low maturity" content rating (Neat-O-Fun 2012). iFart, the equivalent app for the iPhone, reportedly earned its inventor thousands of dollars in 2008 (Hanlon 2008). The underground economy in immature practical joking is apparently alive and well.

To folklorists interested in humor, practical jokes deserve study because they are a truly vernacular, unofficial, or "folk" arena for creative play. At any given moment, the chances are good that somebody near you is involved in a practical joke, plotting another, or regaling friends with stories of tricks that they have played, been taken in by, or heard of. The ready availability of digital cameras and websites like YouTube makes it easy for practical jokers to record their efforts and post them for the enjoyment and commentary of wide audiences. In turn, stories and recordings inspire others to attempt their own trickery.

There are very few professional practical jokers, but a substantial popular culture industry celebrates and supports this pastime. Besides android apps, there are books, film, radio, reality television, and websites all devoted to practical jokes, and all replete with puns, verbal jokes, and cartoon illustrations that bathe the topic in a jocular light (AmazingFX.net and Regan 2008; Jillette and Teller 1989; Van Rensselaer 1941). In the earliest days of television, Alan Funt's *Candid Camera* established a formula for playing elaborate tricks on unsuspecting people and broadcasting the results for the amusement of a mass audience, a formula that continues to be used to great success in shows from *Punk'd* in the United States to *Grand Classics* in Great Britain to *Verstehen Sie Spass* in Germany (Funt and Reed 1994). Around the United States, radio stations similarly entertain their listeners

DOI: 10.7330/9780874219845.c000

with recordings of tricks played on individuals by telephone (Douglas 1996; Richardson 1998). Although these instances have high visibility, they have not supplanted the unofficial, noncommercial folk practice of playing practical jokes—rather, they draw energy from it.

A POOR REPUTATION

Humor scholars, dedicated to understanding jokes of every kind, have paid scant attention to the practical joke, perhaps because it is considered too unsophisticated for serious attention. Even among people who appreciate jokes and other comic genres, practical jokes and pranks are often disparaged. As the compiler of one early joke book put it, "If the pun is the lowest form of wit, the practical joke may be described even more assuredly as the lowest form of humour" (Jerrold 1912, 91). The practical joke "gives no intellectual satisfaction" according to humor scholar Avner Ziv: "For years a variegated industry has supplied players of practical jokes with an apparatus for secret attacks devoid of humorous talent: flowers that spurt water up a person's nose as he bends over to smell them; cigarette boxes from which frogs jump out; jars of mustard whose lids conceal snakes; fake mice designed to look as real as possible, to be placed in such sensitive spots as kitchen drawers; and many more . . . An attraction to this sort of humor is without a doubt connected to the innocence and lack of sophistication characteristic of childhood" (1984, 124, 113). Like Ziv, many sophisticated persons disparage the practical joke as puerile and devoid of skill or talent. The genre is easy to dismiss when considered in the abstract, which usually means with reference to a paradigmatic example like the infamous whoopee cushion or its electronic version, the iFart app. Compared to literary and theatrical genres of humor, folk humor seems simple and unoriginal, and practical jokes rank even lower than verbal jokes from oral tradition because the latter at least approximate a literary form (Marsh 2012, 291–292; Oring 2011).

As a folklorist, I believe that creativity and artistry exist throughout society in humble everyday settings as much as they do in the semisacred arenas that post-Renaissance Western culture has created for art and literature. Perhaps it is this ideological belief in the importance of vernacular art that has led folklorists to pay closer attention to the practical joke than other humor scholars have done. The first attempt to catalog the practical joke and related genres was made by folklorist Richard Tallman (1974). Other folklorists have focused on the repertoire and personal style of outstanding practical jokers (Bauman 2004; Leary 1982; Sawin 2004, 135–155) or on case studies of practical joking in specific contexts (DeNatale 1990; Harlow 1997; Santino 1986; Schmidt 2013).

"A great prank is like art," according to the compiler of a popular book of college pranks, and I agree (Steinberg 1992, ix). However, to appreciate the skill and artistry of the practical joke it is necessary to look at the particulars—particular practical jokes as they are played by particular people at particular times and in particular places. This approach has been used effectively by folklorists with respect to verbal jokes (Leary 1984a, 1), and I will follow it in this book. By studying specific practical jokes, their creators, and their reception by specific audiences, the genre that is so easily disparaged in the abstract is revealed to be a lively expressive play tradition that includes both sophistication and intellectual satisfaction. It is a vernacular art form subject to critical evaluation by both practitioners and audiences, operating under the guidance of local aesthetic and ethical canons. Some practical jokes are better than others, but the best of them demand significant skill and talent, not only to think up but also to execute.

CRUELTY

A more serious objection to practical jokes in general is that they are aggressive and cruel. George Eliot (1883, 101) remarked of practical jokes that "no sympathetic nature can enjoy them," which implies that even for uninvolved observers to countenance a practical joke is evidence of a moral failing. More often, it is the character and motives of practical jokers that are impugned. "I think practical jokes are for the birds," opined Ann Landers. "In my opinion, something is fundamentally wrong with people who enjoy embarrassing or humiliating others and then expect the victim to be 'a good sport' and laugh it off" (Landers 1988). Humor scholar Martin Grotjahn agreed. "The practical joke represents a primitive form of the funny," he wrote, "which often is so cruel and so thinly disguised in its hostility that the sensitive or esthetically minded person can hardly enjoy it" (1957, 40). The fact that practical jokes commonly occur as part of initiation or hazing rituals only intensifies this objection, since the very term *hazing* has come to carry a pejorative connotation (Mechling 2009).

Any play activity that designates one of its major protagonists as a *victim* must contain a heavy dose of aggression, at the very least. A practical joke is always at someone's expense, at least for a brief time. However, whether that aggression amounts to hostility or cruelty is another question. Practical jokes are intended to cause people discomfort but not necessarily distress, embarrassment but not necessarily humiliation, chagrin but not necessarily mortification. Some jokes do cause distress or humiliation, but these are not necessary results. Whether or not the effects of a practical joke go too far to be considered amusing is a judgment made by the audience each time a joke is enacted or retold. Cruelty is a subjective concept, defined variously according to the mores of the day and the social setting. Similarly, hostility refers to the motives of the joker, and motives are always unknowable. Nevertheless, joke audiences and recipients draw conclusions about jokers' intentions, and their determinations have significant and lasting consequences in the social setting.

The cruelty issue can only be decided on a case-by-case basis, and the goal of this study is to elucidate how those decisions are negotiated. Further, the problem of cruelty and hostility in practical jokes mirrors similar problems in all jokes and other humorous genres. The problem is more pointed in practical jokes because they are enacted rather than told or, as Grotjahn (1957, 40) said in his dispraise of the genre, they have less symbolization to disguise their latent hostility. Nevertheless, even an apparently cruel joke is still framed as a joke, and this framing always complicates questions of intentionality and appropriateness. It turns out that questions and arguments about morality are central in the evaluation and effectiveness of jokes of all kinds.

Naturally, I have personal reactions to the jokes recounted in the following pages. Some I find very funny, while others I personally find hard to approve. Still others are merely dull. If some of these subjective feelings leak out in my presentation and analysis, it is neither intentional nor relevant. It is not the job of the humor scholar to be an arbiter of humorousness, to set herself up as an Everywoman whose finely tuned sense of humor can unerringly distinguish the funny from the unfunny or the appropriate from the inappropriate. The scholar's role, instead, is to identify and describe how these determinations are made in specific settings, which is to say, to find out how jokes behave in the wild.

SOURCES AND SCOPE

The major sources for this study are forty-two interviews with jokers and joke targets that I conducted in Bloomington, Indiana, between 1986 and 1988 and in Wellington, New Zealand, in 2005. I also draw on published sources, including memoirs, obituaries, biographies, advice columns, newspaper feature stories, and ethnographic case studies. Folklore archives throughout North America yielded another trove of practical joke narratives and recipes, both traditional and original. YouTube videos posted by practical jokers are another useful source, especially for showing the setup, unfolding, and evaluation of jokes. Finally, I have also drawn on some personal experiences. I am not much of a practical joker myself, but since I have been the target of one or two good fabrications, I have got my revenge by including a couple of these experiences here (see "The Ethnographer Hoaxed" in chapter 11).

It is not always possible for ethnographers to observe practical jokes directly as they happen because most cases are deeply embedded in specific social settings to which only insiders are privy. Instead, most case studies of this genre have relied upon the prank narratives that form part of the microculture of specific small groups. Whether collected in interviews, posted on the Web, or published in books and newspapers, these narratives can substitute for "being there" because they typically include both descriptions of the actual fabrications and detailed accounts of the joke's repercussions and the social and individual characteristics that motivated them. Joke narratives also include the narrator's evaluation of the events, which speaks to both the effectiveness and success of jokes.

Most of the cases presented in the following pages are from the United States or New Zealand. Most of the people I interviewed directly are white and middle class or lower middle class, but the material I draw on from folklore archives also encompasses white working-class individuals. Within this admittedly only mildly heterogeneous corpus, however, it turns out that there is considerable variety in how practical jokes work. Within this aesthetic variety it is difficult to draw broad comparisons based on national culture or class, and it is not my brief to do so. Folklorists have described how the performance style of verbal jokes is influenced by both individual personality and local jocular aesthetics (Bronner 1984; Leary 1984b). I will argue that the same thing applies to practical jokes, not only in terms of repertoire and performance but also regarding how jokes are received and how their humorous qualities are determined. While social class plays a role in forming local joking aesthetics, individual characteristics, regional and occupational settings, and the joking history of the local group are also involved.

OUTLINE

In this book I will examine the creativity, humorousness, and social significance of vernacular practical joking. Chapters 1 and 2 define and catalog the various playful activities encompassed by the terms *prank* and *practical joke*. I will compare practical jokes to other kinds of jokes and suggest a broad definition: practical jokes, broadly conceived, are forms of unilateral play. Within this broad definition are practical jokes more narrowly conceived—especially put-ons, fool's errands, and booby traps—which, drawing on the work of Erving Goffman and Richard Tallman, I define as scripted play activities in which one protagonist is unwittingly contained in the play frame. Chapter 3 is a detailed analysis of the way a single fool's errand manipulates access to information about what is going on. I draw upon Labov and Waletzky's (1967) model of the personal experience narrative to analyze the relationships between the narrated event and several different narratives about it, from the point of view of the jokers, onlookers, and joke target. Chapter 4 explores the relationship between practical jokes and truth and includes an analysis of related folklore genres, the belief legend and the tall tale, that similarly concern themselves with epistemological questions.

Chapters 5 and 6 introduce the question of morality both in jokes generally and in practical jokes particularly. In chapter 5, I explore how jokers use playful fabrications to censure minor wrongdoing as well as how questions of (im)morality arise in the evaluation of their jokes. Chapter 6 argues that morality is a central question in the reception of all jokes, and builds on the humor support and the benign violation models to present a reception theory of humor that incorporates morality, local aesthetics, and play. Chapter 7 focuses on the variety of techniques that the targets of practical jokes can draw upon to show both support for and ambivalence toward their jocular mistreatment.

In chapters 8–10 I investigate the effect that practical jokes have on their social settings. Practical jokes are about relationships; they are deeply socially embedded, arising from, reflecting, and influencing specific relations. While humor support aids solidarity, the withholding of support—the situation for which I have adopted Michael Billig's felicitous term *unlaughter*—tends to heighten group boundaries. Chapter 8 considers how humor support builds solidarity and illustrates the power of the existing relationship to activate the play frame and transform the meanings of behaviors that would otherwise appear cruel or hostile. Chapter 9 is devoted to weddings and initiations, two sites in which ritual practical joking is commonly found today. The incongruous status of those undergoing a rite of passage both motivates and serves as justification for practical jokes, but despite their ritual play / playful ritual framing, targets do not always support these jokes. Initiation jokes are especially vulnerable to unlaughter, and the final case in this chapter considers the relationship between initiation jokes and workplace harassment.

Chapter 10 considers public pranks, specifically media April Fools' Day spoofs and the public practical jokes of university students in England and New Zealand. The targets of public pranks are anonymous but not random; they are selected based on their membership in salient out-groups to play stereotyped roles in public display events that dramatize anxieties held by in-group members about their own social status. Even in public, practical jokes are about relationships. Finally, in chapter 11 I introduce some individual practical jokers, highlighting their different jocular aesthetics and illustrating the roles that practical joking plays in their lives and relationships.

1

What's Practical about Practical Jokes?

It's surprisingly hard to define "practical joke" or its synonym, "prank." It is also difficult to explain what is "practical" about these expressive forms. A good definition must account for a wide variety of pranks and practical jokes, from the simple to the elaborate, from the benign to the malicious. Practical jokes may be personal or anonymous, private or public. Some are tailored for specific individuals and enacted just once while others have been repeated so often that they may be recognized by name, such as the short-sheeted bed, the snipe hunt, or "Going to see the Widow" (Cohen 1951; Grotegut 1955; Stahl and Kirby 1958). For many people, "practical joke" and "prank" conjure up the use of novelties and gag items. "The list is extensive: fake insects, vomit, and animal feces; dribble cups and spoons; foaming sugar; disappearing binoculars; soap and rubber crackers, nuts, eggs, gum, chocolates, and pretzels; dirty and bloody soap; crazy pitch baseballs; useless hinged scissors; exploding pens, cigars, cigarettes, cigarette cases; sneezing and itching powder" (Erard 1991, 1). Yet, while some practical jokes rely on elaborate props and scenery, others are equally effective using no extraverbal means at all. Some pranks involve mess and physical discomfiture of the target while others are more cerebral; some involve extended action sequences, but others can be accomplished in an armchair.

All these activities are playful performances involving the interaction of two parties—trickster and dupe—who have mutually incompatible ideas about what is going on. The involvement of dupes seems to be an essential characteristic of the genre. The role of the dupe is relatively passive: the trickster acts and initiates while the dupe is acted upon.

Dupes play an important role in this genre, as reflected in the abundance of vernacular terms to label them. There are relatively few terms in English for the perpetrators, *trickster* and *joker* being the most common. On the other side is the *victim, fool, dupe,* or *butt* (from the French for "target").[1]

DOI: 10.7330/9780874219845.c001

With the possible exception of *victim*, the names for practical joke dupes are always derogatory. Many traditional metaphorical terms compare them to animals, birds, or fish. In German, an April fool might be an *Aprilochse* (April ox) or *Aprilesel* (April donkey), to give just two possibilities (Wolf-Beranek 1968). The insulting reference to donkeys works in English, too, as witness the English April Fools' Day hoax from 1864 when a London newspaper, the *Evening Star,* announced "a grand exhibition of donkeys" for the following day at the Agricultural Hall. "Early on the morning of April 1st, a large crowd assembled outside the doors of the hall only to discover that they themselves were the donkeys" (quoted in Wight 1927, 40).

Bird metaphors are common in the language of practical joking. In Scotland, the April fool is a *gowk*, that is, a cuckoo, and a traditional practical joke called "hunting the gowk" sends its target from one person to the next in a vain search for an object that does not exist. In general, a naïve or gullible person is sometimes termed a *pigeon*, and the word *dupe* itself derives from the Latin *upupa* (the hoopoe, a bird renowned for its stupidity). *May gosling* is an older English label for the victim of a May Day trick (compare the German *Aprilgans* [April goose]) (Opie and Opie 1959, 256–257). The comparison of dupes to birdbrains probably lies behind the verb *gull*, meaning to cheat or fool someone (that is, to make a gull of them), from which we get the more common word *gullible*.[2]

Fish are commonly represented in the language used to refer to those taken in by practical jokes. In France, Belgium, and Italy, the April fool is an "April fish" (*poisson d'avril* or *pesce d'aprile*); fish motifs predominate in tricks played on this date and appear on a wide variety of greeting cards. Over the centuries several theories have been put forward to explain why fish should be the symbol of April Fools' Day (Dundes 1989), but none observe that the fish theme is also common in the broader vocabulary of practical joking. As fish are caught because they are fooled into swallowing bait, so we speak of a credulous person "swallowing" a false story or falling for it "hook, line, and sinker." In Ireland, *codding* is the current term for playing practical jokes (Harlow 1997). The term *catch*, used for a variety of deceptive routines favored by American children and youth, is another manifestation of the fish metaphor (Roemer 1977).

I talk about *targets* rather than *victims* of practical jokes because the latter term prejudges the outcome of the trickery. The vernacular terminology for the participants in practical joking puts the perpetrators in the active, superior position, but in taking aim at a target it is always possible to miss. While not as derogatory as some of the other terms, *victim* still imputes a passive role to the target of a practical joke, but targets can and do turn the

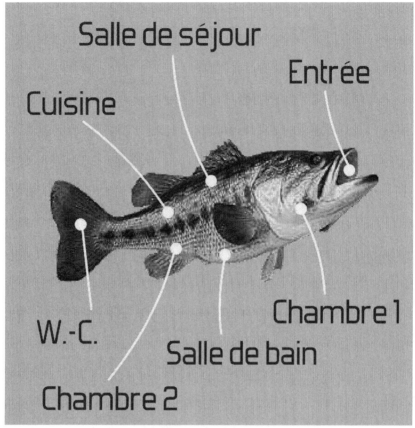

Figure 1.1. "Vous avez gagné une maison á Cannes" (You have won a house in Cannes). French electronic greeting card for April Fool's Day. The front reads, "You have won a house of 110 square metres at Cannes, with an ocean view. Click here for a virtual tour of the house" (Benchmark Group 2013).

tables on tricksters. Further, *victim* prejudges the propriety and humorousness of the genre, whereas debates and negotiations over these questions are at the heart of practically joking.

Riddle jokes and narrative jokes also have targets—blonds, Polacks, JAPs, and many others. However, while the targets of verbal jokes are arguably fictional characters rather than sociological facts (Davies 2011; Oring 2003, 58–70), there can be no doubt that practical jokes, like teases and jocular insults, take aim at real people. No practical joke can exist without a specific, live target or targets.

What makes a target is containment: instead of witnessing a joke or a play activity, the target is unilaterally enclosed in it. Performance and play are framed representations or transformations of reality, but the practical joke requires that one party be unaware of these frames. Because of this lack of awareness, the targets are themselves contained in the performance. Containment and differential framing are what distinguish practical jokes from other jokes, making them both peculiar kinds of performance and peculiar kinds of play. As performance, practical jokes feature protagonists who are acting while not acting. Whereas play is usually thought to be voluntary, practical jokes are unilateral play forms that attempt to compel their targets into play through surprise or trickery.

Narrative and riddle jokes readily lend themselves to frequent decontextualization and recontextualization (Bauman and Briggs 1990) and so spread far and wide; for this reason they are sometimes called "canned" or "prepared" jokes, both terms that underplay the variation and individual creativity that characterize live performance. In contrast, most jocular speech (*joking* as contrasted to *joke telling*) is spontaneous, closely tied to its context of origin, and not often repeated. Practical jokes fall somewhere between these two poles of contextualizaton. A spontaneous practical joke is conceivable but relatively rare; most are planned and scripted in advance. Commonly, this planning and anticipation are half the fun for the jokers. Some pranks are generic, replayed in new settings from tradition, experience, or instructions found in books or on websites. Others are unique, being tailored to the habits, personality, and personal proclivities of specific targets. As with most forms of folklore, however, even the oldest generic pranks offer room for individual variation and style when they are performed.

Many practical jokes appear to exist in imagination only. These have been called *practical joke recipes*: instructions for how to carry out a fabrication (Morrison 1974). Would-be pranksters can find these blueprints by the dozen in popular books (Jillette and Teller 1989), for example, and on websites like April Fool Zone (AmazingFX.net and Regan 2008). Here's an example from a New Zealand online bulletin board with a suggestion for how to liven up a party:

> If you can get a chicken from somewhere (maybe you live rurally?) [this] is quite a good one.
>
> It has to be at a party where everyone is really drunk and the bathroom is quite large, with a toilet at the far end of the room.
>
> First of all, stuff a good base of newspaper as a bedding across the bottom of the toilet basin (so chook [chicken] doesn't get too wet and uncomfortable). And I know it sounds cruel but next, stuff the chicken in the bowl and shut the lid. The chicken will struggle for a few minutes but they generally go quiet after a few minutes in the dark.

Take the light bulb out of the socket and close the door.

Everything going to plan, someone, preferably female will open the
door, try the light, and attempt to cross the room in the dark. When they
open the lid (and certainly when they start pissing on it) the chicken will
fly out and go nuts.[3]

Without more investigation of the readership of these websites and instruction books, it is unclear how often any of these recipes are ever enacted.
Quite possibly, readers have fun simply imagining the possibilities without
going to the trouble of sneaking a live chicken into a party, let alone taking
the risk of startling fellow partygoers.

What is significant for my purposes is that practical joke recipes contain
not only step-by-step instructions for the trickster (First, take your chicken
. . .) but also descriptions of what is supposed to happen next. Frequently
they contain what is essentially a script for how the targets will behave (open
the door, try the light, cross the room in the dark, and open the lid). The
suggestion is that if the jokers carry out their part properly, the targets will
unwittingly follow this script. We are left to imagine the miniature mayhem
that ensues but, "everything going to plan," events will follow the course
as laid out in the recipe. The key is that there is a plan—or rather, a *script*.
I contend that the presence of a script is the second essential ingredient,
alongside a target, in all practical jokes.

PRACTICAL JOKES AS UNILATERAL PLAY

A practical joke is *a scripted, unilateral play performance involving two opposed
parties—trickster and target—with the goal of incorporating the target into play
without his or her knowledge, permission, or both.* I have adopted the some-
what awkward phrase "play performance" rather than "playful performance"
in order to emphasize the nature of the genre as both participatory play and
performance for an audience in equal measure. This definition is broader
than the best existing definitions of the genre in order to account for several
activities that are commonly called either pranks or practical jokes but that
do not fit the usual definitions. These cases will be discussed in detail in the
next chapter.

In my definition deception is not a necessary part of the practical
joke. Since individuals often become targets through trickery and deception, most definitions make playful deceit a central feature (Bauman 1986,
36). For example, Erving Goffman (1974) considered practical jokes one
of several forms of "benign fabrication," defined as "the intentional effort
on the part of one or more individuals to manage activity so that a party

of one or more others will be induced to have a false belief about what it is that is going on" (86). The targets of practical jokes are *contained*, to use Goffman's term, in a framed play activity initiated by others without the targets' knowledge, without their permission, and sometimes without both. Considered more broadly, deceit is a frequent but not necessary element in an effective practical joke. In many cases, it is enough to startle targets with a surprise unilateral move into play.

Most definitions of the practical joke also require the discomfiture of the target, meaning that he or she is caused confusion, embarrassment, or some other mental and/or physical inconvenience or discomfort (Bauman 1986, 36; Tallman 1974, 260). A common assumption is that at a minimum, targets are embarrassed when the joke is revealed to them. The difficulty with this requirement is that there are many perfectly effective and well-received practical jokes with targets who are kept permanently in the dark:

> One mornin' I was gittin' ready to send the general off down there. He come out an' crawled up in th' cockpit an' I strapped him in. He was startin' the airplane up, an' on a T-33 you got a fuel control, you got a starting fuel control on it, an' you switch over to th' main as you're starting. It always made a rumblin' sound as you switched the fuel control over, an' that airplane rumbled, an' the ol' General looked at me an' he said, "Sarge, what's that noise?" I said, "Oh, sir, it ain't nothin' to worry about, it's jest that ol' lumpy fuel." I said, "It's jest a chunk of it went in there." He said, "Oh, okay."
>
> They took off an' they was goin' to New Orleans, an' the next day the General's aide came back. He was a captain. The General had stayed down there, an' the General's aide come back in, an' I parked him. He got outa that airplane a-cussin'. He said, "God damn, Sarge, don't ever, don't ever, tell that General anything like that again. You told that man that cock-and-bull story an' he believed you, an' there wudn't nothin' I could tell him to straighten him out. I tried to explain fuel controls to him all the way to New Orleans, an he didn' believe a damn word I said. He said Sgt. Yount told me it was lumpy fuel. He said git it straightened out. We don't ever want no more lumpy fuel." (Yount 1984, 25)

Angela Yount recorded this personal experience narrative from her grandfather Bill. Quite possibly, the general's containment in this joke might have been unintentional—when Sergeant Yount offered "lumpy fuel" as a joking explanation for the rumbling of the plane, he might have meant it as nothing more than a witticism. But the general treated the joking claim as factual truth and acted on this belief, to the annoyance of his aide. Since to tell the general he had been taken in by a joke would cause the superior officer to lose face, his subordinates wisely decided to keep him in the dark. Arguably, it was the aide who was discomforted by the joke, but the general is the chief target of the joke, the object of ridicule because of his ignorance. The fact that he remains unaware of being ridiculed only adds to the satisfaction of the joker—it is one more dimension of his superior's inferiority. The general's discomfiture, if we can call it that, is that his status is diminished in the eyes of the practical joker and others who are aware of the joke. Practical jokes on the powerful are more likely to be open-ended, because of the greater risk of negative repercussions on subordinate jokers, but this feature does not detract from the satisfaction of the joke in the least.

Revelation is not necessary for a successful practical joke, only the existence of simultaneous, mutually contradictory framings of the activity. Not every practical joke fabrication is revealed, but all are discreditable (Goffman 1974), vulnerable to discovery by those who were contained. The general might believe in lumpy fuel to this day, but since there is no such thing as lumpy fuel, there is always the possibility, however slight, that he will one day find that out. The targets' low status stems from the fact that although their situation is discoverable, they fail to discern it.

AUDIENCES, PERFORMERS, AND SCRIPTS

With or without revelation, embarrassment, or deceit, the targets of practical jokes are the unwitting objects of close scrutiny by an audience. This effect may be achieved by the simple stratagem of pinning a tail, a paper fish, or a "Kick me" sign to the back of a person's clothing to create a situation of differential framing. "Another thing we remember well was sticking tails on him [the headmaster] on April Fools' Day," goes a reminiscence of schooldays in 1874 near Dunedin, New Zealand. "Hilarious laughter used to proceed from the class as he strutted 'round the room with his long dust coat on and the tail sticking onto him" (Sutton-Smith 1981, 208). The language used to describe this prank is telling. The word *strutted* suggests an exaggerated, stylized gait, but we can reasonably assume that the headmaster was not walking any differently than normal since he apparently was unaware of his new appendage. Instead, the children were watching him differently. They thought of him as strutting because they were paying special attention to him. By pinning a tail to his coat, they had temporarily transformed him into an unwitting performer, like an actor strutting on a stage.

Practical jokes are performances in the conventional sense because jokers assume responsibility to an audience for displays of skill (Bauman 1977), these audiences being constituted by observers and sometimes—but not

Figure 1.2. John's tin-foiled desk

always—targets. Digital recording technology has encouraged jokers to find wider audiences by posting pictures and videos of their performances online, where others can view and comment on them. Crucially, however, the practical joke as performance includes both jokers and targets to some degree.

The relative roles of joker and target assume different levels of importance in various types of practical jokes. Often, both joker and target are central performers. In other cases, targets are little more than an audience for the joker's playful displays, but they retain some of the characteristics of a target because the performance is thrust upon them unexpectedly.

At a minimum, the joker him- or herself constitutes an audience of one that keenly watches to see what the target will do, but larger audiences are commonly recruited as well. Later in this work I explore the role of observers in the moral evaluation of pranks, but here I will stress only their function in the performative nature of the genre. One New Zealand joker, whom I call Don, describes how he "tin-foiled" a colleague's desk while the latter was on an overseas business trip. During an hour and a half one night, Don wrapped the entire desk and everything on it—every book, even every individual tea bag—in aluminum foil. He then took a picture of his handiwork. The tin-foiled desk itself was recorded so that it could be displayed as the first part of Don's performance. He emphasized the trouble he had gone to, wrapping every last item on the desk separately and achieving this feat in the course of a single night.

To record the second part of the show, Don and his coworkers borrowed the company video camera, setting it up the night before the owner of the desk, whom I call John, was due to return to work:

> Come Wednesday morning everyone's sitting at their desk, sitting at their desk, and John walks in the door. And it was like, the office stopped. The office just stopped. And everyone was watching him. And you could see right down the end of the hall; there's a lady . . . and you could see her standing up, gawking across to see what this guy was going [to do].
>
> And he walked in, and he was like [*expels breath*] . . . No language . . . you could see, I don't know if he was impressed or pissed off, or what. But it was just like [*expels breath*], head went down; I'll have to get you that video. (Anonymous 2005a)

According to the trickster, not only were all the office staff in the audience, the production staff came up from downstairs to watch too. When his target walked into the office, he walked onto a de facto stage. Quite possibly, everyone was waiting, or hoping, to see John lose his composure and "flood out" in anger or embarrassment (Goffman 1961, 55–61; Goffman 1974, 250–258). But John kept his reaction muted, with no "language" (that is, no bad language—indeed, no speech at all) but only a quiet expulsion of breath. A tin-foiled desk is a booby trap type of prank, one designed to unbalance the target's composure. In this scenario, targets who can keep their poise despite being surprised may claim some success in the contest with the trickster—if not victory, at least a draw.

The distinctive part of the practical joke as performance is that the unwitting or unwilling participation of one of the protagonists is a central element. Practical jokes are based on detailed predictions of how the chosen targets will act in the scripted scenario that the jokers have fabricated. The practical joke is meant to be an enactment of a plan, a script, in which the roles of both jokers and targets are clearly outlined. To be effective, the course of the joke must run in a way that the jokers can plausibly claim is in line with what they expected to happen.

UNILATERAL PLAY

The vernacular discourse about practical jokes repeatedly stresses that they are, or should be, merely play, yet it has been pointed out that "victim" is an odd name for a play partner (Bowman 1982, 69). Scholars of play are unanimous that play is voluntary and that players are aware they are playing (Caillois 1979, 6; Henricks 2006, 162; Huizinga 1950). Compulsory, unilateral play is almost a contradiction in terms. "When more than one participant is involved, all must be freely willing to play, and anyone has the power to refuse an invitation to play or (if he is a participant) to terminate the play once it has begun" (Goffman 1974, 42). Practical jokes, in contrast, work by either surprising their targets with play in unusual or unexpected places or containing them within play without their knowledge. Practical jokers are players, but their targets are playthings, whether briefly or indefinitely.

Play is much more than children's games and make-believe. Adult performance, artistry, fiction, theater—indeed, expressive culture generally— all constitute play broadly conceived (Stewart 1978, 36). Expressive culture is carried out for its own sake, with no obvious immediate purpose beyond the enhancement of experience for participants and audiences. Constituted by a "temporary abolition of the ordinary world" (Huizinga 1950, 12), all play normally depends on metacommunicative signals so it is recognizable as such to participants and audiences (Fry 1968, 125–126). Practical jokes upend this expectation by deliberately hiding play signals from those chosen as targets.

When and if the play frame becomes visible to targets, not all are willing to acquiesce. John Bowman observed an American college fraternity prank in which fraternity members seized female freshmen and forced them onto a mudslide. Some responded by laughing and showing every sign of enjoying it, but others became truly angry: "As she was forced onto it she repeated the following statement quite adamantly the whole way down the slide: 'I am *not* going to have fun, I am *not* going to have fun.' And she didn't. When she reached the bottom she left immediately, letting it be publicly known that she was infuriated by the whole incident" (1982, 70). This example shows that play cannot be obligatory.

Besides crafting effective fabrications, the challenge to practical jokers is to "make sure it's play" (Bowman 1982, 71–72). The task is to construct events that meet the requirements of play for both the jokers and salient others but simultaneously do not look like play to the chosen targets, so that they may be surprised by or contained in the play. So, practical jokes are play that does not look like play but also looks like play. In this, they exemplify the paradox that is inherent in both play and joking forms of metacommunication (Fry 1968).

The concept of unilateral play explains how certain kinds of expressive behavior are considered practical jokes even though they involve little or no trickery. For example, graffiti is commonly labeled either vandalism or prank, and it is usefully understood to be criminal art or art out of place (Stewart 1991, 206–234). As art or something akin to art, it falls into the category of play broadly conceived. The choice between the prank and vandalism labels generally comes down to whether or not the observer agrees with the unilateral move into artistic play initiated by the anonymous graffitist.

In Cibecue, Arizona, on the Fort Apache Reservation, Western Apaches enjoy (or tolerate, depending on whom you ask) a genre of joking performance called "playing the Whiteman." These spontaneous vernacular routines are also instances of unilateral play. Whiteman performances are satirical impersonations that suddenly interrupt everyday ongoing discourse and engage another person, usually a friend or relative, as a silent, sometimes unwilling foil for their performance (Basso 1979). There is no deception in these performances; the foils to the "Whiteman" character are enlisted into brief dramatic scripts knowingly, but without their prior consent, and these efforts elicit annoyance or resigned tolerance at best. The Western Apache describe Whiteman performances as joking, but not as practical jokes. They are scripted playful performance in which one of the protagonists is incorporated into the performance without his or her consent. In this way, those who are present for "Whiteman" impersonations cannot simply watch the show but are pushed into it. When such a thing happens in the Anglo-American world, it is considered a practical joke.

THE PLEASURES OF PRACTICAL JOKING

"Playing" practical jokes has the same sources of fun that are found in play generally. Play worlds lend participants the feeling of control over their surroundings, and "to 'play with' an object is to experience the satisfaction of trying to control it" (Henricks 2006, 186). When they are effective, the scripted or quasi-scripted quality of practical jokes afford tricksters the pleasure of controlling not just their environment but even other people. "I can't really say why, but fooling people into believing things is a lot of fun," explained one college student in California. "Maybe it has to do with being one step ahead of another person—of having a sense of control over what another person thinks. I am always saying things to my sisters in an attempt to trick them" (Maxwell 1994). It is an accomplishment to achieve the predicted script in the face of the target's ignorance of or opposition to the play frame.

However, play that was nothing more than an arena to exert control and skill would soon become boring. Goffman suggests that fun in play derives from a combination of uncertainty of outcome and sanctioned displays of valued skills and attributes (1961, 66–79; see also Henricks 2006, 156–157). Practical joke scripts depend on predicting how targets will act in specified situations, but since targets ideally are unaware of the script they are in, their behavior cannot be totally predicable. Further, since all fabrications are discreditable, the interaction between would-be jokers and potential targets takes the form of a contest whose outcome is never a foregone conclusion (Tallman 1974, 260). Targets who become aware of their situation in time can avoid containment or turn the tables on the jokers. I. Sheldon Posen collected a story about an American summer camp owner/director whom he called Joe. Many summer camps are hotbeds of practical joking, not only among the campers but also among the staff, and Joe was a particularly enthusiastic exponent of the art. One day some of his staff decided to get him back for the many jokes he had played on them. They armed themselves with mustard and ketchup in squeeze bottles, and as Joe walked into the staff lounge they opened fire.

> When he was red and yellow from head to foot, and the staff had finished laughing at him, Joe began to peel off his by-now orange clothes. "Charlie," he said to one of his attackers, "here's your shirt," and he handed out the clothes he was wearing to each one of the staff who had sprayed him. Joe had somehow found out about the impending prank and had walked into the lounge wearing clothes pilfered from his attackers' cabins, over his bathing suit. (Posen 1974, 309)

This legend was repeated among camp staff as exemplifying the model response to an attempted fabrication. The story is a reminder that practical jokes are contests of wits between jokers and their targets.

Another significant source of fun in play is risk, defined as the introduction of elements from the wider world in controlled and disguised form (Goffman 1961, 77). Thus games are enhanced when participants make monetary wagers on the outcome, and physical play is enriched when there is a manageable level of risk to physical safety. Practical jokes share with other joking forms the real-world risks that follow from rule breaking. As unilateral play, practical jokes are inherently transgressive—treating people as playthings, upending metacommunicative standards, eschewing the knowledge or permission of their targets. Such transgressions may be inherently pleasurable to the individual psyches of both those who initiate them and those who are invited to observe—including, sometimes, the targets themselves—but only if the transgression does not go too far. There is always a danger of going beyond the bounds that the audience is willing or able to accept as play, but as jokers knowingly take this risk and seek to manage it, their play experience is enhanced. Chapter 6–8 of this book explores the ways in which jokers, audiences, and targets evaluate the aftermath of practical jokes, when their status as play or as something else is debated, sometimes vigorously.

PLAY AND HUMOR

As their name suggests, practical jokes are also commonly identified as a form of humor. Humor is closely related to play and is often described as a subset of it (Martin 2007, 236; see also Eastman 1972, 15; Fry 1968, 138), but the exact distinction between the two is not always obvious. It does not help to identify humor as play that is funny, for funniness is too contingent to be used as a defining characteristic—instead, it is a moot point that is debated and negotiated by jokers and audiences after the fact. Similarly, not all jokes necessarily elicit laughter. Thus, my definition does not require the practical joke to be funny in either intent or outcome.

Instead, humorous play is to be identified by its formal features rather than by whether or not anyone finds it funny. Play may take either serious or joking forms, the former stressing the illusion of reality and the latter emphasizing unreality: for example, by means of exaggeration and incongruity (Wolfenstein 1978, 56–57). Formally, what makes the practical joke a form of joking play is the way it plays with frames, hiding them from salient participants for prescribed periods or making them ambiguous. To play with frames is to draw attention to them and to the nature of the framed content as a departure from the ordinary world. Frame play serves the same ends as the exaggeration and incongruity of other joke forms.

NOTES

1. Similarly, the person a sting or swindle is aimed at is "the mark."

2. According to the *OED*, the etymology of *gull* is unclear, but the preponderance of other avian metaphors in the vocabulary of deceits and practical jokes lends credence to the idea that the two senses of the word are etymologically related. Similarly, *goosing* may mean to attack like a goose or to turn the victim into a goose.

3. The chicken recipe was posted by "Biff" on www.biggie.co.nz/interaction/forum/viewtopic.php?t=142324 in December 2005 (accessed December 7, 2007). This post is no longer available online.

2

The Types of the Practical Joke

VARIOUS ATTEMPTS HAVE BEEN MADE TO CATEGORIZE PRANKS, practical jokes, and their cousins. Marilyn Jorgensen divided them into malicious types (which she labeled "pranks") or benevolent types ("tricks") (1995). Richard Tallman suggested a classificatory scheme that took into account the number of tricksters and targets, whether the action was active or passive, the intent of the prank (benevolent, initiatory, or malevolent), and the result of the prank (1974, 262–265). Erving Goffman suggested an informal typology of deceits arranged in order of increasing scale and elaborateness: kidding, leg-pulling, practical joking, surprise parties, larks or rags, and corrective hoaxing (1974, 87–92). Finally, practical jokes may be divided into *esoteric* and *exoteric* types, according to whether they are meant to build solidarity or accentuate the social distance between jokers and targets (Smith 1990).

I propose five types, based on the different roles of their targets and on whether their effectiveness requires revelation and/or deception. Unlike contingent criteria like the success or failure of a prank, or opaque ones like the motives of players, these are objective characteristics that are available for analytical observation. These five types are *put-ons, fool's errands, kick-me pranks, booby traps,* and *stunts*.

PUT-ONS

Put-ons, also known as leg-pulls, may arise spontaneously in the course of everyday discourse and contain their targets very briefly. The lumpy fuel joke probably started as a simple put-on. What distinguishes this category of fabrication is that nothing is required of the target beyond a word or phrase that shows he or she believes the fiction; for this reason Richard Tallman (1974, 264) labeled practical jokes of this type "passive pranks."

DOI: 10.7330/9780874219845.c002   21

"Oh, okay," said the general, and this phrase was sufficient to suggest that lumpy fuel had entered his catalog of real things that exist in the world. The effectiveness of this type of fabrication does not require revelation, although in some contexts, this differential state of knowledge may be revealed quickly, before the targets make any adjustments to their external world, let alone other people's.

When visitors ask me what the stuffed animal in my office is, I tell them it is a jackalope.

"What's a jackalope?" they ask.

"A jackalope is a cross between a jackrabbit and an antelope."

"Oh. I never saw one before."

"They're very rare. They come from Wyoming, and only come out at night. If you listen closely out on the prairie, sometimes you can hear them singing [*pause*] 'Home on the Range.'"

While some people recognize that the jackalope is a fictional, folkloric animal (Dorson 1982), others react with wonder or puzzlement. As the one responsible for this instance of the fabrication, I could choose to leave my guests in ignorance, thus creating an open-ended put-on. As rare as jackalopes are, such extended fabrication is unlikely to have any significant effect on the people fooled. But the open-ended fabrication could be discredited at any time, and then they would realize I had toyed with them. Yet to reveal outright that the jackalope was a leg-pull could be construed as rude, even face-threatening. So I build on the initial lie with a bigger one, one that alludes to another poetic text that creates, one hopes, a readily transparent fiction. This tactic allows me to communicate indirectly the fantastical nature of the jackalope without the listeners' having to acknowledge that they'd fallen for the deception.

My jackalope routine edges from a simple put-on into the genre of the tall tale which, in my typology, is simply a longer, elaborated put-on. Tall tales are fictional narratives masquerading as true stories—often as personal experience narratives (Stahl 1977). Piling exaggeration on exaggeration, tall tales move the listener from belief to doubt to disbelief (Bauman 1986, 18–24, 78–111; 2004, 98; Henningsen 1965). Performers tell such tales to fool the stranger or the greenhorn while delighting the insider audience with displays of verbal artistry. Shaggy dog stories and other meta-jokes (jokes that exploit and subvert expectations of the genre, for example, by promising a punch line and failing to deliver) function in similar ways (Brunvand 1963; Utley and Flamm 1969). I consider such jokes varieties of the put-on because all they require from their targets is belief, whether short- or long-lived.

Figure 2.1. The flying jackalope

FOOL'S ERRANDS

Whenever the target moves from passive belief to acting on that belief, we have a fool's errand, one of the earliest recorded forms of practical joke. In "The Birched Schoolboy," an anonymous sixteenth-century poem, the eponymous character excuses his tardiness by claiming that his mother had sent him to milk the ducks—"milke dukkis" (Emerson 1921, 96). This type of practical joke lures its targets into a specific but misguided course of action: for example, venturing on a nocturnal snipe hunt, driving to a nonexistent public event, going to fetch an extraordinary item that does not exist, attempting an impossible task, or rising at dawn to see an extraordinary tool in action. Michael Comes, a twenty-one-year old college student, recounted his experience in an Oregon timber mill:

> When I was working for Louisiana-Pacific, there was a machine down past the sorting chain that was never used during the night shift. When a new person would ask what L-P did with their 6-foot boards, everyone else would tell them that they went down to the machine at the end of the chain and that that was a board stretcher. It took 6-footers and made 8 and 10 footers out of them. Everyone had heard about the board stretcher at one time or another so when asked about it, everyone agreed that it was a marvellous sight and the person should get up at 7 o'clock in the morning to see it work because it only ran from 7 until 8 a.m. I heard that some people actually did come down early in the morning to see the infamous "board stretcher." This happened to me when I started the job in July of 1978. The mill was situated just outside of Tillamook, Oregon in a large, World War Two blimp hangar.
>   There is no known way to stretch wood in any direction. The night shift that I worked on got off at 2 a.m. and you had to make a supreme effort to get up in time to see the board stretcher in motion. The foreman of the day shift usually told the person that they had been fooled and to go home and get some more sleep. (Comes 1978)

Effective fool's errands must find ways to motivate targets to interrupt their everyday activities and act in specific, extraordinary ways. The board stretcher trick relied on curiosity to persuade greenhorns to rise early in the morning, whereas the child who went to milk the ducks was no doubt prompted by his parent's command.

Fool's errands are frequently used in rites of passage for new hires. Frequently they privilege the authority and knowledge of senior workers, who simply instruct their junior targets to fetch a nonexistent tool. Such tools allegedly exist for every occupation and frequently involve "stretchers" for vans, checks, bagels, fences, counters, sheetrock, and more. Considerable creativity goes into inventing nonexistent objects (a leaf repair kit, bumblebee feathers), fictitious variations on real tools (a left-handed crescent wrench, a right-handed screwdriver), and puns on occupationally specific jargon such as 100 feet of shoreline, a box of sprocket holes, a rack of fallopian tubes, or a box of grades. Verbal artistry is clearly manifested in such terms as *flat-footed lathe dog, three-cornered rat-tail file,* or *left-handed flower stretcher.* (Emerson 1921; Honeyman 1959).[1]

Puns and other wordplay in these fabrications cue the joking frame and keep fabrications within the bounds of play. The high incidence of "stretchers" in the set suggests a pun on the idea that the speaker is stretching the truth. The same metaphor gives us the terms *tall tale* and *to pull one's leg*. Such wordplay serves as a potential giveaway to joke targets; like laughter itself, the presence of anything related to joking keys fabrication. More generally, exaggeration is a characteristic of play. According to practical jokers, targets who fail to notice this playful joking frame contribute to their own victimization.

Another way to ensure the targets' compliance is to enlist them in a ritual or a game, both of which depend on voluntary adherence to extensive rules and instructions (Henricks 2006, 13–14; Huizinga 1950, 10). *Catch routines* are a form of fool's errand that exploit people's tendency to follow the rules in such settings. Tricksters give their targets explicit instructions that constitute the joke's "script." Several catches rely on homophones, creating an innocent surface script with a hidden and potentially embarrassing meaning. In the pseudo-initiation rite called "The Royal Order of Siam," American Boy Scout troop leaders instruct neophytes to repeat the phrase "owah tagoo siam" aloud; after several repetitions at increasing tempo the mysterious formula resolves into "Oh, what a goose I am" (Bartos 1979).

Other catches instruct their targets to perform elaborate actions along with the speech play. In the mid-1990s, college students in Nevada targeted drunken friends with "The Sobriety Test":

> The first thing you do when you find this gullible person is to ask them to spell their first name backwards. Once they complete this task (successfully or not), then you ask them to stand in front of you with their arms outstretched. Then ask them to touch their nose with the index finger of their right hand and then with the index finger of their left hand. Then, once you have them going, ask them to take a step backwards, turn around and bend over, placing their hands on their knees making it so their butt is in front of you. This is the best part: ask the person, for the next task, to spell "RUN" five times fast. Thus, the person says "R-U-N," "R-U-N," "R-U-N," "R-U-N," and it slowly becomes 'Are You In." (Neber 1996)

Drunk or not, this catch with an obscene subtext displays the extraordinary disposition that players have to trust their fellows and blindly follow instructions. Exploiting this tendency, the authors of catch routines effectively get others to follow their scripts to the point of embarrassment. The targets of catch routines know they are involved in a game, just not the one they think. Instead, both they and the game they think they are in are contained in a broader play frame that negates the meanings of everything inside it.

Generic pranks constitute another subtype of the fool's errand and simply cue preexisting cultural schemata for everyday activities like answering the phone (Jorgensen 1984) or the door. One such trick, beloved by children in both Britain and the United States, is to knock on doors or ring doorbells then flee as the inhabitants come to answer, leaving them gaping foolishly on the doorstep. Iona and Peter Opie collected more than sixty different names for this game among British children, including "Ring-Bell-Scoot" (Edinburgh), "Knock Down Ginger" (London), and "Bing Bang Skoosh" (Glasgow) (1959, 378–392). This game works because people act predictably. By exploiting this tendency, a child can exert temporary power over an adult, with the added thrill of risking capture and punishment.

A fool's errand that pits two target parties against each other is a *compound practical joke*. Jokers fraudulently cue one script—for example, ordering a pizza delivery—but direct it toward a third unwitting party who must deal with the consequences. Often, but not always, the containment of the first target is merely a tool to get at the third party, who is the joker's primary object.

KICK ME

This trick deserves a type of its own because it requires neither extraordinary action by the target nor revelation of the joke. By a simple stratagem, the target is unwittingly made into a performer for a hidden audience. A sign on one's back, something painted on one's face while asleep, or something similar is all it takes to effect the transformation. This marking serves as a frame, hidden from the dupe but visible to others, that turns his or her every move into an act. As with other fabrications, the humor is enhanced by the targets' ignorance of their objective appearance, and by the incongruity between self-image and what others see.

BOOBY TRAPS

Where a fool's errand uses false auspices to persuade its targets to get up and do something out of the ordinary, an effective booby trap aims only to surprise—sometimes in an unpleasant way but always with the intention of causing loss of composure. Loud unexpected noises or sudden jabs in the backside (*goosing*) are almost certain to elicit a satisfying physical reaction. Someone who is easily startled or reacts strongly to such an attack is labeled *goosy*, apparently another reference to the dupe as a stupid bird. *Goosing* means either to attack like a goose or to turn the victim into a silly goose. I interviewed one colleague who had this tendency and who also had a coworker who loved to play practical jokes. "He also realized that I was easily fooled," she told me. "Once I was concentrating on something he could slip up behind me and I wouldn't know it at all":

> So, first he would do things like coming up behind me in the hallway and tap me of one side of my shoulder and be standing on the other side, so I would look the wrong way and then I'd squeal around and see him; ha-ha. Then he decided that it would be worthwhile to hide behind some of these storage cabinets, of which there are *hundreds* in the archives. And leap out at me, and make me scream, which he did. Always I would let out a blood-curdling yell, as often as three or four times a day. (Cassell 1986)

Part of the humor of goosing is the incongruity between the response and the thing that stimulated it. Considered rationally, a yell or a scream is out of proportion to the severity of the threat. The startle response, however, is a reflex that bypasses the rational faculties. A trickster can generally count on getting a good reaction so long as the coming attack is kept a surprise.

A great variety of booby traps secretly rearrange or otherwise adulterate a portion of their target's everyday environment. At work, jokers coat telephone receivers with grease, fill safety helmets with water, or rearrange the keys on computer keyboards; at home, they put salt in the sugar bowl, loosen the cap on the ketchup bottle, or short-sheet the bed. The office cubicle wrapped in tin foil and the car filled with packing peanuts both belong to the booby trap type. Alternatively, tricksters might lace the target's world with gag items that deliver one unpleasant surprise after another. "A person (hereupon named X) . . . picks up what he thinks is a cracker. X bites the cracker. The cracker is made of soap. X lights the cigarette to rid his mouth of the taste of soap. Halfway smoked, the cigarette explodes. Exhausted, X sits down only to have loud 'poo-poo' noises emanate from under the chair cushion; he picks up the cushion and a cap device explodes" (Erard 1991, 5).

Booby trap jokes tamper with everyday objects so that they are unusable or have unusual effects, and the jokes are effective only if the targets fail to notice these changes and attempt to use them in the normal fashion. While a fool's errand tries to elicit an out-of-the-ordinary response, the effectiveness of a booby trap depends on people's attempts to use everyday objects in everyday ways. The humor lies in the incongruity between these everyday behaviors and their extraordinary consequences, and in the victims' ignorance of the true state of affairs. This type of fabrication requires revelation. Indeed, it is frequently instantaneous. The surprise need not be an unpleasant or messy one—surprise parties belong to this type as well—but astonishment is essential to effectiveness.

Jokers and onlookers who are in on the joke give close scrutiny to the target's uncontained responses after the trap is sprung. The jokers' goal is to cause everyday composure to collapse into surprise, alarm, embarrassment, annoyance, helpless laughter, or a combination of these—in a word, to cause targets to "flood out" (Goffman 1974, 350–358). Having created the fabrication that led to this discomposure, tricksters can take credit for it as well. Scene 1 of the booby trap script shows the targets blithely going about their business, followed by scene 2, in which the same targets show alarm, disgust, or flooding out into helpless laughter. In both scenes, the jokers have transformed targets from competent agents to puppets manipulated by others.

STUNTS

In this category belong play forms with hidden or ambiguous framing that burst unexpectedly into everyday discourse or into public spaces and redefine everything—without warning or permission. These pranks require surprise but not extended deceptions, and while they have audiences, they scarcely have targets in the same sense as other practical jokes. Instead of scrutinizing targets, these pranks direct attention primarily to the creativity and artistry of the pranksters.

The *rags* of British University students (Reeve 1977; Saltzman 2012) and the *hacks* of students at the Massachusetts Institute of Technology (MIT) both belong in this category. MIT hacks are widely celebrated for their impressive constructions designed to be sprung upon the rest of the campus or surrounding areas. Thus, on April Fools' Day in 1998, the MIT web page announced that Disney had made an offer to buy the school for $6.9 billion. School officials realized at once that students had hacked into their computer network, replacing the official home page with one that showed the school's famous Great Dome adorned with Mickey Mouse ears (IHTFP Hack Gallery 1998).

MIT students define a hack as "a clever, benign, and 'ethical' prank or practical joke, which is both challenging for the perpetrators and amusing to the MIT community (and sometimes even the rest of the world!)" (MIT Museum 2012). Like the hack noted above, many target the trademark Great Dome. In what MIT students widely regard as a supreme example of the hacker's art, the MIT community awoke one morning in 1994 to find a campus police cruiser parked on the top of the dome (150 feet above ground), complete with flashing lights and a dummy police officer eating donuts. The car sported a parking ticket that read "No permit for this location" (Peterson 2003, 11–12, 23).

Hacks require students to work in secret to overcome logistical and engineering challenges, and the results draw attention to the anonymous tricksters' ingenuity, creativity, and persistence. Even though the tradition of hacking is well established, audiences do not know in advance when or where the next creative display will appear. Furthermore, MIT rules prohibit climbing on and otherwise adulterating campus buildings, creating the need for secrecy, which adds another layer of difficulty. Hacks are street art in unexpected and illegal places.

Although student hacks and similar activities like these are considered pranks or practical jokes (for example, in Steinberg 1992, 93–120), they appear to have audiences rather than targets. The targets of MIT hacks, if any, are amorphous and abstract. Hackers tilt at authority, the school administration, campus rules, and campus police. Beyond the university environment, public stunts unsettle conventional thinking (Vale and Juno 1987, 75). In practical jokes of this type, targets are always collective and anonymous—anyone who happens to encounter the pranksters' work.

Flash mobs, a fad that began in New York City in 2003, are often described by their organizers as pranks even though there is little if any deception in them. A flash mob is simply a large group of strangers who perform an orchestrated and often pointless action at a predetermined public location (for example, riding the subway without pants or leapfrogging in a department store) and then disperse (McFedries 2003, 56; Wasik 2006). The annual No Pants Subway Ride, now in its twelfth year, is described by its organizers as a prank (Todd 2009). In an interview, the organizer of the 2010 event invoked what he called "the golden rule for a prank": "It should be as fun for the person getting pranked as it is for the prankster" (Simon 2011). Yet when adult play like the No Pants Subway Ride breaks out in public places that are not regularly designated as play spaces, there may be opposition. During the second No Pants ride, the conductor was heard to shout over the PA, "This train is not a playground." On another occasion, the police arrested all participants (although the charges were eventually dismissed) (Improv Everywhere 2013).

Public stunts scarcely require targets in the same way as other practical jokes. However, they do require audiences, who, subjected to these performances out of context and without warning, may react with uncertainty and confusion. Because the pantsless subway riders lack the conventional devices that would frame their activity as theater or play, their behavior appears bizarre, even threatening. Videos taken by stunt participants show some "audience" members reacting with astonishment, uncertainty, and alarm, while others are laughing and enjoying the show (Improv Everywhere

2013). Such stunts turn regular subway riders into audience members rather than players, but as in other practical jokes this transformation is made unilaterally and without prior consent.

Since they often involve little or no deception, many public stunts might seem not to belong with booby traps and fool's errands. At first blush it is surprising that they are called pranks at all, but such is indeed the case. The conundrum is resolved by referring to the broader definition of a practical joke as unilateral play. Flash mobs, hacks, and the like are certainly play, but they are play out of place—in the streets, in the midst of everyday life, sprung on unsuspecting publics. The fool's errand deceives its targets while the stunt merely surprises them, but in every case someone is made to take part in play without his or her consent. Whether or not targets assent to this treatment after the fact is never a predetermined outcome, a point that we will take up at length later on.

NOTE

1. Most of these examples may be found in the files of the University of California–Berkeley Folklore Archives. Folklorists have assigned these traditional practical jokes to motif J2346, "Fool's errand."

3

The Great Drug Bust
Morphology of an April Fools' Joke

PRACTICAL JOKES EXIST IN THE MIND MORE THAN anywhere else. They begin as plans or recipes, predicative scripts that outline what is supposed to happen, but not all of them are enacted. Judging from their numbers, practical joke handbooks and websites are widely read, but it is likely that many readers enjoy them just to imagine the possibilities. When they are enacted, practical jokes are typically fleeting, onetime events, but participants often record them for future replaying and sharing. However, the most widespread way of replaying and sharing practical jokes is in the form of narratives. Whether told by the jokers, their targets, or bystanders, practical joke accounts have a pervasive narrative structure.

The personal experience stories of jokers and targets become part of the joking culture of the group (Fine and De Soucey 2005), and most often do not spread far from the circle of those who were involved or are personally acquainted with those involved. Richard Tallman calls them "purely local" stories (1974, 261). Migratory practical joke stories are far less common and often take the form of legend, recounting events that may never have happened (but even then, the narratives assume the existence of real events). That said, if suitable venues are available, these purely local stories are sometimes shared with wider audiences. Internet video-sharing sites contain some elaborate versions. Just who constitutes the audiences of these vernacular mediated narratives deserves further study.

Another nonlocal venue is the newspaper. The day after All Fools' Day, 1980, Brian Werth, the police reporter at the *Bloomington Herald-Telephone*, posted the following personal narrative under the headline "Reporter Becomes an April Fool":

> I was duped, fooled, double-crossed. Of course, on April fool's Day one is
> supposed to be aware of potentially embarrassing tricks, but this reporter

DOI: 10.7330/9780874219845.c003

was taken in by a particularly thoughtful ruse. Fellow reporters, teaming with a county official at the sheriff's department, gave me a "hot tip" there would be a huge drug bust at Monroe County Airport.

I was instructed to drive there, telling no one else about this, and receive further "instructions" when I arrived. So camera in hand, I whisked out to the airport, keeping my eyes open for suspicious airplanes, police in plain cars and clothes and other possibilities.

I found my way to a building and received my "instructions" in a manila envelope. It was only when I opened the package that I realized, with considerable chagrin, that I was indeed an April Fool. (Werth 1980)

Journalists in all media mark calendar customs, from New Year's Day to Christmas, with special features, sometimes with observations from the occasional folklorist. Features published on April Fools' Day recount famous hoaxes of the past or suggest tricks that readers might try. Other "features" are participatory rather than descriptive, spoofs intended to fool readers (Smith 2009a). These spoofs offer journalists the chance to play, strut their professional skills, and prove that they are "regular guys" by demonstrating their robust sense of humor.

On this occasion Brian takes a different approach, offering an April Fools' story in which he was the dupe rather than the hero. By recounting a personal story taken from the joking culture of the newsroom where he worked, he treats his readers as familiars and honorary insiders. The story is imbued with self-deprecating humor. By telling the joke on himself, Brian implicitly gives readers permission to laugh at his discomfiture. Ridicule is transformed into shared laughter, so readers can rest easy knowing that they are, as the contemporary idiom puts it, laughing not *at* him but *with* him. For his part, Brian gets credited not only for entertaining his audience but also for having a healthy sense of humor himself.

Although brief, Brian's story contains all the minimal requirements for a practical joke narrative: (1) orientation, (2) setup, (3) trick event, (4) discrediting, and (5) evaluation (Bauman 1986, 45). In the orientation section, beginning with the headline, he frames his account as an April Fools' joke, thus priming readers to expect a specific kind of practical joke associated with this date, one that is brief and good-natured and concludes with a definitive formula (Dundes 1989; McEntire 2002).

Richard Bauman suggests that practical joke narratives follow the same structural sequence regardless of whether the storyteller was the prankster or target in the original event (1986, 33–53). Because the structure of the practical joke is a familiar one, narrated versions can follow this structure—departing from the point of view of the narrative persona if necessary so that the backstage setup is recounted before the joke enactment is. "Fellow reporters," Brian writes, "teaming with a county official at the sheriff's department, gave me a 'hot tip' there would be a huge drug bust at Monroe County Airport." Brian only alludes to the setup of the joke, which took place backstage with the collusion of officials from the sheriff's department, but the scare quotes in the next clause indicate what the setup was.

In this sentence and the one following, Brian conveys the setup of this joke, including both his direct experience and the backstage domains that he was not privy to. The scare quotes convey what only the jokers knew: that the "hot tip" and the "instructions" were fake. In written practical joke stories, quotation marks cue the fabrication frame. Viewed from the joker's perspective, the frame quotes are visible and the things contained in them are unreal. They mark a significant difference between what is contained in them and what lies outside them—the gulf between play and reality. From the target's original point of view, the frame was not visible. A hot tip is a police reporter's fondest wish, meaning a big story and professional success; a "hot tip" is a facsimile and has a completely different meaning. The quotes indicate that the reporter was engaged in play, although he did not know it at the time. By interspersing the setup and enactment, practical joke narratives allow their audiences to experience two opposed scripts operating at once—the one that the target is following and another, incompatible with the first, that the jokers have planned and put in place. This structure replicates the original experience of the jokers and those who colluded with them, and this experience of perceiving mutually incompatible scripts in the same text is a necessary precondition for amusement and humor (Raskin 1985).

The trick event and discrediting of the fabrication are also conveyed with economy, but even here the scare quotes appear to reinstate the simultaneous dual framing of what was going on:

> So camera in hand, I whisked out to the airport, keeping my eyes open for suspicious airplanes, police in plain cars and clothes and other possibilities.
> I found my way to a building and received my "instructions" in a manila envelope. It was only when I opened the package that I realized, with considerable chagrin, that I was indeed an April Fool.

Brian does not have to spell out the details of the discrediting, because the structure of April Fools' jokes is so well known that his readers can readily guess what happened: the "instructions" contained a message that simply read something like "Happy April Fools' Day, Brian." The "April

Fool!" formula provides closure to the practical joke much as a punch line marks the end of a narrative joke, but where the latter attempts to make an unpredictable twist, the audience of a practical joke story knows almost exactly what to expect.

The evaluation of personal narratives need not be confined to a separate section at the end, but may be spread throughout. Brian attests to the efficacy of this joke from the very beginning when he says, "I was duped, fooled, double-crossed." He also praises the fabrication as a particularly thoughtful one. However, the evaluation of practical jokes typically does not stop at assessing their efficacy. When we talk about whether a practical joke has worked, the talk can refer to either the trickery at the center of things or its aftermath. These are two separate questions. The first asks whether the joke was effective—did it fool the target, and did events play out according to the joker's script? But the second question refers not to the joke itself but to the post-play (Goffman 1961, 62). Did the aftermath of the joke go according to plan? It turns out that a talent for making fools of people is by no means always matched with ability to manage the consequences. In other words, *effective* practical jokes are not always *successful* ones. An effective joke keeps its targets fooled until the script has run its course. A successful joke is one in which the aftermath also follows the joker's plan. A successful post-play means that jokers have managed things so that relationships with their targets continue in the way they prefer.

As the target of the practical joke he relates, Brian does not directly say what he thought about it, but the fact that he is repeating the story, not to fellow reporters but to the world at large, implies that he approved of it. The story begins and ends with his frank admission that he was an April Fool, implicitly putting the blame on himself for being taken in, and agreeing with the joker's construction of him as an April Fool. Since April Fools' jokes are recognized as being more restrained than some others, to be an April Fool is better than being called simply a fool. An April Fool is a participant in something that, with its elaborate rules, formulae, and restrictions, is clearly framed as play. Supporting this evaluation, Brian's stylistic choices indirectly convey a playful, joking frame. The parallelism and hyperbole in "I was duped, fooled, double-crossed" go beyond the strict requirements of conveying what happened. "Camera in hand," he says, "I whisked out to the airport," describing himself in ironic terms as an ace reporter. These cues move the story from prosaic reporting into a humorous key, suggesting that the writer is in agreement with the jokers in treating the event as just a joke.

BRIAN'S STORY

In addition to the newspaper story, Brian also recounted the drug bust joke to me orally. In the following transcript, the framed portions of the text represent the moments when he was fully contained in the jokers' script. From his point of view, what was happening at those moments was a drug bust at the local airport; he was unaware of the play frame at the time because he was enclosed in it. Surrounding the framed action is everyday life in the newsroom, of which he was aware, and the setup of the joke; as in his published version, Brian takes leave of his narrated persona to describe these backstage domains.

> *I got to work and I was a police reporter. I was told that the sheriff was on the phone for me. So I had a telephone call from the sheriff, who told me that there would be quite a major drug bust at the Monroe County airport, and I was to go drive out to a building out there, receive some instructions in an envelope, and wait there for the bust which was gonna happen.*

Unbeknownst to me, several people in the newsroom had set this up with the county sheriff, and they knew what the call was and what was happening.

> *And so they said, "Brian, what's up?" 'cause I was grabbing my camera and my notebook and running out the door. And I said, "Possibly a big story, can't tell you." You know, I walk out the door thinking I have a great news scoop,*

and I'm sure everybody in the newsroom at the time was just chuckling, ha-ha-ha, laugh laugh laugh.

> *So I drive out there looking for planes, low-flying planes coming in, a lot of police cars, I don't see anything, I get out to the airport, I go to this back area, and there's a woman with a manila envelope; she hands it to me.*

"April Fools', Brian."
No drug bust.
So that was the story there.
    I really was totally surprised up till the point where I opened it up, and it said April Fools' and at that point I just smiled and said, "They got me." (Werth 1987)

The drug bust joke belongs to the fool's errand type of practical joke, one in which the target must be lured into a definite course of action before the fabrication is revealed. The fool's errand type of practical joke has a sequence of six stages: *setup, stimulus, response, discrediting, reframing, postplay*. Brian's experience provides a good view of the structure of a practical joke from the target's point of view.

The *stimulus* was the phone call from the sheriff alerting him to the big event, and his *response* was exactly what one would expect from a good journalist: he rushed to the scene to get the story. Since big crime stories are rare in Bloomington, Indiana, this one looked to be the scoop of the year. He was surprised that there were no signs of the impending event—no planes, no police cars. However, he did not abandon his definition of the situation even though events were not playing out exactly as expected. This tendency of practical joke targets to ignore or explain away things that might discredit the fabrication is another aspect of the way practical jokes exist in the mind. Once a fabricated script has been cued for targets, they tend to normalize the mismatches in that script, construing everything that happens in ways that keep their interpretation of events intact (Dornelles and Garcez 2001). Thus, practical joke fabrications are joint constructs, with contributions by both jokers and targets.

In an April Fools' joke, the *discrediting* and *reframing* stages are virtually simultaneous. The discrediting formula is an unambiguous sign that what had been going on was a joke, and this moment is a watershed that irrevocably changes Brian's understanding of what was happening. It is the moment of truth, literally. In the vernacular expression, he is "let in on the joke." In another sense, he has been "in" the joke from the beginning, and the purpose of the formula is simply to make him aware of the fact. The discrediting stage of a practical joke operates similarly to the way the punch line in a narrative joke reveals an alternative script or interpretation contained in the body of the joke.

The punch line precipitates a *reframing* stage. Brian says that he realized he was an April Fool, but this simple statement covers an extensive replaying and reinterpretation of the salient preceding events not as reality but as fabrication, not seriousness but a joke. Things he had thought strange before—the absence of planes and squad cars—are now explained. The moment of discrediting marks the end of the joke, and the location of a specific, identifiable stimulus helps the previously contained to recognize when and where their containment began. The targets' own actions are also subjected to reframing when a fool's errand is revealed to them; thus Brian was obliged to realize his own role in the fabrication. Once the joke frame was visible, he knew that he had been contained in it, and that for the past few hours he was not so much a newspaper reporter as a representation of a reporter. Further, he realized that during that time he had unwittingly been putting on an entertainment for his fellow reporters back in the newsroom.

A practical joke can be said to be officially over when the first five stages are complete. The fabrication has run its course and been discredited; the target is now "in on" the joke. It is all over but the shouting, but the shouting can be very significant in social terms. In the *post-play* of the joke, targets must come to terms not only with their failure to spot the trickery but also with the fact that friends or family have subjected them to this treatment (Goffman 1974, 89). "At that point," Brian said, "I just smiled and said, 'They got me.'" But the story did not end there:

> I wasn't mad or anything. But then I said, "Well, the best thing to do now is not to go back to the paper, so they can revel in their glory at getting me." So I didn't go back to work that whole day—this was late in the afternoon anyway—so nobody got to see my reaction anyway. In my mind I was thinking, at least they won't get to see me totally chagrined.
>
> I tried to turn it back on somebody, because later that night one of the people that pulled the trick called my house; I said to my wife, "Say that I'm not home and you don't know where I am." Trying to trick him back. But that lasted only for a few seconds. It was a last-gasp attempt to try to get back. (Werth 1987)

This addendum suggests a number of significant things. In many practical jokes, how targets comport themselves in the post-play holds as much interest for the jokers as their contained response did. In the post-play, targets know that their reaction to the fact of being fooled is being watched closely by the jokers and others who colluded with them. To play the game means trying not to show that one is seriously upset or put out. Getting even by turning the trick on the tricksters is one way of dealing with feelings of chagrin or embarrassment while simultaneously disguising them. Thus practical jokes frequently engender more practical jokes.

KURT'S STORY

Kurt Van der Dussen, one of the reporters responsible for the joke on Brian, told me the story from his perspective. The transcript below indicates how he switched back and forth between the trick event and the backstage domain where he and his co-conspirators set it up.

Orientation:
    I can't even remember what year it was; I think around 1971 or so. At the time someone named Randy Williamson still was the county sheriff.

Brian had played some sort of practical trick on someone not that much
longer before; I can't remember what it was. At any rate we planned to put
him in his place.

Setup:
    We called the sheriff—what we did first was we made up a piece of
cardboard that said "April Fools' Day, Brian." And put it in an envelope;
then we called the sheriff on the phone and asked the sheriff whether he
would be willing to take part in this thing with us.
    So at any rate what we did was we had the sheriff call Brian at a pre-
determined time. And meanwhile, the envelope with our sign in it had
been delivered out to Monroe County airport, to the office of the airport
manager.

Stimulus:
    So the sheriff called Brian and: "Brian, we're going to have a big drug
bust out at the airport this afternoon. We are expecting a private plane to
be flying in; we are going to have some police officers out there, hidden,
to capture the people on the plane when they come. And if you want to go
out there and be in on this, we'll tell you where to meet them."

Setup:
    And he was supposed to stress that this was all very secret.

Stimulus:
    "Don't tell anyone about it, and when you get out there, go to the air-
port manager's office and they will give you an envelope, and the envelope
will give you instructions where to find us at the airport. When you get out
there you won't see us."

Setup:
    So we got that all set up.

Stimulus:
    And at the appointed time the sheriff called Brian on the phone; and
everyone in the newsroom knew about it, sitting there trying to play innocent.

Response:
    Brian answered the phone:
    "Yeah. Uh-huh, uh-huh." You know he's getting real excited about it.
    So he gets off the phone and someone says to him casually, "What's go-
ing on, Brian?"
    "Can't tell you, can't tell anyone."
    So Brian [*laughs*] at the appointed time, which was something like one
or two o'clock in the afternoon, Brian mysteriously leaves the newsroom,
drives all the way over to the county airport, goes to the airport manager's
office, and sure enough there's an envelope waiting for him.

Discrediting:
>He opens it up and here's this big card which says "April Fools'."[*Laughs*]

Post-play:
>So Brian disappeared for the rest of the day. Never came back to the paper. And by then we were beginning to feel kinda bad about the whole thing. So, around four or five that night I called his house and I got his wife [at] home.
>"Is Brian there?"
>"No, he never got home."
>So, we thought, where's Brian? So I called later on in the night, and she said, "No, Brian hasn't showed up."
>Well, it turned out that Brian had shown up, and he was getting back at us by leading us to believe he had gone out and done something rash because of the embarrassment.
>But at any rate he was very embarrassed about it. He vowed to get back at me the next year, so the next year I went up to Indianapolis to play golf on April Fools' Day, so that he couldn't *possibly* get back at me.
>At any rate, that's the other version of the Brian joke. (Van der Dussen 1987)

The *orientation* section of a practical joke story, according to Bauman, "sets out the factors that bring the participants into place for the practical joke to be recounted and that provide the means . . . for enacting it" (1986, 45). However, these stories commonly also begin with information that sets out not just the means but also the motive for the joke. Kurt not only sets the date and introduces the players, he also explains that the target of the joke had played tricks on someone else and that "we planned to put him in his place." There is a folk morality governing the playing of practical jokes within small groups according to which anyone who plays jokes on others should expect the same treatment. Other practical joke stories mention salient parts of the target's character and behavior. These details not only explain why the joke to be recounted was enacted but also provide the justification for it. Practical jokes seem to need excuses, a point to which we will return when we come to Kurt's evaluation of his fabrication.

The *setup* of this joke was fairly elaborate: concocting the story, making up the sign, enlisting the help of the county sheriff, giving the sheriff a detailed script of what to say, and so on. This preparation took place in backstage domains that Brian was not privy to, but as one of the jokers, Kurt had direct knowledge of it. However, he also gives the sheriff's extended speech and describes Brian's actions after leaving the newsroom, both events that he would not have observed directly. Everything in the joke was scripted, with Kurt as dramaturge; the sheriff, the clerk at the airport, and the other reporters as players; and Brian as the chief, albeit unwitting, protagonist. Brian was onstage only briefly—between getting the sheriff's phone call and the moment he left the newsroom—but that was enough for the jokers and the audience to enjoy. Jokers could have found out from Brian what happened after he left their sight, but they would not need to since the joke script already predicted the essential events.

The heart of any fool's errand, and the central point in the stories about them, is the point when the fabrication is enacted and the target/actor embarks on the play. In their stories both Kurt and Brian mark this moment with direct speech, as if the joke script is unfolding before our eyes:

> Kurt:
> Brian answered the phone:
> "Yeah. Uh-huh, uh-huh." You know he's getting real excited about it.
> So he gets off the phone and someone says to him casually, "What's going on, Brian?"
> "Can't tell you, can't tell anyone."
> So Brian [*laughs*] at the appointed time, which was something like one or two o'clock in the afternoon, Brian mysteriously leaves the newsroom, drives all the way over to the county airport, goes to the airport manager's office, and sure enough there's an envelope waiting for him.

> Brian:
> And so they said, "Brian, what's up?" 'cause I was grabbing my camera and my notebook and running out the door. And I said, "Possibly a big story, can't tell you." You know, I walk out the door thinking I have a great news scoop, and I'm sure everybody in the newsroom at the time was just chuckling, ha-ha-ha, laugh laugh laugh.

Both narrators switch into direct speech at this juncture, marking the moment with special importance. These speeches portray the joke target following the script with vim and enthusiasm—the perfect outcome of any fool's errand. A third version of the joke, published in the *Herald-Times* by another reporter some years later, also highlights this juncture with particular artistry:

> When he got off the phone, he excitedly told us he had something really hot going on, but it was confidential. "You'll see," he said smugly.
> An hour or so later the sheriff called the reporter back and gave him his instructions: drive out to the airport, go to the manager's office and further

instructions would be waiting for him there. "This is it," the reporter announced, stuffing his note pad into his back pocket as he rushed toward the door.

The rest of us could barely conceal our grins, and once the reporter was out the door we laughed ourselves silly. He took the hook like a mackerel and we could almost hear the winding sound of the spinning reel, pulling him in.

Once at the airport, he was handed a manila envelope. Inside, the message read: "You're an April Fool!" and it was signed by all of us.

Heh, heh, heh. (Leonard 1990)

In this story, as in those told by the joker and the target, the central part of the practical joke is framed with laughter, either actual or reported. The first laughter moment coincides with breakthroughs into direct speech, both marking the key moment in the practical joke enactment when the joke takes off and the target reaches the depths of his containment.

The significance of laughter is often ambiguous—in this story, it could signal ridicule of the target, but it might also be sympathetic. This is also the point in a practical joke enactment when jokers and audiences report the most difficulty in keeping a straight face, as Leonard reports in this case. In narrative jokes, laughter is commonly said to be caused when the punch line surprises the audience by revealing a hidden script. In practical jokes, tricksters and audiences laugh even though the joke holds no surprises for them. They know not only that the discrediting trigger will occur but also what form it will take. The only uncertainty is *when* the discrediting will occur. Instead, their laughter while the enactment is under way is caused by the fact that at this juncture, they can see two opposed scripts in play. One script is real, actual, plausible, or possible, while the other is unreal, nonexistent, implausible, or impossible (Raskin 1985). Common sense holds that two mutually opposed scripts cannot exist in parallel indefinitely; the longer that situation continues and the more obvious the target's containment becomes, the more tension arises in observers, who wonder when this impossible situation will be resolved.

In all three stories, laughter erupts again after the discrediting punch line, marking the closure of the containment. Laughter has an evaluative function in practical joke stories, pointing out the moments where the effectiveness of the joke is most visible and when the fabrication is discredited, making the joke frame visible to all. Laughter thus frames the central part of the joke in which the target is acting while contained. This delicious opposition of opposed scripts is what the practical joke is all about. The setup exists only to create this, and the post-play is all about evaluating it. The final laughter (or smiling, as the case may be) marks the end of the joke and the beginning of the post-play.

There is no reframing stage in Kurt's story because for him and his fellow players the joke's framing was never in doubt. His account of the post-play begins with Brian's attempt to fool the jokers into thinking their joke had backfired and that he had "done something rash." As Kurt tells it, this effort was effective; when it became clear that their target was not going to return that day, the jokers began to feel some twinges of guilt. This was the only time that they were uncertain about what was happening out of their sight. "Where's Brian?" they asked themselves—because Brian had departed from their secret script.

Kurt ends his story with a coda (Labov and Waletzky 1967, 33–40) to bring us up to the present, with Brian once more inside the social orbit of the newsroom, embarrassed but playfully threatening revenge. Describing how he foiled any such counterattack by staying away from work the next April Fools' Day, Kurt leaves us with a portrait of friends and colleagues enjoying a competitive game whose rules specified that Brian had the right to retaliate with a practical joke of his own so long as he did so within the confines of another April First. By implicitly pointing to these unspoken but well-understood rules, Kurt suggests that the drug bust joke and its aftermath were a form of play.

At the end of his story, Kurt offered an *evaluation* of the joke:

> The great thing was we got the sheriff to go along with this thing, so completely. He did a great job when he called Brian up, he just had Brian convinced that they were going to have the biggest drug bust in Bloomington history out at the airport. We told the sheriff just what we wanted him to say; in fact the sheriff sent a squad car down to pick up the envelope and a police officer took the envelope out to the airport. I forget whether we called the airport or not, to tell the airport manager what was going on.
>
> But at any rate I always wish I could have seen Brian's face when he went all the way out to the airport and opened this thing up expecting to find out where to meet these guys at the airport, and finding out that the whole thing was a joke. (Van der Dussen 1987)

As performances, practical jokes are subject to audience critique. In the first instance, the audience members are the jokers and other players, who evaluate their own performance and those of fellow players. Efficacy can refer to the actions of the jokers and anyone who colludes with them. Kurt takes credit for securing the help of the sheriff and praises the latter's acting ability. The sheriff had the toughest role in the joke because he had to relay a detailed scripted message to the target directly, convincingly, and in a way that would impel him to act, since without the role of the ace reporter this joke script would have been a failure. Further, the sheriff had to avoid giving away anything that would signal a state of play, a feat that was rendered easier by using the phone as a medium. The sheriff did a "great job," according to the director of this play, because "he had Brian convinced," causing Brian to respond in accordance with the script.

"I always wish I could have seen Brian's face," Kurt says. This lament, almost formulaic in stories of jokes that are discredited offstage, is another evaluative device: it suggests that even though they cannot witness the target's emotional discomfiture directly, they assert that it must have been powerful, too powerful to be suppressed or hidden. Targets will often strive to keep their reactions muted so as to deprive jokers of the satisfaction of seeing them discomforted. Brian's solution was to stay away from the newsroom so the jokers could not "revel in their glory at getting me."

However, the evaluation of a practical joke does not stop at establishing its efficacy. Whether the evaluation is made by the target or, as here, by the joker, it includes not only the effectiveness of the fabrication but also its success in social terms, that is, the success of the post-play. Kurt concluded:

> It worked. Fortunately he got back at us a little bit by making us think that he was so ashamed of himself that he was out hiding somewhere and wouldn't even go home; when the whole time he was sitting at home; and we were all feeling progressively more guilty about doing this. I was pleased with it on the whole.
>
> So to send the poor guy all the way out to the airport—it's probably a fifteen-minute drive out there—to send somebody on a wild goose chase like that and then to be for nothing; I mean, if you can play a joke on a guy in the newsroom, that's one thing, but to send him driving all over the place, I began thinking perhaps we had overdone it a little bit. So when he got back at us by raising our guilt factor considerably, I felt he was entitled to that. (Van der Dussen 1987)

To achieve a joke that is successful as well as effective, jokers must choose the right target. Efficacy requires an accurate prediction of the targets' response when contained, but success depends on knowing how they will react after their containment is discredited. If the goal of the post-play is to have targets join in the play, jokers must take care to keep the fabrication within the bounds of what that person can handle. (I stress *if* because some jokes are not intended to have their targets laugh along.) When the post-play does not go according to plan, even though the central script went off perfectly, the joke is said to have backfired. Brian's post-play was a fabricated backfire.

Kurt's comments about the post-play have a moralistic tone and return us to the observation that practical jokes require justification. He welcomed Brian's post-play, once it was revealed as fabrication itself, because it showed that although embarrassed, he was not so overcome that he could not respond in a spirit of play. However, the post-play also raised moral questions about the joke—perhaps indeed the jokers had gone "too far." Accordingly, Kurt found it "fortunate" that Brian had succeeded in getting back at them because he was "entitled" to inflict some discomfort on those who had discomforted him. Just as Kurt introduces the drug bust joke with the justification that Brian had been playing jokes on others and so needed to be put in his place, the tricksters who ensured that Brian got his deserts deserved to "get theirs" in turn.

4

Lies, Damned Lies, and Legends

THERE IS A CLOSE RELATIONSHIP BETWEEN PRACTICAL JOKING and legend. Both genres involve construction of truth claims: the practical joke is based on differential knowledge, whereas the legend is based on differential belief. The practical joke provokes its targets to say or do something that displays an erroneous belief[1] that is belied by the knowledge of the jokers. Similarly, legends make listeners and proponents state and debate their beliefs. "Telling a legend is the time to confess," according to Dégh and Vázsonyi. "To confess, to ascertain, to argue for or against, to assert or refute: this is the time of dispute. The dispute takes place on different levels and on different fronts in which the legend teller discusses his belief with himself, but mostly with a real or imaginary incredulous audience" (1973, 5). The legend process is always a debate because the genre is inherently based on the real or purported existence of differential belief. The legend assumes that someone, somewhere believed the claims it makes are true (Dégh and Vázsonyi 1976, 119), but it also assumes that someone, somewhere either doubts or does not believe the same claim (Oring 1990, 164).

Some legends seem to have been designed from the beginning as jokes. Take the fabulous, legendary snipe. In the Berkeley Folklore Archives I found the following typical description, which was used on family camping trips in northern California around 1980:

> Snipes are little animals the size of guinea pigs that are furry and cute. They run fast, hop, and jump around near the lake at night. They are nocturnal, so they only come out at night and they go by the lake to drink water. Snipes are able to jump high enough that they can "fly" a couple of feet above ground, similar to flying fish in the ocean. Most snipes are gray, but some are brown.
>
> Snipes are attracted to the noise of sticks banging against paper bags, so to catch one you walk around near the lake at night banging a stick inside a paper bag. (Salter 1998)

DOI: 10.7330/9780874219845.c004

According to twentieth-century American folklore, as recorded in the hold-ings in the Berkeley Folklore Archives, science does not agree whether the snipe is a bird, a mammal, a fish, or an insect. Descriptions range from the plain ("A bird that chirps, 'Snipe'") to the fabulous:

- something that looks like a cross between a jackrabbit and a squirrel
- a bird that looks something like a squirrel, with one red and one green eye
- a little black bird-like creature with furry feathers; it only comes out at night when there is a full moon
- a creature about the size of a squirrel, with six legs, scales, wings, and ears like a rabbit
- "You'll know one when you see one"

The imagination and verbal artistry in these descriptions signal the play frame. Other fabulous creatures of North American comic legend are described in similarly creative ways, and many rejoice in names that sound like jokes: guyuscutus, hodag, jackalope, side hill galute, sidehill gouger, whiffenpoof, or wiffenpoofendorf (Dorson 1982, 1–7; Taft 1983, 390; Smyly 1970). For those who have heard them before, these accounts are performances to be appreciated for their comical names, artful accumulation of detail, and other verbal artistry. Comic legends about fabulous fauna resemble tall tales—cre-ative untruths that have been aestheticized and elevated to the level of perfor-mance. The tall tale is a particularly elaborate version of the put-on, designed to elicit then increasingly challenge the belief of the listener. "At some point in their telling, tall tales begin to challenge the belief of the hearer as they transcend the bounds of credibility and shift into the hyperbole central to the genre," according to Richard Bauman. "They move the hearer from a sense that 'this is true' to a stage of wondering 'is this true?' to the conclusion 'this is not true'" (2004, 98). The difference between a tall tale and a more everyday put-on is the degree of hyperbole that characterizes the former, and the fact that listeners are not persuaded to act on their mistaken beliefs.

What puts comic legends into practical joke territory is that they are told as true to the uninitiated. If it stops there, we have a put-on or possibly a tall tale, in which nothing is demanded of the listener besides belief. The details that entertain the initiated only enhance veracity for the greenhorns. Instead of verbal art, they see only empirical accuracy. However, the creative portrayal of the snipe or its kin is often a setup for a *snipe hunt* (motif J 2349.6*), a fool's errand type of practical joke attested in the United States since at least 1847 (Smith 1957). Having laid the groundwork with accounts of the creature and its habits, jokers lead the dupes into the woods at night and leave them there, armed with sacks and other implements, promising to beat the bushes to drive the prey toward them. The jokers return to camp, leaving their targets alone in the dark woods—and in the dark epistemologically—until they either give up or figure out their error (Ellis 1981; Salter 1998; Posen 1974). When similar comic legends are enacted as practical jokes in other parts of the world, the identity and description of the mythical prey differs while the structure of the fabrication is unchanged from North American versions (Chartois 1945).

The snipe hunt is a potentially open-ended fabrication. Instead of a definitive discrediting, jokers leave targets to figure out for themselves that they have been contained. Targets are likely to follow the same progression from credulity through uncertainty to disbelief that the hearers of the tall tale do. Further, their physical location replicates on the physical plane what is happening on the epistemological plane (Dundes 1989). Left alone literally "holding the bag," targets are in the dark both literally and figuratively. For some, light dawns as they figure out they have been had and make their way back to the rest of the group. Those who simply give up may be let in on the joke upon their return, but still others never find out the truth. Donald Cox recalled a case from his childhood in the early 1940s in Clawson, Utah, where newcomers were regularly persuaded to go out hunting for side hill galutes:

> There was a Bush kid who came to help Calvin Jensen and he was twelve or thirteen years old . . . We would set him out there on the hill with a gunnysack and a stick and we'd tell him that these side hill galutes couldn't get away from him cause they could only run around the hill one way, because of the short leg on one side and the long leg on the other side. So we'd walk off in the dark, of course, and go on home, and he'd sit there from the time we left him until almost daybreak and then go home. Now he was working for Calvin Jensen and Calvin would get him up about six o'clock in the morning because he was paying him fifty cents a day and he wanted to get his money's worth out of him . . . He told my Dad, "Ya know, that Bush kid's not worth a darn, he's sleepy all the time." We did that to him day after day, and he never did catch on! (Hussey 1996)

Mr. Cox did not explain why he and his friends chose to treat "that Bush kid" this way, whether he was an outsider, a newcomer to the community, or simply someone whom they wanted to pick on. By never revealing the secret to him, they effectively kept him in the status of an outsider, drawing a symbolic boundary between themselves and him.

The comic legend is at best a pseudo-legend, based on containment of some to the amusement of others. Stories about snipe and jackalopes are not true legends unless the joking frame remains hidden or ambiguous, thus providing the motive for debates about the truth of the account. Sometimes the lie escapes from the boundaries of the joke, and targets go their whole lives believing in the existence of snipe. In the early nineteenth century John James Audubon fed fellow naturalist Constantine Rafinesque stories of the nonexistent Devil Jack Diamond fish. The scales of this fish, he said, were shaped like cut diamonds and hard enough to repel rifle bullets; when dried, they could strike fire from steel. None the wiser, Rafinesque included a serious account of this creature in his treatise on the fishes of the Ohio River, giving it the scientific name *Litholepis adamantinus*, and other travelers repeated his report (Audubon 1831, 455–460; Boatright 1971, 74; Rafinesque 1899, 140–141).

A common setting for a snipe hunt is a camping trip, a time when urban or suburban dwellers venture into the wild, or at least the outdoors. The novelty of this setting is part of the fun for campers, but it is also a situation where they may expect to encounter the unknown, creating a mixture of fascination and awe that makes them willing and credulous audiences for tall tales and legends. Urban campers replicate in a small way the experience that European frontiersmen, travelers, and colonists had in the New World. To enter a new world is to enter a new domain of knowledge that challenges standards of truth and absurdity, making it difficult to preserve distinctions between completely fictitious tales, exaggerated descriptions, and amazing but true stories. Practical jokes and legends alike flourish on such epistemological frontiers.

The joke, in contrast to the legend, assumes that certainty is possible. The open-ended trick might transform the pseudo-legend into the real thing, but most practical jokes are based on the idea that the truth is known. When the fabricated snipe is discredited, targets rarely if ever dispute the reality that jokers have unveiled. Jokers view their targets' experience as a progress from error to enlightenment, from falsehood to truth. Their amusement stems from the incongruity between their knowledge and the dupe's error, because they know that of course there are no such things as snipe. But truth is relative, and the truth about snipe is constructed locally and socially. If they consulted their dictionaries, many snipe boosters would be surprised to learn that snipe do exist—they are a small, undistinguished species of North American waterfowl.[2] However, the scientifically endorsed ornithological truth has no impact on the effectiveness of the joke. The practical joke depends not on a difference between truth and error but simply on differential beliefs, one sanctioned by the local group represented by the jokers, and another that they invent and then discredit. The truth into which targets are brought at the close of the joke is the local version, the one accepted by the majority.

TRUTH STRANGER THAN FICTION

Since Rafinesque was in the "New" World, he fully expected to encounter things that were strange and incongruous; indeed, it is likely that the chance of such encounters was exactly what motivated his visit. In such a setting, he was primed to believe in the reality of the Devil Jack Diamond fish, and his desire to discover just such novel fauna would have made him more inclined to believe Audubon's fabrication. Novelties and anomalies are more likely to be greeted with skepticism when they appear in the midst of the familiar, everyday world. When the first platypus skins were sent from Australia to British museums, naturalists dismissed them as an obvious hoax. A fur-bearing, warm-blooded, and egg-laying creature, the platypus was a paradox: was it a bird? a reptile? a mammal? Confronted with a puzzle that confounded their classification systems, naturalists found a solution by positing a taxidermist's hoax, similar to the fake "mermaids" that mariners had long manufactured to fool the unwary (Hall 1999; Ritvo 1997).

Similarly, when extraordinary things happen, it is not uncommon for people to think that they might be practical jokes. A gas station clerk held up in an armed robbery thinks at first it is a practical joke: "When two men burst into the BP Dundee service station in Invercargill on Saturday night, forecourt attendant Willie Fraser thought it was his prankster workmates playing a practical joke" (Southland Times 1998). Another example:

> Doctors may be expensive, but a $3.7 million medical bill for a blow to the head is enough to give anyone a headache.
> Auckland chef Mark Redknap (27) could not believe his eyes when he got a bill from a debt collection agency for $3.7m.
> Southern Cross had asked College Credit Management to collect $34 from Redknap for treatment for concussion from an indoor soccer game.
> But a typing error saw the $34 turn into a bill for $3.7m.
> "I thought it was a practical joke," Redknap says. (Tyler 1996)

When the extraordinary enters the everyday, people seek explanations. Armed holdups are relatively rare in New Zealand, so one way to discount the danger is to conclude that what is happening is not real. In fact, the "I thought it was a practical joke" response by people innocently caught up in such events is a way of stressing how extraordinary and frightening the events were. A $37 million bill for a simple medical procedure is incongruous and unexpected. Mr. Redknap could not believe it. The amount deviated from his expectations of how interest accumulates, so he looked for another category in which to place the letter. The practical joke category was relevant because absurdities like these are to be expected in play.

Sometimes everyday events take on the features of a *Monty Python* script. This was the experience of a New Zealand couple living in the Auckland suburb of Greenhithe:

> Lisa and Tim Nickel were painting the outside of their partly built Greenhithe home on Sunday afternoon when their work was cut short.
>
> A security guard walked on to their property and handed them a North Shore City Council notice ordering them to stop making excessive noise for 72 hours. To their dismay, they were told someone had complained.
>
> The couple, who were being helped by Mrs Nickel's father, were hand-painting. They had no machinery going and no radio on . . . The couple thought someone was playing a practical joke on them, especially when the security guard asked them to stir the paint quietly. (Thomson 2002)

"Truth is stranger than fiction," the saying goes, yet we don't believe it. The very fact that we need a proverb to remind us of this suggests that in our day-to-day thinking, we expect reality and truth to be familiar, not strange. By explaining strange phenomena and extraordinary events as fabrications we preserve the illusion that *somebody* is in control, even if we are not.

Susan Stewart suggests that nonsense, including its varieties of disorder and absurdity, "gives us a place to store any mysterious gaps in our systems of order" (1978, 5). Practical jokes are manufactured nonsense. To admit that platypuses simply don't fit, or that ordinances against noisy paint are simply nonsense, is to give up on our capacities to categorize the universe. Explaining the unexplained as a fabrication avoids that resignation because it preserves the idea that someone, somewhere, is in control. If the incongruities before us are fabrications, they are not real and therefore no further explanation or modification to our expectations are necessary.

Given this proclivity to suspect fabrication, practical jokers must design their creations to avoid obvious absurdities. However, jokers also include absurdities in jokes as built-in play signals and discrediting cues. A popular compound practical joke is ordering pizzas by phone to be delivered to an unwitting target. Many pizza delivery businesses get two to three such orders every day, so employees are on the alert for bogus orders. "We've had our share of people ordering pizzas for nonexistent people or for people they don't like," one told me. "Weird-sounding orders are suspect." "Hold the anchovies" is a frequent stock phrase in the American popular press whenever the pizza business is being talked about (Wiley 1999). The perception is that the little salty fish are not a popular choice on pizzas in this country (although they may be more in favor in other countries) ("Eat It: Anchovies" 2008). Accordingly, pizza company workers recognize that orders with anchovies are unusual, and therefore suspicious. More than once I was told, "If the order is fake, they order anchovies."

This observation may be another example of the tendency to explain anomalies as fabrications. However, it is possible that practical jokers who phone in bogus orders do include the anchovies, even though this choice might tend to discredit the trick and cause the fabrication to fail. Some absurdity is necessary to ensure that the fabrication stays within the realm of play. If the absurd anchovies are present, the implied argument is that the targets should have recognized the trick; if they do not, the fault lies with them. While I do not have direct experience of people who phone in bogus pizza orders, this suggestion is based on observations from many other practical jokes.

THE SOCIAL CONSTRUCTION OF ABSURDITY

The joker's task is to create a fabrication that is obviously untrue—that is, "absurd"—but that does not obviously appear to be untrue. Specifically, this feat is achieved by means of untruths that are obvious absurdities to insiders but are beyond the knowledge of the targets. A common frame of knowledge among the jokers and the audiences is assumed, as is a lack of common knowledge with the target population. Any esoteric knowledge is ripe for playful exploitation. Take statistical jargon, for example. Some faculty in the political science department at Florida State University once fooled some of their colleagues by announcing a lecture by a fictitious job candidate:

> So-and-so from the University of New Mexico is coming in, will do an "Analysis of Most Cubes of Warfare over the History of Mankind" or something. "Most cube analysis," which is an absurd notion, technically it's a pun itself, which nobody in the department would get . . .
>
> Then it turned out that two faculty members showed up for the nonexistent colloquium and sat in an empty room for ten minutes before they figured out that something was wrong . . . That one worked. That one was a lot of fun. (Anonymous 1986)

As the joker explained to me, those "who knew their statistics" would have seen through this fabrication, because the expression "most cubes analysis" is meaningless. "But to a person who didn't know any statistics," he explained, "it sounded like statistical jargon . . . 'Least squares' is the expression; it is very, very common throughout the social sciences, least squares analysis. Everyday kind of thing. But the sciences are split right down the middle so half would never get the joke, and the other half would. They'd know it was ludicrous" (Anonymous 1986).

This open-ended fool's errand exploits the epistemological divide between quantitative and qualitative social scientists. The former, familiar with statistical methods, would know that "most cubes analysis" is a non-existent term and would recognize it as a play on the authentic technical phrase "least squares," both of which would qualify the fabricated lecture title as "absurd." To the uninitiated, however, "most cubes analysis" is no more nonsensical than "least squares analysis." Since my own knowledge of statistics is vanishingly small, when I first heard this story, I briefly wondered whether my informant—a political scientist—was not pulling my leg about the term. (He wasn't.) By these means, the jokers succeeded in creating a fabrication that was simultaneously absurd and not absurd.

Presumably, the colleagues who were fooled by the bogus title and showed up for the nonexistent lecture recognized that they did not really know what it meant but chose—probably not for the first time—to hide their ignorance and trust that their quantitative colleagues were making a bona fide contribution to the field even though they did not expect to understand the details. Fabrications are effective in part because people are generally ready to trust the word of others as to what is true and what is absurd. Much of our knowledge of the world comes not from direct experience but from what we accept from experts, authorities, friends, and colleagues.

LEGENDS AND LIES

Hoaxes, practical jokes, and humor make regular appearances in ongoing legend processes. It has been suggested that the defining characteristic of the legend genre is the performance of truth (Oring 2008), but the complete legend process also includes proponents of the various dimensions of untruth. As F. G. Bailey has pointed out, there are three kinds of untruth: "what we condemn (lies), what we regret (error), and what we may enjoy (fiction)" (1991, 10), and in vernacular discourse the three are frequently confused. A typical website listing the "Top 25 Web Hoaxes and Pranks" includes well-known urban legends, e-mail chain letters, and the Nigerian e-mail scam (Bass 2007). Similarly, the *Museum of Hoaxes* bills itself as a compilation of "Pranks, Stunts, Deceptions, and Other Wonderful Stories Contrived for the Public," thus mixing lies and fictions in the same pot. To add errors to the mix, the book begins with a "Gullibility Test" that invites readers to distinguish between popular errors ("Thomas Crapper invented the toilet") and what it designates as outlandish but true facts ("Turtles never die of old age") (Boese 2002, ix–xi). These popular works mix the three varieties of untruth together, whereby the lies of the hoaxer become the errors of the gullible, and all are served up framed as fictions, or possible fictions, for the entertainment of the reader.

In the legend debate, nonbelievers and skeptics might argue that the legend proposition is simply an error, but another common tactic is to assert that the proposition under debate is a lie or a hoax. "Hoax" is used for any fabrication that achieves wide circulation, especially if the source is unknown. Excepting the absence of a personal relationship between perpetrators and targets, benign hoaxes are structurally indistinguishable from any other practical joke, and they may take the forms of ether put-ons or fool's errands. This popular confusion of hoax and legend occurs because the first kind of untruth (lies and fabrications) is generally preferred to the second (error). Gullibility and ignorance are thought to be closely entwined, but gullibility is more readily limited and pinned on others because the concept assumes the deliberate actions of someone doing the gulling.

The corollary of calling legends hoaxes is that proponents are treated as fools or liars, which can cause offense and threaten to take the debate into a physical arena (Toelken 1996, 317–318). Despite the potential social fallout from this approach, the legend-hoax confusion reflects a desire for epistemological certainty, based on the belief that truth and untruth are, in theory, readily distinguishable. If the legend proponent's error is due to his or her containment in a fabrication, even if the source is unknown, then this assumption is left unscathed. What the legend proponent puts forward as unusual, anomalous, or incongruous, pushing the boundaries between the everyday and the unknown, the skeptic can safely return to the taken-for-granted everyday world where absurdities are obvious and constructed.

FOLK SKEPTICISM AND NEGATIVE LEGENDS

Practical jokes also enter ongoing legend processes directly when legends are enacted by pseudo-ostension, that is, when individuals enact a legend that they do not themselves believe in order to make fools of others who do (Dégh and Vázsonyi 1983, 19). Wherever differential knowledge or beliefs coexist, there is also fodder for practical jokers like Boyd Trask from Newfoundland:

> There were other mischief nights . . . when we played tricks on fellows who were scared to go home alone. I recall one such fellow. John thought he loved my cousin Mary; he had the habit of following her home nighttime. Really, he was a bit of a nuisance. He would stay down her way until after dark and then pretend that he saw her home. Yet coming home in the dark he was very much afraid. One night we decided to give him a bit of a scare. We made a very good substitute for a devil, worked it puppet fashion, and waited for him. This was on the north side; he had to go to the south side. We found two old cellars along the loneliest part of the road, one on either side. There we hid and waited.
>
> Soon John came whistling and singing. One could easily tell that he was scared stiff. The puppet was lying on the ground, and the moon was just beginning to rise. When he got within reasonable distance my friend and I began to manipulate the devilish-looking puppet. John made quite a rear [noise or yell]. "Lord Jesus, who are you? I never done notin' to you! I'm not afraid of ya!" etc. In the meantime he would be squaring off to the puppet, pretending he was going to hit it, and backing up when we maneuvered the puppet close to him.
>
> Finally, he got mad and decided to pass. As he did we almost succeeded in putting the puppet's arms around John's neck. He nearly fainted. In the scuffle he ended up on the right side of the puppet and started to run for home. We hauled the puppet to the side of the road and began to make all kinds of queer noises. John was in bed for a week attended by the doctor from Bonavista; he didn't bother to chase my cousin again. (Trask 1967, 4)[3]

The motive for this practical joke was twofold: to stop John from following cousin Mary home, and to make fun of him for being "scared to go home alone." His fear of the dark was both a means and a justification for his victimization. The joke is represented as having been very effective—John was so frightened, the narrator implies, that he was confined to bed and needed medical care. The post-play was also successful, in that he stopped his unwanted attentions to cousin Mary. The implication is that this change of heart was because of what happened to him that dark night, although precisely how he would have connected the two is left unexplained.

The legend proposition that is enacted in this trick is not spelled out but can be implied: that devils are real, and that they physically attack travelers on the road at night. From the point of view of the jokers, the discrepancy between John's fear and the harmlessness of a mere puppet was laughable.

Since they never let him in on the joke, they kept him in the status of an outsider, where they could mock his fear and the superstitious beliefs on which it was based. However, the jokers and their target shared a common frame of reference that included ideas about what made an object "devilish-looking."

Pseudo-ostensive legends in the form of practical jokes or hoaxes are not uncommon. Such tricks may index the presence of folk skepticism (Roper 2012), but this label must be applied with care. Mr. Trask wrote this account of his personal experience as part of an English paper that was deposited in the MUNFLA Folklore Archives in 1967. In the same paper, he described members of a local family "who were famous for telling tall tales and ghost stories, yet they were very afraid of ghosts themselves. They were especially afraid of queer noises heard after dark" (Trask 1967). "As boys, we used to play window tricks on them," Trask explained. He described their variant of the widespread game of "window tapping," in which children use homemade devices to make strange noises on the outside of windows from a distance (Opie and Opie 1959, 389–390; Story, Kirwin, and Widdowson 1990):

> When Mrs. Tilley heard the noise she would put up the blind, see nothing, and lower it again. After a few times, she would open the door. We would hear her say: "You cannot frighten me, I didn't hurtie. I never did notin' to you, I'm not afraid'v e." As soon as she went in we would repeat the trick. On one such occasion we kept it up until nearly daylight with the entire family staying up all night half scared to death. The next day Mrs. Tilley would tell a very ghostly story to her neighbors about what she heard and saw the night before. On one occasion the neighbors already knew that I was one of the culprits. (Trask 1967, 3)

It would be hasty to conclude from these stories that Boyd and his teenage friends did not themselves believe in devils or ghosts at all. Just as there are many varieties of belief, all mutable and fluctuating (Dégh and Vázsonyi 1976), so there are degrees and diversities of skepticism. Quite possibly, Mr. Trask and his fellow tricksters chose their targets not because they believed in otherworldly beings but because they believed in them *too much* or were excessively fearful of them.

The two practical jokes were negative legends, arising from the legend climate, based on the same frame of reference, and contributing to it. As such, they did not necessarily put a stop to the legend dialectic. Even if Mrs. Tilley and John learned that their spooky experiences were only teenage practical jokes, there is no guarantee that either one would have changed her or his overall beliefs as a result. There was no ghost or devil that time, but nothing in the enacted negative legend rules out the possibility of real supernatural attacks another time. Far from quashing the legend dialectic, some pseudo-ostensive negative legends simply add fuel to it. When two artists came forward in the early 1990s and confessed to having created dozens of "crop circles" in England and elsewhere as a hoax, the revelation was only incorporated into the ongoing legend (Dégh 2001, 320–321; see also Dégh and Vázsonyi 1973, 25–26).

Both practical jokes and legends are explorations of epistemological limits. The legend climate opposes received truths and its natural process is to provoke debate and raise questions: "Is the order of the world really as we learned to know it? . . . Do we know all the forces that regulate the universe and our life, or are there hidden dimensions that can divert the causal, rational flow of things?" (Dégh 2001, 2). In the living legend process, these questions do not admit of easy answers. In contrast, practical jokes promise epistemological certainty, positing a clear distinction between truth/reality and untruth/absurdity, and mocking those who confuse them. Only a close look will show that jokes also undermine this promise, regularly creating untruths, or fabricating truths that are, for short time, truth.

The comic "appears within everyday life, momentarily transforms the latter, then quickly disappears again" (Berger 1997, 11). The verbal joke is an alternative to reality that is briefly inserted into reality, a finite, bounded domain within which we may experience incongruity, absurdity, even chaos, in an enjoyable way (Fry 1992, 230–231). Whereas the legend process is an attempt to grapple with these domains and understand them, jokes tame them so that they may be safely enjoyed for their own sake. Jokes achieve this realm of safety by means of extensive framing devices.

A practical joke may be the most dangerous species of the comic because its frames are deliberately kept ambiguous and fluid. Participants and observers alike are forcibly reminded not only that joking boundaries and play frames are there, but also that these boundaries are themselves human constructions, as revealed by the relative ease with which jokers can hide or reveal them. To play practical jokes, then, is to do humor without a safety net.

NOTES

1. Once knowledge is defined as erroneous, it instantly resolves into "belief."

2. At least one practical joker recorded in the Berkeley Folklore Archives described the mythical snipe exactly like the real snipe: "a black and white bird, like a sandpiper." If this description was used like the others to fool the uninitiated, it was doubly a fabrication.

3. The names in this story have been changed.

5

The (Im)morality of the Practical Joke

A DRINKING PROBLEM

Bᴇʀɴɪᴇ ᴀɴᴅ ʜɪs ꜰᴇʟʟᴏᴡ ᴡᴀʀᴇʜᴏᴜsᴇ ᴡᴏʀᴋᴇʀs had a problem. It concerned one of their coworkers, Perry.

> I'll tell you a really good practical joke. Like one time there was this guy, he was actually the nephew of Rocky Marciano [the prizefighter], his name was Perry Marciano. And, he was kind of, kind of a built guy—not really athletic, but kind of a stocky guy. He'd eat anything—anything in sight. So we'd all have lunch, and you know, we'd have lunch and he'd scarf down whatever he'd brought and after everybody's done he'd be, "You done with that? You done with that? You done with that? You got any extra . . ." or whatever.
>
> So he had this habit of um, he'd take, like we'd get sodas in the summertime, and it'd be super hot, and this would be inside the warehouse [where we worked] at night, pulling candy orders, and he'd like drink out of somebody's soda. You know, try to like, down half of it when they weren't looking. And the other guys would always catch him and he'd think they weren't looking.
>
> So we took a soda, poured it in a glass, so the can was still cold, and filled it up with castor oil. And so we went over there and two of us were watching him where he couldn't see us watching him and he's looking around a little bit, and he picks up the can and he just like, chugs it and tries to get half of it down. And then, proceeds to puke in a box. (Maxwell 1994)

Like most practical joke narratives, Bernie's story begins with an orientation that describes the target of the joke in some detail. More to the point, he describes Perry's bad habits of begging for food and stealing drinks, thus providing both the means and the motive for the trickery.

Many people would find such a trick both cruel and distasteful. Yet although the impact on the victim was extremely unpleasant, the student who recorded Bernie's story for the Berkeley Folklore Archives excused the

DOI: 10.7330/9780874219845.c005

cruelty because Perry "had it coming." "Practical jokes can seem kind of mean if they are directed at the innocent," he commented, "but when you get someone with a practical joke when they are doing something wrong, which actually causes the planned result of the joke, it has an especially delicious result." The deliciousness lies especially in the sense of poetic justice, which makes the target the victim not so much of a practical joke as of his own bad habits and weaknesses. The implication is that since it was Perry's own misbehavior that made the trick work, responsibility for the outcome fell on him.

The student's comment expresses the folk morality of the practical joke in a nutshell. In the first place, the target is thought to have deserved this rough treatment for his petty theft. He suffered a minor punishment for a minor crime. Second, he had only himself to blame—if he had stuck to drinking from his own soda can, he never would have fallen into the trap. The joke is a little morality play (Basso 1979, 76) in which wrongdoing is punished and group norms triumph, all in a framed and highlighted setting that draws special attention and can be replayed later for both enjoyment and instruction.

Bernie never tells us who thought up the idea of replacing the soda to trick the wrongdoer, and he never identifies the joker (which might have been him). Instead he says, "*We* took a soda . . ." and "*The guys* at the warehouse figured they'd settle the score." In his story, the entire group is united and jointly responsible for giving the wrongdoer what he deserves. The practical joker serves as the agent of group morality, providing vicarious satisfaction for everyone who is in on the joke. We cannot be certain that Perry got the message, but Bernie and the others certainly did. Most likely stories about this and other jokes on the hapless soda snitcher became part of their joking culture (Fine and De Soucey 2005), and retelling them allowed the jokers to enjoy the pleasure of imagining poetic justice at work again and again.

Most people have probably had to cope with coworkers like Perry who have irritating personal habits. Although constantly begging for food and sneaking drinks out of other people's sodas are minor infractions of the social code, they are still difficult to deal with. The issues are not significant enough to lay a formal complaint, and many would be loath to confront the miscreant directly. Both actions would threaten the veneer of harmonious social interaction that small groups prefer whenever possible (Fine and De Soucey 2005, 9, 17). Yet, it is frustrating to silently put up with these constant irritations.

A tailored practical joke offers a way out of this social dilemma. If we cannot correct the miscreant, we can at least enjoy the feeling of manipulating him. When people feel powerless either to escape or to change the minor offenders in their midst, the practical joke makes the situation more palatable by reframing it as a humorous script. The trickster tailors his fabrication to exploit the target's annoying habits, in the hope that the target will behave true to type. If the joke works, the greedy soda thief acts just like a greedy soda thief, but the joke frame makes this annoyance just a part of the joker's script—something that can be turned off and on at will. Irritating behavior becomes just a bit of playacting that we can laugh at.

TEACHING THEM A LESSON

The castor oil in place of soda trick was not the first time Bernie and his coworkers had targeted Perry the scrounger. Another time, they liberally dosed a soda with laxative and waited for him to sneak a drink from it, with predictable results. Bernie concludes this story by saying, "We kinda cured ol' Perry of his scrounging habit" (Maxwell 1994). The idea that a practical joke is meant to teach the target a lesson and send him or her a message from the group is widespread. In fact, it is almost taken for granted that any practical joke must have been tailored to send a subtle message of social sanction. This expectation is so widespread that it is subject to playful reversal itself, as in the following story from a British university department:

> What they [department colleagues] did was to send the colleague a series of defunct clocks through the internal post using old preused envelopes and boxes that had random original departmental addresses and putting them into the out-trays of other departments randomly. It had no meaning. They had no grudge against him nor wished to do anything other than baffle him and in time amuse him. He was well liked and respected and an extrovert who went in for self-mockery. He tried to find out who was sending them and failed.
>
> He also tried to see a meaning in it, such as "Your time is up." The clocks were of no distinction or value, just cheap clocks that his colleagues had round the house that no longer worked. When these ran out they got some from a charity shop . . .
>
> It was not malicious. Rather it was because he could be guaranteed to talk about it. If he had been a quiet introvert and just kept it all to himself there would have been no amusement, but he would come in to the coffee room and say laughingly, "I got another bloody clock today. Who is doing it? What does it mean?" (anonymous personal communication, December 30, 2007)

This example of a metapractical joke took place in the archaeology department of Reading University. The joke had no connection to any particular habit of the target, but it caused him to spend a lot of time trying to determine what the intended message could be. His colleagues created this unsolvable puzzle for him by playing upon the belief that every practical joke must have a point. Erving Goffman describes *corrective hoaxing* as a separate category of benign fabrications, usually with a public audience and "often with the object of making a moral point" (1974, 90–91). However, making a moral point is by no means confined to public hoaxes but is clearly a characteristic of almost all practical jokes.

What is less clear is who gets the point. In Bernie's story, the implication is that the scrounger mended his ways after realizing that he had been targeted with a joke and figuring out that the jokers were sending him a message that they disapproved of his behavior. However, Bernie hedges this suggestion when he says "We *kinda* cured" him. Social groups must find ways to regulate the behavior of their members, but direct social control is costly in social terms. Joking provides an excellent vehicle for communicating messages of social sanction indirectly (Emerson 1969; Fine and De Soucey 2005). People turn to practical jokes and other forms of humorous communication because these genres offer deniability to both message senders and message recipients. If the joke targets get the point, this revelation happens privately, so the message was sent and received without anyone having to acknowledge it.

Practical jokes teach lessons to a variety of audiences, but the joke targets are only one such audience. Since the examples considered here are all open-ended fabrications, it is impossible to be certain whether the targets even realized they had been fooled, let alone were led to see the error of their ways. Nevertheless, all the jokes were completely successful because they conveyed enjoyable lessons to the bystander audiences and to other group members who heard the stories. Both the original jokes and the narratives depicted the punishment of one who had repeatedly transgressed group norms, thus reaffirming those norms for the audience while also affording the pleasure of watching poetic justice unfold.

WRONGDOING CAN BE FUNNY

Part of the appeal of practical jokes and stories about them is that they satisfy our thirst for poetic justice on small-time wrongdoers. Time and again, they are aimed at people guilty of inappropriate or mildly illegal behavior. Drinking unlawfully after hours provides another example. The following reminiscence comes from the West Coast in New Zealand, an area once well known for its amiable disregard of licensing laws. When the police staged a raid, customers simply ran out the back door. Joyce Beumelburg, who grew up in the 1930s next to a pub called the Aussie, remembers watching people scurry away at night when the police came knocking:

> As children in the thirties we often saw scattered figures racing down from the Aussie, through our front gate after dark, and shooting up the hill to hide in the long grass or clamber up a tall tree growing on the lawn in an endeavour to escape the law. We thought it was most entertaining and would never dream of splitting on them. Sometimes though, my father, who had a madcap sense of fun, would drape himself in a policeman's cape acquired from somewhere and scare the living daylights out of after-hours drinkers and the publican of the Aussie by knocking imperiously on the side door, later telling us with glee about the resulting scramble. (Sullivan 1999, 37–39)

The sight of these miscreants running from the law gave the children pleasure as they compared their own safe position to the other people's alarm. To these onlookers, the pain suffered by the dupes was slight, and in any case they deserved it. The punishment fit the crime. To scoff at licensing laws was only a minor infraction, and the justice meted out by the practical joker was a passing discomfort only. Since the violation was minor, and the punishment of the offenders was on the same scale, the scene aroused amusement rather than outrage.

While West Coasters would not dream of turning the scofflaws in to the police, they were not above tormenting them a little with a practical joke. We may sympathize with the victims, but on the other hand, they were breaking the law. A practical joke acquires the character of poetic justice when the victims bring about their own victimization. The after-hours drinkers knew they were breaking the law, and presumably felt a modicum of guilt and apprehension at the possibility of getting caught. The trickster simply exploited those feelings. The wrongdoers effectively punished themselves because their apprehension encouraged them to mistake a man in a cape for the police and subject themselves to panic and fright—to poetic justice, in other words.

After-hours drinking was an appropriate target for a practical joke because on the West Coast the whole topic was inherently comic. Even before their father played his trick, Joyce and her siblings found the sight of the offenders running from the law entertaining, not shocking. Similarly, New Zealand has numerous jokes and funny stories about West Coast pubs

(Brednich 2003, 150–153; McNeish 1984, 201, 215, 219, 225). Humor theory offers some ideas as to why these jokes exist. For example, Mary Douglas suggested that a joke in the social situation inevitably calls for a joke to reflect it in the expressive domain (1975). I think that there is a joke in the social situation any time an absurdity or incongruity exists, whether in the social, cognitive, or emotional domain. For New Zealanders, and especially West Coasters, the incongruity lay in their ambivalent feelings about after-hours drinking. On one hand, people believed that the law should be respected in general, but at the same time they recognized that some laws are asinine. (At the time, New Zealand licensing laws mandated that all bars close at six p.m. daily.) Respect for the rule of law was countered by a love of beer and by the demands of local solidarity against the intrusions of the distant state, and for many people these conflicting feelings existed virtually simultaneously.

PLAYING ON WEAKNESS

Part of the practical joker's art lies in tailoring fabrications to exploit the specific habits, foibles, and personalities of the targets. The closer the fit, the better the joke. The following example is told by a professor who was in charge of a data lab staffed by graduate students:

> One of the things about the graduate student [Douglas] who pulled this joke is he's always hitting on undergraduates. We've tried to stop it, given him lectures and all that, but that's been the tendency in the past.
>
> He had a note left in his office, when he was supposed to have been there. He wasn't. During his office hours. And it was in what looked like a woman's handwriting, and it was filthy. "Sorry I missed you, I had wanted to blankety blankety blank." All kinds of sexual stuff, very, very explicit, written throughout it. "I only wish I had the courage to come and face you again; it took all I could today; I'm sorry I missed you. Yours forever."
>
> And so there was this picture of this woman who was mad to do all kinds of mad passionate love with Douglas. Probably a student but it wasn't absolutely clear from the note. And was probably afraid to ever get her courage up again.
>
> He was going crazy. Had anybody seen her? Who was it?
>
> He was ragging everybody in the department about this thing. He just wouldn't stop. And finally somebody said they probably don't exist. Finally he was probably thinking this was a practical joke, [and] who would do that.

As is often the case with tailored practical jokes, this fabrication was never unambiguously revealed to the target. "So what did Doug think when he realized?" I asked.

> He never knew. He doesn't know yet. Last time we talked about it, nobody was sure that it was a practical joke. It could have been real. But it was so ludicrous, so out of character for anything [at this university] . . . Most of us, once you decide it was probably a practical joke and say yeah, of course. But Douglas wants this to be true so much [*laughs*]; it really played on his weakness.
>
> So that was a good one. I like that. (Anonymous 1986)

The narrator in this case was part of the bystander audience, and he begins the story by describing the habitual infractions exploited by the unknown joker. He rates the joke highly ("that was a good one") because it "played on" a specific weakness of the target—in this case, his habit of inappropriately propositioning undergraduates. Direct sanctions ("we'd given him lectures and all that" had failed to change his behavior, making it ripe for treatment in a practical joke. The point was not to change his behavior—indeed, in this case it is uncertain that he ever realized he had been contained—but to dramatize it for the rest of the group. The joke tells a story that is satisfying and repeatable because of the way it displays bad behavior being punished. The moral of the story apparently never reached the person who needed it most, but it was there for the rest of the group. My anonymous informant related the story with pleasure. Retelling the story lets him laugh at Douglas all over again, and also lets him affirm his moral stance toward the subject of the joke.

Effective practical jokes transform their targets into caricatures of themselves. These enacted caricatures are not flattering; they throw a spotlight on weaknesses, not strengths. The target's flaws provide not only the means and the subject of the joke but also the excuse. The point of the story about Douglas is that his flawed personality made him easy prey for a note that was "ludicrous," something that "most of us" would see through. This enactment of his personality is considered authentic and accurate because he did not realize he was in the spotlight.

According to the logic of the practical joke, targets are not acting but simply being themselves, unwittingly putting their personal flaws on display for others to mock. Human behavior is influenced by both the external environment and internal motives that stem from an individual's personality and character. Normally, it is not easy to disentangle the relative importance of external and internal influences, but the practical joke simplifies things by substituting a bogus external stimulus for a part of the real environment.

This move removes the effect of the environment from the equation, leaving just pure personality at work. The logic of the practical joke thus asserts that when targets are taken in and respond to fake stimuli, they show themselves as they really are.

Beyond the specific weakness of the joke target, tailored practical jokes embody another criticism about the gap between the way targets view themselves and the way others see them. Plato argued that such self-ignorance is the essence of the ridiculous and that we laugh at those who consider themselves better, smarter, or stronger than we know them to be (Morreall 1983, 4; 1987, 10). Douglas was laughable and thus deserving of being a target not just because of a personal failing but because he was ignorant of this aspect of his own character. According to the narrator, this self-ignorance was the reason he never spotted the joke, but this did not spoil the teller's estimation of the joke in the least.

Plato's theory focused on idiosyncratic forms of self-ignorance, but the practical joke points to a fundamental self-deception common to all—the fond belief that we are active agents in our own lives. Practical joke targets believe that they are in control of their actions, but the joker's circle knows differently—they see not active agents but hapless targets being manipulated and following a script devised by others. A common metaphor for the person who is taken in by a fabrication compares them to a fish on a line; the phrase is some variation on "They swallowed it hook, line, and sinker." Practical jokes replace agency with scripted behavior, and the fact that joke targets regularly fail to notice this switch makes them ridiculous and throws the whole notion of agency into doubt.

SPEAKING PIE TO POWER

"Speaking Pie to Power" was the motto of the Biotic Baking Brigade (BBB), a loose-knit political activist movement dedicated to playful attacks on world leaders and celebrities by means of cream pies. At their height in the late 1990s, the group "pied" CEOs, public figures, and elected officials, with targets ranging from Microsoft founder Bill Gates to the king of Sweden. These stunts were intended to attract media attention so the pranksters could explain which corporate crime had motivated this "just dessert." Bill Gates was a target because his company sells millions of products that are environmentally harmful; Milton Friedman was pied for the influence of his "fascist" free market economic theories, and so on. The Biotic Baking Brigade and its imitators around the world used public pranks to draw attention to their political messages.

Public pieing is a ludic attack on authority, a highly visible ritual reversal of the normal distribution of power. As one blogger explains, "The VIP covered in cream, spluttering and sticky, briefly out of control, is suddenly no longer any different from us. He is removed from the rarified air of beings who matter more than we do and becomes human again . . . just another schlub with pie on his face" (hyperbolic pants explosion 2006). The cover of the BBB's book *Pie Any Means Necessary* exemplifies this ritual reversal (Biotic Baking Brigade 2004). It shows a well-dressed man in the act of being pied. With his face obscured by the contents of a custard pie, his celebrity status is temporarily obliterated, rendering him "just another schlub with pie on his face." This phrase recalls "to have egg on one's face," the vernacular expression for being embarrassed or being caught in error or wrongdoing, which is precisely what the public pieing of a VIP is intended to do—call public attention to corporate crimes. The prank briefly breaks through the control wielded by the powerful over their public image. The pranksters, represented on the book cover by an anonymous arm clad in a proletarian brown suede jacket, enjoy a moment of victory over their political opponents, and millions of similarly disempowered audiences share in it.

It is not uncommon to target those in authority with practical jokes, but these subversions of power relations are usually either anonymous and/or open-ended, or confined to occasions that confer traditionally sanctioned license. Traditionally, Carnival in Europe was a time when satire of public figures was expected and tolerated to some degree. Similarly, Halloween conveys traditional license on youth to play tricks on the adults who normally wield power over them, while April Fools' Day offers a similar license to children (Leary 1979; Opie and Opie 1959, 244–245; Santino 1994; Tuleja 1994). In the workplace, practical jokers who challenge the hierarchy serve as trickster-heroes for fellow workers, and their exploits become the stuff of the local joking culture, providing feelings of vicarious triumph for other workers (Santino 1978, 169). The humor culture specific to each workplace determines how much subversive humor occurs, but open practical joking across status lines is found only when the status differential between boss and subordinate is relatively low (Santino 1986).

Public pieings are public, closed fabrications—their targets are fully aware of having been targeted—and these stunts lack the protection of any traditionally sanctioned license. Accordingly, the Biotic Baking Brigade carefully aestheticizes its activities by means of puns, humor, and careful attention to pie recipes. The choice of this particular form of ritual degradation is no accident. Pieing is technically battery, but it is also a staple of slapstick comedy appropriated for another domain. The BBB's rhetoric is peppered with puns: "Rules of Crumb," "Cream and Punishment," "Operation Dessert Storm," "Let Slip the Pies of War" (Biotic Baking Brigade 2004). These corny jokes provide ludic cover for the group's activities without completely masking its aggressive motives. Borrowing Gregory Bateson's felicitous formulation, the BBB's playful nip clearly denotes a bite, and it might also denote what the bite denotes (1972, 180). This is play with a bite to it.

According to the BBB, most targets do not treat their pieing as joke. Three of the group's members went to prison in 1999 after being convicted of battery for targeting San Francisco mayor Willie Brown. The mayor was technically right, but in the court of public opinion he was morally wrong. The anger and protests of the VIPs with pie on their faces become a second joke that shows them in their true colors. Angry responses are interpreted by pranksters and their sympathizers as inelasticity, humorlessness, a crucial inability to see oneself as others do. The last quality is referenced by the adjective "pompous," often applied to the targets of pieing, and indeed to any practical joke targets who are in positions of power. Pomposity is self-ignorance, a trait that is humorous in itself but that also calls for ridicule and correction by means of a prank. When targets still cannot see themselves objectively after their pieing, the pranksters are vindicated. They claimed that their targets are pompous, and the aftermath shows this pomposity in action.

The playful tactics of the Biotic Baking Brigade fall into the category that I have labeled stunts—public, unilateral play events. They are also a form of culture *jamming*, the appropriation of mass media by political activists to subvert corporate control of the information environment and show up the truth behind the branding. Jamming techniques include graffiti, subversion of billboards, mock advertisements, performance art, hijacking public media events, and pranks. Notable examples include the Great Barbie Hack of 1989, when activists switched the computer chips in talking Barbie and GI Joe dolls to reveal the gender-based stereotyping of the toys, and the Bhopal hoax of 2004, when pranksters impersonated officials from Dow Chemical and publicly announced that the company accepted full responsibility for the chemical spill disaster in Bhopal, India (Paterson and Bindra 2004). Culture jamming has been called "rhetorical ju-jitsu" turning the power of the mighty against themselves. Opponents are few, under-resourced, and without ready access to power so instead of attacking their opponents head on, they focus their energies to subverting the symbolic environment (Harold 2004, 191).

Culture jamming draws from the Situationists and other avant-garde artists who also employ public pranks to surprise, disorient, and shake up conventional thought (Vale and Juno 1987, 176–79). Activist culture jammers hope to instill moments of epiphany that will lead to changes in thinking and hopefully in behavior. A spokesman for the culture jam movement proclaimed that it aspired to be a major social movement that would "change the way we interact with the mass media and the way in which meaning is produced in our society" (Lasn 2000, xi). However, culture jams have not lived up to this revolutionary promise. Corporate power has hardly been slowed by their pranks—instead, corporations have appropriated culture jam methods, including pranks, to their own ends. As in interpersonal practical jokes intended to convey messages to miscreants, the humorous frame both promotes and undermines the communicative goal. With its playful attacks and cartoonish revolutionary figures, the Biotic Baking Brigade does not just ridicule the powerful; it is a burlesque of activism itself.

The chief value of culture jamming lies not in its persuasive power but in its fun. Fun is a tactic for protesters to cue the play frame, but it is also a significant part of the message. So long as the jammer stays in character as a fool, angry reactions rebound on the target. The jammer's emotional control contrasts with the target's loss of it (Wettergren 2009). Further, the act of planning, preparing, and carrying out public pranks is fun in itself, and pranksters enjoy the solidarity-enhancing pleasure of shared transgression. In politics, as in art and in everyday life, play is its own reward.

RUNNING THROUGH OUR PROGRAMS

The wrongdoings pilloried by practical jokes are habitual ones—Perry repeatedly sneaked other people's drinks; Douglas was "always" hitting on undergraduates, and so on. This predictability is essential to effective practical joking. The joker's art consists in anticipating what the target will do in a particular situation, creating a bogus version of that situation, and sitting back to watch the predicted behavior play out. Accordingly, not just bad habits but any habits are grist for the practical joker's mill.

Henri Bergson suggested that the essence of humor is "something mechanical encrusted on the living," or "mechanical inelasticity" (1956, 92, 67). This original theory is sometimes viewed as being primarily applicable to the humor of physical clumsiness (for example, Billig 2005, 111), but the moral discourse of the practical joke is a reminder that Bergson was equally interested in "inelasticity of character" (1956, 73). Indeed, some of his ideas are echoed in the phraseology of the vernacular discourse about practical jokes. In British English, for instance, a practical joke is often called a *wind-up,* suggesting that the target is made to behave like a clockwork toy.

Similarly, Bergson suggested that "all *character* is comic, provided we mean by character the *ready-made* element in our personality, that mechanical element which resembles a piece of clockwork wound up once for all and capable of working automatically" (1956, 156). Practical jokes highlight what he called "the easy automatism of acquired habits" (72). The purpose of laughter, he felt, is to correct the tendency to follow habit unthinkingly, because those who do so lack the alertness and responsiveness to their surroundings that life demands. Overreliance on habit is more appropriate for a machine than a living creature and so calls for correction.

Today we might express the same thought by drawing a metaphor to computers. For example, a friend told me of a joke that she and her fellow office workers played on the abusive and demanding professor for whom they worked. The boss had a mania for order and would yell at the staff for failing to place objects precisely as he wanted them. After he had left one evening, the office staff subtly rearranged everything on his desk. Nothing was obviously tampered with, but everything was slightly out of its accustomed place. The next morning, as they went in to talk to him on some pretext or other, they could see him unconsciously moving everything back into its proper place as he talked. It was very satisfying to watch him unwittingly follow their script. As my friend put it, "It was great to stand there and watch him run through his program" (Nancy Michael, personal communication). Bergson would have said the boss was comical because he was acting mechanically instead of noticing what was going on and adapting to the change.

According to Bergson's theory, the moral of the practical joke is that any habitual behavior pursued unreflectively leads to foolish behavior and makes us vulnerable. This lesson relates not just to tailored fabrications but to all practical jokes, even the simplest and most generic ones such as short-sheeting a bed, putting salt in the sugar bowl, or daubing a telephone handset with ink. Jokers can play generic tricks like this on people they do not know at all because they can count on the fact that much of everyday human behavior consists of unreflective habit. They can safely assume that people climb into bed without checking it first, automatically spoon the contents of the sugar bowl into their coffee, and mechanically pick up the receiver when the phone rings. Practical jokers assume that human behavior is predictable, and they succeed when they correctly identify and exploit that predictability. Jokers defend their manipulation of others because, they say, they merely encourage us to follow our own scripts—whether those peculiar to our individual personalities or those that we share with most other members of society. All the joker does is push our buttons—and we, like machines, lurch into motion.

SCRIPTED BEHAVIOR

I have suggested that practical jokes are the enactment of scripts planned and predicted by jokers, in which one party is ideally unaware that he or she is following a script. To be effective, jokers need only tap into the generic scripts that govern much of our everyday lives. Routine activities are normally carried out without thinking. We do not need to figure out what to do each time the phone rings; instead, we simply follow the familiar routine that we have learned for this situation. Cognitive scientists argue that much of our everyday activity is made possible because it is based on routines, or *scripts*, that serve as mental shortcuts or templates to manage everyday life. Indeed, it is difficult to imagine how we could function day to day without these routines. Scripts enable us to make sense of situations, providing ready-made frameworks that tell us what is going on here and what our role in the action should be.[1]

While scripts are useful shortcuts, the practical joke points out that there are times when it is better to be flexible and depart from the script. The following story from a graduate student in folklore suggests that even the simple routine for dialing a telephone number can be followed too rigidly:

> Have you talked to John yet? He is the king of practical jokes. Not just scaring, but making the other person a fool. He rushed over to me one day and said, "Nancy, I've got this 800 number you can call" . . . it was something like a folklore hotline that you could ask questions about superstitions or anything relating to folklore and get an answer. Something *barely* plausible but enough that you would be curious about it. So he gave me this number, wrote it down and said, "Go dial this number." So, while he was standing there, trying to act blasé, I rushed to the phone and dialed a number that did not have enough digits in it. And so you ended up with this "wah-wah" on the phone; incorrect. And he just fell all over and just laughed, laughed . . . He just thought it was hysterical.
> *What did you think?*
> I just laughed. And the thing was as I was dialing the number I thought, "there's something wrong with this number, it doesn't have enough digits," but I dialed it anyway, just . . . to carry on doing it, even though I *knew* on a certain level that it was not going to work. (McEntire 2002)

It is very telling that the target admits she dialed the number anyway, "just to carry on doing it." She followed the script even though she knew it was inappropriate. In Bergson's terms, the joke highlighted the human tendency to behave mechanically. "The laughable element," he said, "consists of a certain *mechanical inelasticity*, just where one would expect to find

the wideawake adaptability and the living pliableness of a human being"
(1956, 67).

Practical jokes highlight the limitations of our reliance on familiar
scripts. Once we have embarked on a script, we tend to want to stay with
it. Sizing up a situation, we decide that a particular script is applicable and
thereafter may overlook evidence that our initial estimation was in error.
For this reason, practical joke targets fail to notice the built-in discrediting
signals in the joke or discount them simply because they are not part of the
operative script. This tendency provides opportunities for practical jokers
to pile one absurdity on another to see how far they can push the limits of
the fabrication. For example, John Duenez and his wife had a friend, Cindy,
who had been waiting three days to hear the outcome of her application
for credit at a furniture store. He phoned her, disguising his voice, and pre-
tended to be the store's credit manager. "Your application is approved," he
told her, "but we just need one or two more things from you." In an interview, he told me some of the things he asked for:

> A medical exam for one. A complete medical exam.
> *She went along with that?*
> Yeah. This was a medical exam, a dental history, a family tree, an IQ
> test, an objective goal for the next twelve years, as far as her finances were
> concerned, income tax records for the past eight years, and, three quarts of
> blood.
> *She fell for that too?*
> I lost it when I said three quarts of blood [*laughs*].

Cindy was so anxious to get credit, John told me, that she would agree to
anything the bogus credit manager asked for. So he kept elaborating the
requirements until "it came down to the ridiculous part, and she was willing to do it. Just to have her financial statement go through and be A-1"
(Duenez and Duenez 1987).

As the joke played out, John's wife was listening on the extension and
"rolling on the floor," giving into laughter at the incongruity between what
she knew was going on and Cindy's blissful ignorance of it (Duenez and
Duenez 1987). So long as he stayed in character, John was operating in two
interaction frames at once—the one he shared with his wife, in which they
were playing a practical joke, and the bogus one that he and Cindy were
jointly constructing of an interaction between customer and store manager.
When the incongruity between the different frames became too great for
him to bear, he too burst into laughter, finally revealing to the target what
all the "ridiculous" demands had failed to do.

This joke demonstrates targets' strong tendency either not to notice or to discount play cues that would have revealed the fabricated frame. If anyone had directly suggested that a medical exam and an IQ test were requirements for a credit application, Cindy would have laughed it off, but once she had framed the conversation as a credit application she normalized as a part of that frame things that she would have recognized as absurdities in another context (Dornelles and Garcez 2001, 1707). Faced with incongruities, dupes find ways to make sense of them in ways that fit their current interpretation of events. With a strong enough interpretive frame, even laughter may sometimes be ignored or explained away.

The power of scripts in our everyday understandings of the world means that no practical joker constructs a fabrication single-handedly. Fabrications exist primarily in the mind. Neither elaborate props nor teams of actors are essential for effective containment; instead, practical jokes succeed because their targets unwittingly collude in building and sustaining the fabricated world. These false world pictures (Jones 1957) can be so robust that they withstand all but the most direct discrediting strategies.

Another moral of the practical joke, then, is to critique the human tendency to use mental shortcuts. If we insist on them too much, they become blinders, limiting our alertness to the world around us and curtailing our adaptability. Practical jokes take advantage of and critique our propensity to go on automatic pilot. If we act too unreflectively, we can get into trouble. Useful as they are, neither cultural nor individual scripts absolve us of the need to pay attention to what's going on around us. The practical joke is a salutary warning to all of us not to go through life merely running through our programs.

NOTES

1. Other theorists use the terms *schema* and *frame* to refer to the same concept. Victor Raskin suggests that some scripts are peculiar to small groups or even to individuals (1985, 51).

6

All Jokes Are Bad if They Are Any Good

Humor Support and Unlaughter

THE AMBIGUOUS TRICKSTER

THERE IS PLENTY OF MORALITY AND IMMORALITY, blame and justification to go around in practical jokes, but it is not just the joke targets who come in for scrutiny. Practical jokers also find themselves under a negative moralistic gaze. New Zealand columnist Rosemary McLeod expresses the opinions of many: "I've always seen people who play practical jokes as bullies in disguise," she wrote. "Their humour is not about self-recognition, or even insightful recognition of the human condition; it's just about humiliating other people" (2003, 6).

Some practical jokers themselves comment on the nastiness of their play. "Gosh, these are all quite dark, these examples!" said Tack Daniel after recounting some of his practical jokes to me in an interview (2005). "I'm a bad one to go pulling jokes on people," confessed another (Sawin 2004, 135). Sometimes the joker feels regret for the mistreatment she or he extends to others. "I played a practical joke on some County Waterford men," confesses a folklorist:

> The prank was so successful that, despite my amusement, I regret-
> ted my participation in what I then decided had been not funny, but
> unkind. The next day I was visiting with some acquaintances who had
> already heard of what I had pulled over on the lads, told me the story
> of it, expressed their appreciation and admiration, and asked me to tell
> them the story of it. When I confided that I actually felt badly about it,
> they reassured me that it had all been done in fun, and that the victims,
> who were somewhat self-important, had deserved to be cut down a bit.
> (Harlow 1997, 162n122)

In this case, the joker's friends were quick to turn blame for the situation away from her and onto the targets. The trickery was acceptable, they argued, because the targets deserved it—not for a specific act of wrongdoing but for the more general fault of self-importance. If this defense did not

DOI: 10.7330/9780874219845.c006

remove all the blame from the shamefaced joker, it did succeed in distributing right and wrong more evenly between the parties.

Practical joke narratives are filled with moralistic themes precisely because the jokes themselves cannot help but be transgressive on both the logical and social levels. Logically, they topple the everyday expectation that truth and untruth are or should be readily distinguishable, and they upend the assumptions of the natural attitude, according to which the way an actor sees his or her current situation is the way things objectively are. On the social plane, they violate norms that sanction deceit and require clear frames and prior permission for excursions into play. The targets of practical jokes are subject to ridicule and embarrassment, and on top of that some jokes also subject them to trouble, discomfort, and mess. In the practical joke narratives these violations of everyday norms are balanced against the alleged errors, wrongdoings, and character flaws of the targets.

As useful as a well-aimed practical joke is in "teaching a lesson" to petty offenders and providing solace to their long-suffering colleagues, the joke itself is also tinged with wrongdoing. The practical joker cannot claim to be entirely on the side of right. However much the victims deserve it, fooling them involves violating everyday norms of honesty and respectful behavior, leaving the trickster vulnerable to censure. Thus we rejoice when practical jokes backfire, turning the trickster into the fool. Previously, I quoted the story of the summer camp director who got wind of campers' plans to ambush him with mustard and ketchup; he achieved legendary status after he turned the joke back on his would-be tormentors (Posen 1974, 309). Whether or not this story really happened, it and others like it, in which practical jokes are turned against their creators, are satisfying because they depict the jokers as wrongdoers who get their comeuppance. In the same way that practical joke narratives depict how the character flaws of targets lead them to victimize themselves, so stories about the comeuppance of jokers blame them for their own discomfiture.

Similar reactions are aroused by stories about swindlers, imposters, and confidence tricksters, all of whom use deception and fabrication to lure people into contributing to their own victimization. Condemnation of the criminals is mixed with sneaking admiration for their creativity and a suspicion that the victims largely had themselves to blame. The imposter "reveals his fellow-men's failings and vices by using them as the very basis of his schemes . . . He may not be a better man than his victims, but he certainly invites more sympathy" (Lehrburger 1966, 9–10).

The practical joker is closer to swindlers and other tricksters than to heroes, more Bugs Bunny than Superman. Tricksters are familiar figures in mythology and folklore around the world and are represented in contemporary American culture by such characters as Bugs Bunny (Abrams and Sutton-Smith 1977) and the Blues Brothers. They violate taboos with impunity and appear to show no concern for others. The Blues Brothers, for example, leave a broad path of destruction in their wake with their amiable disregard for law and propriety—but they also save the orphanage. While the cinema audience roots for them and enjoys their antics on the screen, they would not invite such people into their homes.

Like the trickster, the practical joker is an ambiguous figure and arouses ambivalent feelings. He is hero and troublemaker, cheater and cheated, cunning and foolish, rule breaker and enforcer of group norms. Like all tricksters, he is neither purely good nor irredeemably bad but exists playfully between morality and immorality. The difference is that practical jokers are not characters in myth and not safely confined to stage or screen; instead, they are all around us and can break into our lives at any time and without warning. The trickster's domain is "a tolerated margin of mess" (Babcock-Abrahams 1975), but it is easier to tolerate mess when it is safely framed in a story, within a ritual, or on a stage than when it erupts into real life.

FOWL PLAY

Whether practical or verbal, jokes rarely occur alone. Where there is one, others often follow, creating a comic climate in which examples of various humor genres multiply. Thus, written accounts of practical jokes often include the liberal use of puns, whether they are in joke books or in newspapers like the *Christchurch Press*:

> Readers wondering what the flap was in Sydenham on Sunday may be surprised to hear it was caused by a rooster parading with what appeared to be explosive canisters strapped to its body. Police were called to Huxley Street at 10:30am by a member of the public who had seen a chicken with canisters taped under each wing and wires protruding. The bird "played chicken with us for a wee while," before he was herded up a driveway, the home evacuated, and the army's improvised explosive device squad called in, said Senior Sergeant Ian Freeman. With the rooster having gone to "the big chookery in the sky," the contents of the canisters were found to be harmless.
>
> Unfortunately the chook was the victim of a not very funny practical joke. (King 2003)

The police sergeant's colloquial language and puns on a poultry theme all suggest that he found the situation amusing. The colloquial New Zealand term *chook* adds to the effect, especially with the whimsical reference to "the big chookery in the sky." The reporter amplifies this jocular tone with a punning headline and still more puns in the story, all sticking to the same theme. Normally, using puns to talk about a practical joke would suggest that the speaker was amused by it, but in the last line he undercuts this impression by calling it "not very funny." This closing highlights another side of the story: a hoax bomb threat, a home evacuated, the police and the army bomb squad's time wasted, and an innocent rooster destroyed. To see the funny side of the story, one has to find a way to put these serious considerations aside and view the scene in the spirit of play. The playful vision allows us to appreciate the incongruity in the scene: on one side, the impressive forces of the police and the army, bristling with equipment; and on the other side . . . a chicken.

THREE SCHOOLS OF HUMOR THEORY

There are three schools of thought that offer competing theories about what makes us laugh in stories like this one. The oldest and most predominant ones are the aggression school and the incongruity school. The aggression school stresses the dark side of humor and the underlying cruelty of laughter. At their most reductionist, theories in this school consider superiority and aggression the essential and defining characteristic of all humor. "There is no laughter without a butt, and no butt without a message about a risible inferiority," says F. H. Buckley (2003, xi). "What is necessary and sufficient to cause laughter is a combination of a loser, a victim of derision or ridicule, with suddenness of loss," according to Charles Gruner (1978, 31).

There can be no doubt that any activity in which one of the protagonists is commonly designated as the "victim" must involve aggression, if not hostility. The chicken in this story is a victim, certainly. However, if the affair was a practical joke, then there must have been a human target—presumably, the police and the bomb squad, who were called out for no good reason. Aggression theories do not offer a good explanation for the fact that the targets of practical jokes, like the police sergeant here, often laugh along.

The incongruity school has won wide acceptance in recent years. Such theories argue that under certain conditions the perception of incongruity produces the feeling of mirth or amusement (Morreall 1983, 15–19; 1989). The semantic theory of jokes is a narrower application of this idea, arguing that every joke comprises two opposed semantic scripts—one that appears on the surface and another that is revealed in the punch line (Raskin 1985).

Our story contains an amusing incongruity between the imaginary bomb threat and the reality of a single unarmed chicken.

An effective practical joke is constituted by competing simultaneous scripts—one visible to the jokers and audiences, and another known to the targets. However, by no means every effective joke is successful in winning audience support—especially not from its targets. Script opposition describes the necessary but not the sufficient conditions for amusement. Any joke is vulnerable to failure even if it is well formed at a structural level, and practical jokes are especially vulnerable because they have live targets who may be asked to join in the laughter at their own expense, a feat that, understandably, many of them find difficult. Incongruity theories also do not address the motives of jokers or those who laugh with them, and they leave aside issues about the ethics and morality of jokes, even though such questions arise in the reception of jokes more than in any other genre (Kramer 2011, 147).

The argument between the aggression and incongruity schools of humor is never-ending, which suggests that there is something about humor that includes both elements. Certainly, there is something about practical jokes that encourages this view. The aggression in practical jokes is mitigated by playfulness and aesthetic elaboration, both of which signal more benign motives. The essence of the practical joke is a mixture of the benign and the aggressive. To reduce this complex mix to a single element, whether one chooses aggression or innocent fun, is to lose the essential nature of the genre. Practical jokes are in fun, but they are not all in fun. To comprehend them properly means being comfortable with the possibility of mixed motives.

This approach to the practical joke rests on a third school of thought, dubbed the benign violation theory of humor. It represents a middle way between incongruity and aggression theories and is a major advance on both. It argues that amusement depends upon of a state of affective absurdity in the observer that arises when a situation violates a norm or principle to which the observer is committed but which he or she is simultaneously able to view as normal, tolerable, or acceptable (Mannell and La Fave 1976; McGraw and Warren 2010; Veatch 1998). Jokes include some transgression that the jokers have framed as play. In performing the joke, they invite audiences to adopt a similar playful attitude and tolerate the transgression, if only for a moment. The violations in jokes are amusing if and only if the audience can find a way to permit them through a temporary playful suspension of its everyday values. To take the playful attitude implies a temporary suspension of one's values and norms—in fantasy/play, these are not salient (Mannell and La Fave 1976, 235). A suspension of everyday norms is necessary to appreciate jokes precisely because jokes generally involve the deliberate violation of some norm or other. Indeed, many jokes break several norms at once.

It matters that the protagonist in this story was a chicken. Chickens seem to be inherently funny, and the reason they are is that we care about them, but we do not care too much. If a beloved family pet was destroyed in a hoax bomb threat, fewer people would find the story funny. Substitute a cockroach for the chicken, and the humor likewise vanishes, because most of us do not care at all about the life of an insect—unless it is a beloved family pet. We have strong affective commitment to the norm against killing human beings and almost none against killing insects, but our commitment to the life of a chicken falls somewhere in between. The degree of audience commitment to the norm that the joke violates is important; too much, and the audience is unlikely to find it amusing. Too little, and the joke is merely corny.

The reporter of the fowl play story follows the sergeant on the scene in treating the affair as a joke, but he retracts this attitude with his final comment: "The chook was the victim of a not very funny practical joke." When a joke violates the norm with respect to a chicken, many people can playfully shelve it, but this action does not wipe out our commitment to the norm. Amusement requires a temporary abandonment of our everyday norms, but the emphasis is on "temporary"; the attitude we adopt when we support a joke is only in play. Hedges like the conclusion to "Fowl Play" underline this message, reminding observers that our appreciation of the joke does not reflect our real attitudes. The result is a perfectly ambiguous response that supports and condemns the joke in equal measure, signaling the affective absurdity that is the essential characteristic of amusement.

PLAYFUL, ARTFUL TRANSGRESSION

The benign violation theory makes the moral and ethical dimension of jokes central to the understanding of humor, which mirrors, and explains, the frequency with which jokes of all kinds arouse moral and ethical arguments. It also explains the gap between the effective and the successful performance of jokes. A joke performance that is perfectly executed as to content and form may be hilarious to one audience but fall completely flat with another, or even with the same recipient on different occasions. If amusement is a subjective state of affective absurdity, then humorousness is in the eye of the beholder. Whereas aggression and superiority theories focus on the hidden motives of jokers, and script opposition theory applies only to the logic of joke texts, benign violation locates humorousness or its absence in the reception of jokes and appropriately restores agency to their audiences.

The playful element in the production and reception of jokes is sometimes downplayed by scholars. My analysis in the following pages emphasizes that jokes are best understood as a variety of play. Their transgression may take the form of ridicule, superiority, hostility, or simply violations of logic (script opposition is a transgression of this type), but the play frame supplied by the joking form signals that these motives may not be what they seem. Jokes are bounded boundary smashing and rule-governed rule bashing. Humor depends upon boundaries—if there were no limits, there would be no humor (Lockyer and Pickering 2005, 14). Jokes constitute *artful* and *playful transgression* of boundaries. Aesthetic elaboration, traditional formulae, and careful management of the performance post-play all contribute to the playful suspension of everyday norms that is the hallmark of humor, but jokers cannot take this suspension for granted.

UNLAUGHTER

It is useful to draw a distinction between effectiveness and success in joke performance, because the two do not always occur together. An effective joke is simply one that is performed or enacted well. In a practical joke, effectiveness means that the jokers' fabrication played out as expected and the relevant targets were fooled according to plan. Success, on the other hand, means winning humor support from salient audiences. It is theoretically possible for an in effective, ill-formed joke to achieve success; if it is an in-group performance and the performer is a well-integrated group member, the audience might offer a show of support, including laughter, if only to avoid hurting the performer. In other words, humor support can be merely a show; we generally have no independent evidence of what is going on in the recipient's head or heart.

The next example is a joke that is effective but not successful. The story was told to me by Rob Mills, a resident of Brown County, a rural area in Indiana, whose family regularly played practical jokes on each other:

> One of the jokes that Russ played on John was putting green food coloring in some home brew, 'cause John had developed this system of brewing beer; and he had a refrigerator with a tap on it and everything. So he put green food coloring in his beer, and it worked especially well, because John later had a friend over who was from out of town and he wanted to impress

him with this system, with the tap. So he started taking some beer out of the tap and it came out green. (*Laughs*) "Oh, God, what's happened?" So it was impressive but not in the way he had intended. He couldn't figure out what was going on. He did figure it out later because there had been several jokes going on; the tradition had been established by then.

Sometimes when the family gets together we tell joke stories. The green beer joke has not been talked about. I guess John didn't appreciate it very much. That must have been in the midseventies. I don't think he enjoyed it. He probably got them back. (Mills 1987)

Initially, John did not recognize that the incident was a joke ("What's happened?"). He recognized it later ("he did figure it out") because this joke was one of a series of reciprocal tricks that had been going on in the family. However, he did not "appreciate it."

Here is a family of confirmed practical jokers. They regularly play jokes on each other and share stories about them. In this context, it is very telling that the green beer joke has not been talked about, even though it "worked especially well." This silence suggests that in the family's opinion, it was a failed joke. Why? Because John was an audience whose humor support was desired and salient but not forthcoming.

Sociologist Michael Billig has coined the term *unlaughter* to refer to these situations, meaning "a display of not laughing when laughter might otherwise be expected, hoped for or demanded" (2005, 192). This concept usefully distinguishes the absence of humor support (Hay 2001) from the mere absence of laughter. Most of our daily activities are not accompanied by laughter, and this absence is neither remarkable nor significant. But, after a joke, the absence of laughter or other support is very meaningful. Because every joke is transgressive, the absence of support is an implicit accusation against the joker for having violated some norm or moral code. Recognizing, or suspecting, that John did not appreciate the joke played on him, the jokers could not dodge the fact that they had embarrassed him in front of his friends on a subject that was dear to him.

In a recent analysis of rape joke arguments on the Internet, Elise Kramer makes this startling observation: "Disagreement . . . [is] a necessary component of humor: those who find a joke funny and those who do not are mutually constitutive groups that cannot exist without each other" (2011, 163). Public arguments about the morality of jokes are common (Lewis 2006a) and the anonymity of Internet communications makes such disputes more widespread and more vituperative than they would be in face-to-face settings (Blank 2013). But Kramer is talking about something more central to the nature of humor. Disagreement is not a contingent, potential outcome of jokes but a necessary, constituent part of them. Laughter rests on the hypothetical existence of others who are not laughing or would not laugh if they were aware of the joke. To support a joke is to acknowledge that there is some norm violation toward which one is willing to take a playful attitude. Accordingly, humor support necessarily involves noticing transgression, and to notice a transgression is to posit the existence of someone who would object to it.

Unlaughter can open up the disagreement at the heart of the joke. In small high-context groups, like families, such disagreements can be divisive and are often avoided. In these settings jokers take pains to ensure that their targets can support the joke and "laugh along." When John did not offer a show of support for the green beer joke, the joke was deemed a failure and was removed from the family repertoire to avoid more divisive unlaughter. Management of unlaughter in in-group settings boils down to avoiding it wherever possible and minimizing it when it does occur.

THE COMMENCEMENT EXERCISE

Successful joking requires that joker manage the post-play so that salient audiences show support for the joke, but not every joker can do well at this task, sometimes not even when the joking is set within a long-term close relationship:

> While dressing for my son's commencement exercises, the phone rang. My husband answered, talked for a few minutes and came into the dressing room where I was finishing my makeup. With a stricken look, he said, "You don't have to bother getting ready. John failed the exam." After this statement, there was a 60-second pause while he studied my face for a reaction.
>
> My hands started to shake and tears began to stream down my cheeks. I was completely shattered. The feelings of despair and disappointment were overwhelming . . .
>
> After a minute, my husband says, "April Fool!" (It was June.) "Do you want to know who really called?" At that point I was too sick to care.
>
> What kind of person would pull such a joke on his wife? This is not the first time he has done this sort of thing to me. And when I become angry, he sulks, sometimes for weeks at a time, and refuses to speak to me. (Landers 1990)

The husband's spur-of-the-moment deception was very effective in that it fooled his wife completely, eliciting an emotional response that provided unambiguous evidence of her containment. However, success—measured by the ability of the salient audience to support the joke—was noticeably lacking. Since only two people were present for this joke, the only audience the husband had to manage was the target herself, and here he appears to have been a spectacular failure because she was too upset to offer any kind of humor support. The joke toyed with a topic to which she had a deep affective commitment, not easily put aside with a playful attitude. Further, her husband misused the "April Fool" play signal by applying it out of season.

Enthusiastic practical jokers pride themselves on choosing their targets judiciously, knowing who can take a joke, avoiding those who cannot, and recognizing which topics are available for playful manipulation and which are not. One frequent trickster told me he would never play a joke on his wife because "she doesn't like that kind of banter," but the husband in this story seems to have had a tin ear when it came to choosing his target. The relationship between joker and target is the most important factor in the target's evaluation of a joke as well as in the joker's decision to play it. This relationship lends targets the information needed to ascertain the joker's motives—benign intent is more likely to be attributed to a close friend. Further, the relative value of the relationship influences targets' decisions about whether to support jokes at their expense. Humor support strengthens the relationship, but lack of support has the opposite effect.

Some spouses would have suppressed their upset feelings for the sake of domestic harmony, but this case suggests a more antagonistic joking pattern. In stark contrast to joking relationships that are strengthened by the exchange and support of practical jokes and other forms of humor, the fact that this husband continues to play jokes on his wife even though she does not support them suggests hostility that he is probably not consciously aware of. His silent treatment is a passive-aggressive response to the censure implied by the wife's unlaughter. Her unlaughter rebuffs his invitation to treat a norm transgression playfully, and without the play frame the transgressions of both joke and joker are thrown into relief. Without humor support, the joker is left out in the cold.

Commenting on the deadly international furor over the "Mohammed cartoons" published in a Danish newspaper in 2006, Paul Lewis observed that "humor brings people together except when it tears them apart" (2006b, A4). Unlaughter has powerful social effects up to and including lawsuits, implosion of political careers, and international incidents. The source of this divisive power is that unlaughter withholds the permission that all jokes seek, thus censuring the joker. In January 2015, unlaughter reached an extremist apex when gunmen slaughtered staff at a satirical newspaper in Paris for lampooning Islam. More than withholding support, such attacks seek to punish the creators of humor that the attackers find not merely offensive, but blasphemous (Bilefsky and de la Baum 2015).

EXOTERIC JOKING

Unlaughter is a better word than *failed humor* because in certain kinds of practical jokes, it is not a sign of failure. When the target of the joke is an outsider, his or her support is not always considered necessary. On the contrary, jokers may deliberately provoke unlaughter from unpopular targets or outsiders in order to amplify their exclusion and heighten group boundaries (Smith 2009b). In these scenarios, the vernacular ideology or humor justifies exclusion because so long as jokers can assume they have humor support from the rest of the group, then the problem can be said to lie with the individual who is not laughing. If the jokers have support from salient audiences, unlaughter may be interpreted as a sign of some lack or failure in the target. This supposed flaw, often labeled simply "no sense of humor," may index a myriad of other personality problems (Wickberg 1998, 84–98). Paradoxically, another method of excluding undesirables is to omit them from the in-group joking exchanges entirely (Plester and Sayers 2007), but the exclusionary effect is the same. Exclusionary joking is by no means always failed joking.

When joke targets are chosen based not on their ability to take a joke but simply because they are perceived as outsiders (see, for example, DeNatale 1990), we have an exoteric joking tradition. Here, unlaughter from the outsider indicates a successful joke. The traditional pranks played by adolescents on adults at Halloween are a good example of this exoteric dynamic:

> We were out last year, Halloween was a Saturday, next morning we were just walking around, and corned a house early in the morning.
> And woke everyone up. They all came outside.
> It was pretty funny. They were screaming.
>
> But there was no damage done to the house at all. (Cobra Patrol 1982)

This little story, told by the members of a Boy Scout troop in Bloomington, Indiana, refers to "corning"—the act of throwing dried corn kernels against a house wall or porch to create a racket and startle the inhabitants. The impotent rage indexed by the term "screaming" in this story is the expected, indeed scripted, by the preteen pranksters. Evidence from other Halloween pranksters suggests that their goal is not just to get a reaction but to elicit displays of unlaughter—the more out of control, the better. One group of Indiana friends told me that they took particular care to throw their eggs and tomatoes at police cars because "you had the most fun with them. 'Cause they'd chase you." Another prankster complained, "No one cared, in my hometown, if you threw corn at their porch. They'd get up in the morning and sweep it off." In this tradition, indifference, let alone humor support, is a disappointment.

Like all practical jokes, Halloween pranks exploit predictable behavior. They are intended to irritate the irritable by taking aim at those who can be relied upon to take the joke badly (Santino 1998, 47). In jokes of this type, unlaughter is not an accidental response but another part—indeed, the most salient part—of the jokers' script. The victims' negative response to their jokes is framed as just another joke, another predictable scripted reaction engineered by the jokers to show up their targets.

In exoteric joking the differential responses—humor support from some, unlaughter from salient others—mark the perceived differences between social groups. While some targets are chosen because they are known to be irritable, others are picked simply because they belong to the class of property-owning, status-wielding adults that the tricksters are excluded from, and the pranks temporarily reverse the power relations between the two groups (Leary 1979). So long as the jokers can avoid being caught, the unlaughter of their targets merely underlines the social distinctions between the insiders and outsiders.

7

The Rhetoric of Humor Support

JUST ANOTHER OFFICE PRANK

THE TIN-FOILED DESK IS CURRENTLY A POPULAR PRACTICAL joke among the millions of people who spend their working hours in offices or cubicles. Any office worker who goes on vacation or even takes a day off might return to find desk, office, or cubicle lovingly wrapped in aluminum foil or newspaper, or otherwise adulterated by coworkers. Although not an original joke—videos, images, and detailed instructions are readily available on the Internet—tin-foiling still offers room for variation, style, and creative elaboration. Tin-foiling is an example of what I call the booby trap subtype of practical joke. An effective performance requires a more or less elaborate backstage setup that is suddenly sprung on the (hopefully) unsuspecting target. The target's response at that moment is the climax of the joke, often recorded for YouTube immortality. A particularly elaborate version from Slovenia documents the entire thing as if it were a feature film from Twentieth Century Fox (Loooooooka 2010). Table 7.1 is my transcript of this video, including titles, soundtrack, and the on-screen visuals.

There are many such tin-foiling prank videos on YouTube, but this one is especially elaborately produced. Like verbal practical joke narratives, the video follows the phase structure of the practical joke (Bauman 1986). It begins with an orientation as to time and place and an account of the precipitating events—the boss leaves and the workers are motivated by videos that they have seen on YouTube to pull the "newspaper prank." The backstage setup follows, then, after a dramatic pause, the boss returns and the prank is enacted. The post-play follows immediately, consisting of almost two minutes of the boss circling his office and laughing. "Funny as fucking hell," he declares. The video ends with an evaluative comment: "Almost perfect." If the goal was to get a laugh from the boss, then this joke was a clear success.

DOI: 10.7330/9780874219845.c007

Table 7.1

Time	Titles	Video	Soundtrack
0.0	[Fades in] Dork Productions presents "Another office prank"		Twentieth Century Fox Fanfare
0:12	[Typewriter effect] Date: 4.2.2010Time: MU?Location: Lju-bljana (Slovenia)Yes It's in Europe. Not a former Soviet Union country.		Sound of manual typewriter
0:38	[Fades in] The Story:		
0:43	[Fades in] Boss goes to Cuba for 9 days. Co-workers and friends decide they really like those youtube newspa-per pranks		
0:50	[Fades in] The Setup:		
0:54– 1:10		Sped-up video shows several young men wrapping office con-tents in newspaper	"Yakety Sax"
1:11	Smelly slippers checked!	Still of slippers wrapped in newspaper	
1:16		Sped-up video as above	
1:38	[Fades in] The boss's Chair (keeping it red!)	Still of office chair wrapped in newspaper with red paper squares being taped along it	
1:40	[Fades in] Checked!		
1:43		Sped-up video contin-ues; the floor has been covered with newspa-per and a line of red paper squares has been added leading from the door to the desk	

continued on next page

Table 7.1—*continued*

Time	Titles	Video	Soundtrack
1:46	[Fades in] Welcome back sign	Still of "welcome back boss" written in yellow	
1:48	[Fades in] Checked!	Post-Its on newspaper-covered wall	
1:53		Still of two pranksters posing in the wrapped office, giving thumbs-up sign	
1:56		Black screen	Silence
2:00	Camera, lights, ACTION!	Video of empty wrapped office. Door opens; boss enters; he bursts into laughter	
2:24	[Fades in] Upon entering, the Star Wars Imperial song was played and he received an SMS with "Smile. You're on Candid Camera"		
2:31		Video of boss laughing, walking back and forth and looking around. He picks up objects and replaces them. Laughter occasionally interspersed with indecipherable speech	The Imperial March ("Darth Vader's Theme") is heard playing in the background from 2:31–3:08
3:38		He stops laughing, pulls out his chair, spots something under the desk, and begins laughing again.	
3:59		Boss sits in chair, pulls out his cell phone and says into it: "Funny as fucking hell." Still laughing.	

continued on next page

Table 7.1—*continued*

Time	Titles	Video	Soundtrack
4:09	Black screen		Silence
4:12	[Fades in] Oh yeah . . . we also replaced his windows shell with a custom console program and disabled safe mode . . .		
4:18	[Fades in] But somehow I managed to f%$k up the taping . . . Ah well. Almost perfect!		

The practical joke documented here had multiple audiences, and the jokers employed a variety of methods to secure laughter from each. For the YouTube public, the video contained several culturally specific devices intended to signal that what watchers are viewing is intended as a joke. One such signal is the incongruous hyperbole in introducing "Another Office Prank" with a grand fanfare and a title sequence modeled after Star Wars. Two other widely recognized comedy cues are the quick tempo in the setup section of the video and a soundtrack featuring "Yakety Sax," familiar as the theme music from the well-known comedy series *The Benny Hill Show*. The 565 "thumbs-up" votes compared to 31 "thumbs-down" on YouTube suggest that the majority of viewers got the joke.

Then there is the audience of one—the target of the joke. The jokers could count their work a success because their target laughed. In the vernacular discourse, a common rule of thumb for identifying a successful practical joke is one in which the targets can laugh along. To wrap the boss's office in newspaper violates accepted norms for proper behavior in the workplace. It is disrespectful of a superordinate, an invasion of semiprivate space, and an obstacle to the demands of the work day. Many of the 151 online comments that this video received praised the boss's forbearance in deciding to laugh rather than to fire the jokers. Given this risk, it is not surprising that the jokers added cues to encourage his agreement. The "welcome back boss" sign on the wall signaled that the joke had a benign intent. The "red carpet" made from paper and the "Imperial March" from *Star Wars* both used comic hyperbole to flatter him playfully while also signaling that he was still the boss. The jokers also sent him a text message that said "Smile. You're on Candid Camera." This formula, used in Alan Funt's reality television show (1948–2004) to close and reveal fabrications to their targets, has become a byword—apparently an international one—for a practical joke or for a comic situation generally.

The benign violation model of humor suggests that the boss had a choice. He could take seriously the violation of his workspace and the fact that his subordinates had played a joke on him, or he could treat the incident as humorous. To take the latter course he had to temporarily suspend his attachment to the norms that had been broken, or bring to bear alternative norms that would make these violations acceptable (McGraw and Warren 2010). Other values that might have contributed to this choice include the desirability of balancing work with play; of maintaining informal and friendly relations at work; and of showing that one has a good sense of humor. The last of these, commonly understood as the importance of not taking oneself too seriously, is one of the most highly valued personal attributes in the modern world (Wickberg 1998, 89–98), and it plays a significant role every time practical joke targets become joke audiences.

THE RHETORIC OF LAUGHTER

When people become aware that they have been contained in a practical joke, their response can be quite complex. "Another Office Prank" shows someone who seems unable to commit to any particular course of action for the time being; he circles, he picks up objects then sets them back down, he moves back and forth, periodically erupting in loud laughter. As Wallace Chafe points out, laughter literally incapacitates any other action (2007). Considering all that the target of a booby trap joke must cope with at the moment of enactment, doing nothing is not a bad strategy.

It has been suggested that psychological distance can help audiences treat a joking violation as benign (McGraw et al. 2012). When the recipients are themselves the targets of the joke, not just symbolically but physically and immediately, psychological distance is a tall order. The situation is complicated by the fact that the target usually understands that his or her reaction is being closely watched, and judged, by an audience constituted by the jokers and their supporters. "Helpless" laughter can be strategically useful in this situation. In the vernacular ideology of humor, laughter signals amusement. When the person laughing is the target of the joke, it is read as a sign of a healthy sense of humor as well as that the person is a "good sport." Several YouTube comments on this video praise the boss for reacting the way he did. In truth, neither we nor the jokers can know for certain everything that was going through his mind for the full two minutes, but his laughter papers over these details, leading to the impression that the joke was a complete success, conveying approbation to everyone involved.

DELAYED LAUGHTER

The importance of laughter as a sign of humor success is illustrated by a case in which the laughter almost did not happen. I got the following story from a forty-three-year-old secretary in a university department who was well known for playing April Fools' Day jokes on everyone in the department, including the faculty. She and a student collaborator used a hoax phone call to play a trick on a professor one April Fools' Day. The trick was completely effective, but its success in winning the support of the target was in doubt:

> He'd just gotten a computer and he had a grant. He'd been doing all his research on the computer, everything. And I had a student call up and pretend that she was from Research and Graduate Development. And she called him up and said that they had to recall his computer. And he's working on a deadline; he has to get this stuff out. She said that there was a part wrong in it that if you left it on it could explode and that they had to recall it immediately and they'd come over and pick it up.
>
> And he went on—of course he was getting upset—and said, "Over my dead body you're going to get this computer" [*laughs*]. And she went on and on—she did a fantastic job—she did it. I had a heck of a time getting her to do it—mainly because she didn't know the faculty member really that well—but once she got on the phone and started doing it, it was unbelievable; she was a great little actress. And she went on and said there was some question about it; they had to return the computer. And he was getting more and more upset.
>
> And finally she . . . said, "Well, just a moment, you can talk to my supervisor about it" [and handed the phone to me]. And I got on the phone and I said, "April Fools'." There was *dead silence*. And then he said, "Oh" [*laughs*].
>
> And then he started laughing. And I *think* maybe he thought it was funny afterwards; at the time he didn't, I'm sure. Now I don't know how he feels about it; I don't know if he liked that joke or not. (Aten 1986; see also McEntire 2002, 142–143)

The vernacular ideology of humor treats laughter as a more or less automatic response to exposure to a funny joke. Some humor scholars similarly hold that laughter is subject only to weak conscious control and therefore unfalsifiable (Buckley 2003, 178–190; Provine 2000, 49–53).[1] Given this common set of assumptions about laughter, any delay plants the suspicion that the laughter is not genuine, which in turn signals a failed joke and reflects on the joker (Fine 1984, 85). Thus, when the joker told me this story years after the event, she was not certain that her target really supported it. But the rhetorical power of laughter is such that even with a delay, it allows the target and the joker to carry on as if the joke were a complete success. The target's laughter might have been forced, as my interviewee suspected, but the fact that he laughed at all conveyed a semblance of amusement, allowing everyone to treat the joke as a success. Even forced laughter was to the target's credit, as it showed that he valued solidarity with the joker more than his personal dignity.

THE MEANING OF AMUSEMENT

There is something imperious about the way jokes seek responses from their audiences ("Smile! You're on Candid Camera" is an imperative.) While all performers desire an audience, those who perform jokes need audiences in a way that specialists in other genres do not. The benign violation model explains why jokers demand immediate responses from their audiences. It is not just laughter that they crave but *humor support*. Jennifer Hay proposed this term to designate the looked-for responses to jokes because, as she observed, laughter is just one of many ways to respond positively to jokes (2001). Her choice of the term *support* is very telling, I think. Why would we assume that humorous performances require support, specifically? I propose that it is the inherent transgression of jokes that makes support necessary. The benign violation model suggests that since the perception of something at once reprehensible and amusing is at the heart of all jokes, a joke must be not only recognized but also permitted (Douglas 1975, 98). Jokers have some awareness that they have played with norm violation and so they seek support from others that these violations are somehow tolerable or acceptable. Failure to show support for a joke censures the joker because it strips away the playful and artful frame to reveal the underlying transgression as simply a violation of a norm.

Jokes thus put their audiences on the spot. As Giselinde Kuipers has observed, "The joke teller puts pressure on his audience to laugh; the audience feels obligated to answer the humorous tone by smiling or laughing" (2006, 58). One source of this pressure is the general belief that a good sense of humor is virtually an indispensable personal characteristic. When the audience is also the target of the joke, the same vernacular ideology of humor expects that one display the ability to laugh at oneself. When joker and audience are known to each other as relatives, friends, or coworkers, then another source of pressure is the desire to maintain social harmony; lack of support implies criticism of the joker and reveals the underlying argument implied by the joke. When the person from whom humor support is sought has just been targeted by a practical joke, the pressure is increased still further because targets are under close scrutiny by another audience made up of the jokers and their supporters.

THE TARGET'S DILEMMA

Susie Duenez was a thirty-one-year-old mother, a former nurse and full-time homemaker in Indianapolis, married to a man who was a frequent practical joker. In a telephone interview, she told me about a joke her best friend, Cindy, had played on her:

> A couple of years ago I had gone for a pregnancy test, and thought I was pregnant and I went, and I just could not wait to get the results back, and I had the doctor put a release on it, which means—it was a blood test and so you could call the lab that week and find out the results.
>
> And so I called, and they didn't have the results, and they weren't done with it, and I kept calling, and I kept telling her [Cindy], "Oh, I can't wait to find this out, I'm so anxious." So she knew that I was—and I must have called down there, I don't know, a few times, and never had the results and finally the guy said, "I tell you what," says, "I will call you. It will be shortly, within an hour or two; I will call you if I can get it done before midnight." So I says, "Ohh, that will be wonderful," I says. "You really would do that for me?" He says, "Yes."
>
> So meanwhile, Cindy called me—you know, my friend—and it was a girl [on the phone]; I didn't think much of it, [although] I had talked to this guy and he was the one that was going to call me, and she said, "This is the medical lab." "Yes?" I said—didn't recognize the voice at all—and she told me that I was pregnant. And I said, "I *am*?!"
>
> I fell for it hook, line, and sinker and I was so excited; and it turned out I *wasn't*; and then when I found out that it was her I . . . I guess when it turned out I wasn't and I wanted to be pregnant it was a real big letdown. I went *crazy* thinking I was, how wonderful, and then to find out it was *her*, it was like . . . it was almost like a slap below the belt, you know what I mean; it was . . .
>
> *Kinda mean?*
>
> Just a little bit. Not a lot; just a little bit. Yeah, it kinda was; I wanted it so bad. But I wasn't angry, as far as not wanting to speak to her or nothing like that. (Duenez and Duenez 1987)

It would be difficult to say Susie was amused by this joke on her. Yet she does not condemn the joke either. In general, she was a practical joke fan—she came from a family of practical jokers, her husband was a frequent practical joker, and she supported and encouraged his trickery, even when she was its target. If anyone could be expected to laugh along at a practical joke, it was she, but in this case her feelings were complex and ambivalent.

Susie indicates that she appreciated the joke, at least partly, because she stresses that she was completely taken in by it (using the common formula "I fell for it hook, line, and sinker"). She explains that she missed the clues that might have discredited the joke—the caller was a woman, not the man she had spoken to before; and she failed to recognize her best friend's voice. These details in her narrative indicate that she found the joke well formed and effective. It worked; but was it okay?

Susie's account of her reaction to the joke shows very mixed feelings about it. When she likens her feelings of disappointment at the end of the joke to being hit with a physical blow, "a slap below the belt," she gives notice that she also found the joke a violation. However, she hedges this notice—it was "almost like" a slap. At my prompting, she allowed that it was *just a little bit* mean, emphasizing that it was just a little bit, then dialing up the outrage by stating, "Yeah, it kinda was" mean. However, her next statement includes still one more hedge: "I wasn't angry, as far as not wanting to speak to her or nothing like that." Her conclusion communicates the same ambivalence as the previous statements: first claiming that she was not angry at all but immediately implying that she might have been at least a little angry—just not so much as to break off the friendship.

While she appreciated the joke, Susie could not agree with it, at least not completely. To deny her negative feelings would be to deny that there was something transgressive in the joke and to deny her affective commitment to its subject. Humor arises out of mixed feelings, but to directly acknowledge ambivalence in this setting would have risked a tear in the social fabric. Instead, she got even by enlisting her practical joker husband to play a trick on Cindy (that joke and its post-play are recounted in an earlier chapter).

The series of hedges and reversals in the evaluation portion of this narrative offers a view into the dilemma that practical joke targets face when they are let in on the joke. On one hand, the general cultural commitment to being able to laugh at oneself pressures targets to play along with the jokes. Further, when the joker is a close friend, targets are likely to feel motivated to avoid the criticism and resulting social disharmony that outright lack of support would engender. Susie felt anger, just not very much. The fact that the joker was a good friend would also help mitigate these negative feelings because she could reasonably surmise that her best friend's motives were benign. Thus, the social context provided both the motive and the means for her to show support for the joke.

Humor support of a joking transgression does not obliterate the transgression; instead, the humorous attitude lies in a simultaneous acknowledgment and acceptance of transgression. The benign violation model suggests that violations are recognized but considered benign, but often the process is more complex than that. Veatch (1998) stresses that the necessary condition of amusement is affective absurdity, in which the violation is noted and simultaneously found tolerable. Thus, to support a joke does not necessarily mean canceling or obliterating the violation within it. Susie could not be expected to abandon her strong desire to start a family just because her friend joked with her about it. Nor did she fail to notice that this trick violated everyday expectations of fair treatment by others.

"Getting even" is a common way for a target to respond to a practical joke. Answering one joke with another is a display of humor support but, like laughter, this strategy also provides cover for more complex feelings. By replying to her friend's practical joke with another one, Susie showed acceptance and appreciation while simultaneously acting on her more negative feelings. Like laughter, joke reciprocity papers over any possible negativity. The playful cover that the first joker used to seek permission is extended into a reciprocal joke, allowing the target to express both support and disagreement at the same time and using the inherent ambiguity of the play frame to mirror her affective ambivalence.

HUMOR SUPPORT STRATEGIES

Audiences have a variety of strategies at their command to communicate their support of jokes, including but not limited to laughter and replying with more jokes (Hay 2001). One common approach is aestheticizing the joke (Fine and Wood 2010)—that is, pointing out its effectiveness, creativity, and skillful construction. Alternatively, in a strategy found particularly frequently when the audience in question is also the joke target, support may be indicated in a ritualized, formulaic display of anger. All these tactics are in the spirit of the play frame that the jokers initiated—"playing along" with a joke. The joking frame conveys role distance to jokers, allowing them to suggest that they don't really mean what they are saying (Fine 1984), but playful support conveys role distance to the audience, reminding everyone that their support of the joke's violation is itself playful and not necessarily a reflection of their true attitudes and feelings.

Aestheticizing Strategies

John Johnson, a professor and frequent April Fools' Day joker, describes a joke he played on one of his graduate students:

> Speaking of Bob, one day I did convince him that I was going to leave academics. Because I was burned out. And I had him going for about fifteen minutes before I pointed out that it was April Fools' Day.
> *What did he do then?*
> He rolled on the ground, of course. I mean, he and I have pulled so many off on each other that once the plug is pulled, he knows what's going on. (Johnson 1986)

To be considered successful, April Fools' Day jokes between friends need the support of their targets. This joker uses the "rolled on the ground" formula to index the success of his joke because his target supported it enthusiastically. The traditional metaphor "rolling on the floor laughing" (ROTFL in digital social media communications) describes someone who is physically incapacitated by hearty laughter. Contemporary middle-class Anglo-American adults like John and Bob generally do not show humor support by laughing until they can no longer stand up, although it appears that it is a culturally approved humor support strategy among the Mbuti people, for example (Turnbull 1962, 44). Metaphorically, however, the formula is based on the idea that the volume and amount of physical involvement in laughter index the degree of support. In fact we do not know precisely how Bob signaled his amusement, but what matters is that the joker had no doubts about his target's support.

When I asked Bob about this trick, he adopted another humor support strategy. "That was a good one," he said enthusiastically, and went on to describe what a good acting job John had done:

> I believed him; he was real good; he was a real good actor. He was very convincing. He took me into his office and went into some stuff about he just couldn't take it anymore, he was fed up with it. He seemed very upset. He seemed genuinely upset. Almost to the point of crying. Really put it across real well.

Later, he said, "I got upset when John told me he was leaving academia, but when it's over, you laugh. You say, 'Jesus Christ, you got me again'" (Harrah-Conforth 1986).

Instead of blaming the joker for fooling them, practical joke targets often blame themselves. Phrases like "You got me" or "I don't believe I fell for that" are formulaic ways for targets to admit that they contributed to their own containment. Acknowledging the target's gullibility mitigates the joker's transgression, rendering it a benign violation. At the same time targets can downplay their own failures by praising the skillful execution of the fabrication that fooled them.

Even unoriginal jokes like tin-foiling a colleague's office cubicle carry potential for varying degrees of elaboration and creativity. An elaborate practical joke increases the possibilities that targets and other audiences have for aesthetic critique. One target literally applauded the jokers who had carefully foiled his cubicle: "Bravo; well done," he said, and soon after: "This is a masterpiece" (Marsh 2012, 297). He playfully treated the joke as an artistic event, borrowing the audience rituals familiar from classical music performances. Another target responded by carefully collecting all the tin foil from her cubicle and, with help from coworkers, forming it into a large ball, which she mounted, photographed, and posted online for others to admire (Marsh 2012, 298f; Piotrowski 1996). Thus, she answered one artistic work with another. Strategies like these convey humor support by implying that the jokes were artistic creations worthy of aesthetic critique; like laughter itself, this approach also diverts attention from any possible remnants of disapproval or disagreement that targets may feel.

The relationship between aesthetic appreciation and humorous appreciation of jokes is complex. Disagreement normally trumps aestheticization, but aesthetic considerations can encourage a joke audience to agree with a joke. To come to terms with the fact that someone found it acceptable to play a joke on them, targets must ascertain what the joker's motive was. Signs that jokers have expended time, trouble, and resources are read as evidence of their benign intentions. A carefully executed fabrication belongs more unambiguously to the realm of artistry; it calls attention to itself as a fabrication and a construction, thus inviting an aesthetic response. Contrariwise, sloppy and slapdash execution may suggest that the jokers' motives are less friendly, decreasing the likelihood that targets will respond with humor support.

Explicit emphasis on the aesthetic qualities of a joke implies agreement. Targets who are upset by their discomfiture and onlooker audiences who find it ethically objectionable are unlikely to critique or even notice the finer points of the joke. If performances of either jokes or other artistic genres are too transgressive, their aesthetic qualities become irrelevant. To take any kind of aesthetic approach to an immoral performance may be

considered immoral itself, because aestheticization implies agreement. By
the same token, disagreement on moral or ethical grounds trumps any aesthetic considerations.

In humorous genres, however, transgression itself can be an evaluative
yardstick so long as salient audiences are able to adopt a playful attitude
toward it. "Boldness" and "nerve" are positive qualities in practical jokers
when they effectively carry off the fine balancing act between norm violation and playful framing that characterizes humor.

Playful Ritualized Anger

Professor Johnson counted April Fools' Day as one of his favorite holidays.
Others in his department called him "the king of practical jokers." He would
not play jokes on his wife, he explained, because "she doesn't like that kind
of banter," but students, staff, and colleagues on campus were fair game:

> I pulled one on Jude; it was really funny. Jude is Patrick's secretary in
> African studies. I saw her and her family in the van over at the Credit
> Union one April Fools' Day. And I come up to Jude and I say, "Is Patrick
> angry at you or something?" She says, "No, I don't think so, why?" I says,
> "Well, he just called me, and he was *ranting* on the telephone. I couldn't
> understand; he *really* is mad at you. What did you do?"
>
> And she's sitting there *petrified*, you know, 'cause this is her *job* we're
> talking about—you know, he's the *boss*. So I says, "I think you ought to go
> back to the office or something 'cause he's really mad about something."
>
> So then I turn around and walk toward the Credit Union door. She's
> sitting in the van. And I stop and I turn around and I say, "Oh, by the way,
> Jude," and she says, "Yeah?" and I says, "April Fools'!" [*laughs*]
>
> I thought she was going to come out of the car with a stick or some-
> thing. She really blew up.
>
> *She didn't like it, then?*
>
> Oh, well, no, she thought it was funny. She didn't get angry. But it's
> that initial reaction, it's not real anger but it's . . . bantering, I guess you
> would say. (Johnson 1986)

Jokers know full well they run a risk of angering their targets, and when
John said "she really blew up," I thought it meant Jude was seriously angry.
He thought quite the opposite.

Humor support requires the playful suspension of everyday norms and
values (Mannell and La Fave 1976), but the playfulness of that suspension is sometimes overlooked in humor theory. Jude's response to the April
Fools' Day joke was a playful, exaggerated display of anger: "I thought she
was going to come out of the car with a stick." Exaggeration is a typical

metacommunicative signal of play, which suggests that Jude was playacting at being mad. Jude's tormentor got the message; he recognized that it was bantering, not real anger, and he read it as humor support.

Jude's bantering anger response explains a puzzling phrase I heard from another joker. Bruce, a thirty-seven-year old musician, archivist, and graduate student, was a compulsive practical joker who liked to scare his coworkers by grabbing their hands in the dark, but he thought his targets took the jokes reasonably well: "Well," he told me, "they'd be mad, but it wasn't an angry mad" (Harrah-Conforth 1986). "Mad" but not "angry mad" recalls Gregory Bateson's classic formulation of play, the playful nip that denotes the bite, but does not denote what the bite denotes (Bateson 1972, 180). "Not angry mad" denotes anger, but does not denote what anger denotes.

Besides mock anger, practical joke targets very often resort to formulaic threats of retaliation. Susie Duenez, whom we met earlier in this chapter, describes the post-play of a practical joke in which her husband had fooled her friend into thinking he was the credit manager from a furniture store:

> She didn't have any doubts, when he was doing it, that it wasn't the furniture company, and so therefore when she found out that it was him, I think she just felt so . . . she wasn't mad; she was not angry, it was kinda like, "I can't believe you did this" and, "I am going to pay him back some way. I owe you one." She laughed, and it was like, "I'm gonna owe you one." That was really her attitude; it wasn't one of anger, like, "I hate you for this." I think for a split second it was one of, "Ohhh I can't believe I fell for this." (Duenez and Duenez 1987)

Several conventional humor support strategies are evident here, including laughter, self-deprecation ("I can't believe I fell for this"), and praise for the joker's boldness ("I can't believe you did this," which indexes both the audacity of the joker and the violation in his deceptive play). There is also mock anger and a promise to get even. "I owe you one" is a formula commonly used by Americans in this situation; in New Zealand, the equivalent expression is "You'll keep," meaning that the speaker will find a way to get back at their tormenter eventually. It matters not in the least whether these threats are ever carried out; the ambiguous but playfully covered message has been delivered.

These ritualized threats are one of the cultural resources available to joke targets for conveying playful humor support. They are the practical joke equivalent of the formulaic, exaggerated groan that greets an outrageous pun. Both responses express humor support but not unconditional acceptance. The groan conveys appreciation for the pun but also annoyance for such an obvious departure from the norms of serious discourse. Similarly, the play anger of the practical joke target conveys agreement with the joke but is also a reminder that he or she recognizes the inherent transgression. The ambiguity of play accommodates the affective absurdity of simultaneous commitment to a norm and temporary departure from that commitment.

APPRECIATION, AGREEMENT, AND PLAY

In her model of the pragmatics of humor support, Jennifer Hay (2001) suggested that recognition and understanding are followed by appreciation and sometimes by agreement. "Agreement" may be the same thing as the permission that jokers seek for the inherent norm violations in their performances, and "appreciation" usually means amusement in vernacular talk about joke reception. According to the benign violation model of humor, appreciation (that is, amusement) does not happen in the absence of agreement. Hay argues that it is possible to be both amused and offended by a joke: that is, to appreciate it but not agree with the messages associated with it (72), but on the face of it the benign violation model rules this possibility out.

The humor support strategies of practical joke targets put the emphasis back on the playfulness of jokes *and* the reception of jokes (Mannell and La Fave 1976). Targets may answer jokes with more jokes, with aesthetic critique, or with ritualized, playful threats, and each of these choices treats the jokes as playful, artistic transgression. The serious dimension of a joke is not obliterated by its humorous framing, and audiences are aware that others might read their support of the joke as serious support for its transgression: that is, that their appreciation of the joke reflects their true attitudes and feelings. The benign violation theory of humor should be adjusted to recognize that the permission extended to a joke by an audience is itself framed as play. The norm suspension required for amusement is playful and temporary, suggesting that the audience's regular commitment to the relevant rules continues undiminished. Like jokes themselves, humor support belongs to the realm of play, not reality.

RESTORING AGENCY TO THE JOKE AUDIENCE

In suggesting that humor support is thoughtful and conventional, I am not claiming that genuine amusement does not exist. Of course it does. I am suggesting that amusement and its expression in social settings are complex accomplishments. If practical joke targets are any example, amusement may be accomplished swiftly or gradually; a joke that was not really funny to the person at the time may become so in retrospect. Further, amusement is not an all-or-nothing response. Humor support is touched by the play frame just as joke performances are, and this framing gives joke audiences multiple options for nuanced responses. Since joke audiences, especially joke targets, are fully aware that their responses are being monitored and judged according to prevailing ideas about what the sense of humor is and how it works, and since they are equally aware of the risk that transgressive ideas contained in jokes might be attributed to them (a problem that has been dubbed the "moral stickiness" of jokes [Fine and Wood 2010, 313]), they not unreasonably choose their responses in strategic ways.

Amusement is not something that happens to us when we are exposed to jokes or other funny things. Instead, amusement is something we do, sometimes consciously and deliberately, sometimes less so. One is not amused *by* a joke but amused *at* it; the quality of funniness lies not in the joke itself but in the perceiver, and audiences are not at the mercy of the joke but choose when and how to respond with displays of mirth. These suggestions run counter to the vernacular model of humor in which laughter is a virtually automatic response to amusement that is only loosely subject to personal control or cultural convention. In this conventional model of joke reception, any suggestion that the audience response is made by choice—indeed, the very concept of a humor support *strategy* itself—carries implications that the response cannot be genuine. Joke performances are the only cultural sphere that denies agency to the audience to such a degree. In contrast, audience applause at a classical music concert is ritualized and governed by definite conventions. People applaud until the conductor and soloists have left the stage, they may continue for two or three encores, they cheer when certain performers are acknowledged, and so on. Yet none of this artificiality is taken to suggest that the audience's approval is inauthentic. The idea that genuine responses to jokes are beyond individual control or cultural convention is itself a cultural convention.

NOTE

1. Other scholars reject the notion that laughter is a reflex (Billig 2005, 189–192; Mulkay 1988, 93–107; Smith 2008).

8

"That Was Why We Were Such Good Mates"

GETTING EVEN: THE DYNAMICS OF RECIPROCITY

TIME AND AGAIN, PRACTICAL JOKE VICTIMS RESPOND to their discomfiture with retaliation in kind, leading to sequences of reciprocal trickery that may take on a life of their own. The typical dynamic is illustrated by the following stories from a Newfoundland paper mill. Our source is Bob Saunders (pseudonym), a fifty-one-year old steam plant engineer, who was hit one night with a practical joke by other shift workers. The story began when he took a catnap during his shift, a minor and common transgression that workers both winked at and considered fair game for playful exploitation. While he slept, three fellow workers tied Bob's legs firmly to the chair . . . then they turned on the alarms. Waking with a start, he tried to jump up and promptly fell over, landing painfully on his elbows.

Every small group has its own style of joking, usually learned through observation and practice rather than explicit instruction. Local guidelines boost certain humorous genres over others, lay down who is an appropriate target, and specify the limits of the play frame (DeNatale 1990; Holmes and Marra 2002; Leary 1984b). The local joke aesthetic also provides rules on how to display humor support, including the approved forms of retaliatory practical joking. Among Bob's fellow shift workers in the mill, the conventional response of practical joke targets was to chase after the jokers and get even with them. One by one, Bob chased down his tormentors, soaking one with a hose and dousing another with what appeared to be hot water. That left just one:

> And then only one more guy I had to get and he was watching me all
> night. That was my best buddy, James Fisher, . . . I had to get him. I said,
> "I don't know how I'm going to get him." So, then every move he watched
> me. So, when we went down to the washroom to get ready to go home, he

 DOI: 10.7330/9780874219845.c008

was there dressed, you know, he was watching every move and there was no way I was going to get him.

So, this young casual guy came in and he was wearing his hard hat. So, when James wasn't looking I motioned to him, "Okay, leave your hard hat here by the sink." So, that's what he did. He didn't know what was going on, but he knew I wanted his hard hat for some reason.

So, I took out the lining and I filled the hard hat full of water, just walked over towards my locker with the hard hat. So, James looked at me and couldn't see nothing out of, you know, nothing amiss, right? So, he went on putting on his shoes and I just put the hat on his head, water and all. So, he was with all his new clothes on.

He got half mad over it even though he was my best friend. He practically almost got mad over it, right? But when he realized what he had done to me, you know, he laughed at it, right? (Small 1999, 158)

Humor support in the form of playful retaliation can paper over a target's mixed feelings. Bob described the joke on him as "a bad joke in a way because I could have broke my two arms' (158). He had a reason to feel aggrieved because the risk of serious injury put the prank beyond the locally allowed limits of play, but the same local rules also prescribed what kind of response was appropriate: answering one joke with another without delay, physically chasing after the miscreants, and using water as the main play material. In this mill, as Bob remarked, "Water was a lot of it because water is suppose to be harmless" (157). His retaliation conformed to the local joking aesthetic, where pranks were low in fabrication or trickery but high in the amount of physical mess they caused. In the paper mill, booby traps involving glue, water, wood chips, and the like were the order of the day.

Playful retaliation also extended the unilateral play of the original practical joke, transforming it into a shared, competitive game. According to the rules for joking in the mill, James knew he was marked for retaliation. He had to be ever vigilant for some trick from his former target, who was watching closely for any opening in his opponent's defenses. It was a playful contest for both of them, a game that they apparently played with great absorption for the space of one work shift.

In the post-play section of his narrative, Bob speculates about what was going through his target's mind. James's response to the playful assault on his person was neither simple nor unthinking. At first, "He got half mad over it even though he was my best friend," implying that their friendship was one of the things that ought to have persuaded him to laugh along. However, Bob suggests, what tipped the balance was the joking context, namely, the fact that James had played an edgy joke on his friend earlier in the shift. Bob surmised that James knew the local morality of joking, which expected him to support Bob's practical joke because he, James, was guilty of playing a joke on Bob not long before. Having started the play sequence, he was required to assent to its continuation. Failure to do so would be grounds for further sanction from the group.

Folk morality has a special disdain for people who play jokes on others but object when the shoe is on the other foot. In American English such people are often described with the formula "They can dish it out, but they can't take it." Bob Saunders described another coworker who fell into this personality type:

> But, like another one of the guys, one night when they played a joke on me, and I saw him coming. We used to have those fire extinguishers, those big old fire extinguishers. So, in the meantime I had it brought over by the desk making out I was asleep. So, he come in and he come and stood right by me, looking at me and he was going to pour the water in my eyes and I just tipped it up . . . And I just let it go and shot at his face and it scared the hell right out of him. He really got mad. He really got mad. He was one of those guys [who] loved, you know, doing things to you but don't dare do anything back to him. Like us guys it would be give and take, you know, you get me, I get you, you know, some other day, some other time. You know, it's all in fun. But some guys, like, you know, they sort of didn't want to be jokes played back at [*sic*]. But, you know, you had to do it. (Small 1999, 108)

This man's unambiguous "really got mad" violated the local ideal of reciprocal joking, described as "You get me, I get you . . . some other day, some other time." In this pattern, coworkers take turns "dishing it out" and "taking it"—alternately aiming and receiving practical jokes. Although the actual patterns of who jokes and who is targeted may not always be as even as Bob's words suggest, reciprocity and equilibrium describe the ideal model of workplace joking, conveying the impression that everyone is jointly involved in creating and maintaining an ongoing play frame. When somebody "really gets mad" and breaks the chain of reciprocal joking, it challenges the "all in fun" message previously sustained by everyone.

CHICKENS AND MORE CHICKENS: RULES OF RECIPROCITY

In all genres of joking, a common way to show humor support is to build on the original joke or answer it with another one. With oral narrative and riddle jokes reciprocity can take the form of rapid-fire exchanges, creating situations that have been described as "humor orgies" (Fry 1968, 106–109). In contrast, reciprocal practical joke sequences sometimes extend over months or even years. Rob Mills, a thirty-six-year old, college-educated carpenter, described such a series of practical jokes between himself and his brothers John and Russ, all of whom lived in Brown County, Indiana. The series began one evening in the Halloween season when John and his wife drove to the neighboring town of Bloomington to attend the annual Halloween performance by Dennis James. Rob begins by describing the *materia iocosa,* the primary ingredients for the prank:

> John lived out in the country, in Brown County, and had chickens. And one thing about chickens is they love to make nests where there's a shady spot and it's covered: a little nook. And they seem to be able to tell when cars are about ready to be added to the junk pile. And they find a window open and they enter and make a nest. So John had an old Chevrolet station wagon that was approaching the end of its life, so he'd occasionally find chickens laying. You don't care about the car as much so you leave the windows open. So he was used to finding chickens in his car.
>
> So he went to Bloomington once, in the Chevrolet station wagon, to a concert, Dennis James. And Russ and Bill gathered up his chickens, 'cause it was night, they were easy to catch; took them to Bloomington and put them in his Chevrolet station wagon.
>
> *All of them?*
>
> I think it was all of them; it was about a dozen chickens. And so John and his wife, Maggie, came out of the concert and went over to their car, and there were chickens in the car, and they thought, "Oh, big deal, there are chickens in the car—wait a minute, we're in Bloomington!" [*laughs*]. So they had to drive home with chickens roosting in their car.
>
> Which started some chicken jokes. Another Halloween night we came home, Cathy and I, to our trailer, from Bloomington; we'd been to the Dennis James concert. And it happened enough that pranks had been played on that night that we were a little wary about what we were going to find. We opened the door to the trailer, and there were no lights on inside, but we could see some kind of shape in the doorway. So we were pretty cautious. What John had done is piled up chairs and boxes and put a rooster up on top. Hoping that we'd open the door and start in and the rooster'd crow, and there'd be a big scramble and a mess.
>
> So that didn't really get us. But we didn't take the rooster back that night. So early in the morning, the rooster starts crowing. Real early. So it got us then. (Mills 1987)

The "chicken jokes" sequence began one Halloween, which, like April Fools' Day, is recognized in the United States as an appropriate time for practical joking. When the original joke is tied to an annual calendar custom, the unspoken rules suggest that retaliation may follow a year later and still be recognized as belonging to the sequence. In contrast, in Bob Saunders's paper mill joking retaliation was expected to follow immediately if at all possible.

Local joking cultures supply the guidelines for practical joke sequences, but across different groups and different joking styles some common tendencies may be observed. Each joke tends to match the preceding one in style or theme while also seeking to best it in ingenuity or impact. Compliance with the local joking aesthetic is the norm—a hard hat filled with water is answered with another booby-trapped tool rather than a telephone prank. If the original trick relied on persuasion and verbal trickery rather than physical props, the retaliatory joke will use similar means. Further, the competitive edge is usually blunted: it is desirable to do the opponent one better, but not ten times better—the latter would threaten the valence of the play frame. These constraints encourage humor support from both targets and onlookers in the group. Finally, some series, like the Brown County chicken jokes, add the additional constraint of confining each joke in the series not just to the same style but to the same ingredients. These arbitrary limits add an arbitrary constraint to the tricksters' creativity, which increases the challenge but also highlights the gamelike nature of the series.

Both competition and morality fuel these reciprocal practical joking sequences. The genre offers unlimited possibilities for creatively topping any joke. Each successive joke creates another competitive edge that motivates a response. At a more fundamental level, each joke adds a fresh infusion of transgression, creating a moral imbalance that demands redress. A similar dynamic may be observed in the exchanges of verbal jokes (Fry 1968, 106–109). Practical joke series grow in part because the parties never attain exact moral equilibrium.

FINDING THE LIMITS OF HUMOROUS PLAY

Specifying the limits of play is a crucial function of the local joking aesthetic. As an example, consider the following account of a reciprocal joke sequence between two men in a small dairy-farming district in New Zealand. The story comes from an obituary of a man named Bill Hathorne in the *Nelson Mail* in 1997. The location is Anakiwa, a small village in the Marlborough Sounds, home of the Outward Bound School where Bill had worked as the maintenance man:

> He was a great practical joker, quick to initiate reprisals if anyone played
> a practical joke on him. Once a Linkwater valley dairy farmer was silly

enough to remove a set of steps outside a gypsy caravan . . . while Bill was inside living it up at a party. They all laughed, particularly the farmer, when Bill came to leave, opened the caravan door and fell 1.5m to the ground.

Next morning the farmer went out to milk his 200 or so cows. Imagine his surprise when he found someone had been in his unlocked cowshed before him and totally dismantled the milking machine. Hathorne had struck again. (Grady 1997)

Did these jokes go too far? Considered in the abstract, both scholars and lay commentators are happy to provide rules of thumb as to the proper limits of jokes (for example, Morreall 1983, 110). If the rule of thumb is to avoid jokes that are costly or dangerous, both jokes in this series went too far. Causing someone to fall one and half meters could have resulted in significant injury. Likewise, dismantling a farmer's milking machine could impact his economic well-being. Although the machine could be put back together, it would take some trouble, especially with a herd of 200 impatient cows waiting. Viewed objectively, both jokes arguably go beyond the limits.

Yet it seems that the original audiences to these jokes supported them. Since a newspaper obituary is not the place to raise disagreements, the inclusion of these stories in Bill's obituary suggests that they were a part of the local joking repertoire and that his acquaintances supported the jokes. The local dairy-farming audience was able to draw on its specialized knowledge, within which milking machines are as familiar as expensive computer workstations are to scholars and office workers. Because of this familiarity, a rural community would more readily countenance playful tampering with this equipment, even though it is expensive and economically important, and such pranks involving costly farm equipment are a traditional part of wedding shivarees, for example (Greenhill 1989). Similarly, practical jokes on computer workstations are common among office workers.

In in-group practical joking, an important criterion for deciding a joke's success is whether or not the target supports it. The local bystander audience would have been influenced to support the physically dangerous joke on Bill because he seemed to support it himself. Despite sustaining a dangerous fall, he kept his composure and replied with a practical joke that exceeded the original in daring, effort, and impact, thus making him the winner in what everyone understood as a contest. With attention diverted to this contest of audacity and wit, no one need ask whether he was really amused at falling several feet to the ground. The humorous mode (Mulkay 1988) leaves such questions unasked and unanswered, allowing reciprocal joking to paper over any actual hurts and dissensions in the joint accomplishment of social solidarity.

Readers who are not a part of the little community of Anakiwa might find this sequence of jokes inappropriate and not at all funny. Although it is a truism in humor theory that distance tends to enable amusement (McGraw et al. 2012), this case illustrates that, as the vernacular saying has it, sometimes you just have to be there to see the funny side. If amusement depends upon a violation that is considered acceptable, humorousness is in the eye of the beholder, not an objective measurable quality inherent in the joke. As a consequence, "nothing is funny to everyone and anything seems potentially funny to someone" and "humor lies neither in laughter nor in jokes but only in the minds of men" (La Fave, Haddad, and Maesen 1976, 85, 83). The playful violations of jokes are trivial, not inherently, but only if the beholder adopts a playful attitude toward them.

The suitability of a practical joke—indeed, of any joke—is not dependent on staying within the rules. On the contrary, jokes depend upon the existence of some norm that is violated. The limits of humorousness and seriousness are socially constructed, locally and temporarily. The joker who laughs alone is one who has failed to win support for his or her joke from a salient audience, and it is the audience's response that is the greatest determinant of the final assessment of a joke's humorousness (Zijderveld 1983, 34). The limits of humor are set by the local joking aesthetic and the immediate social situation, but it is the audience's definition of play that decides the matter.

Hathorne's antagonist is not named in the newspaper account, but it is assumed that the two knew each other. In fact, they knew each other well enough that Hathorne knew who had removed the caravan steps and caused his fall. Similarly, Bob Saunders knew precisely who had tied him to his chair as he napped, and he considered one of them his best friend. The precise social context—specifically, the relationship between the joker and his or her target—is a significant factor in the target's decision of whether or not to support a practical joke. Within the right relationship, the limits of play can be stretched very far indeed.

New Zealanders Rod and Lee shared this kind of relationship. In his autobiography Lee recalled a time during a trip to Thailand when they were dining out with two women friends. Finding some unfamiliar things that resembled green beans in his soup, he asked the others what they were. "All three confirmed that they were green beans," he said, so:

> I ate them. They weren't. I thought I'd been napalmed. It was the hottest thing I'd ever bit into . . . My lips went numb for hours and I couldn't taste anything until the next day. My taste buds were razed. I don't blame Rod

for it at all. Well, I do actually. I mean, he knew what he was doing when he called it a green bean, it's just that I would have done exactly the same thing to him if the positions were reversed. He knew it too and that was why we were such good mates. (Hughes 1999, 133)

"I don't blame Rod for it at all" is an expression of humor support, but a playful one, as underlined by the retraction: "Well, I do actually." The phrase "that was why we were such good mates" articulates the way that reciprocal joking both builds and displays solidarity between friends. When two people can playfully mistreat each other in this way without anyone getting angry, jointly sustaining a play frame over actions that others would find serious, it is taken as proof that they are true friends—good mates. They can joke with each other because they are good mates and the fact that they joke in this way also makes them good mates.

Rod and Lee, enjoying special license to treat each other with joking disrespect, are in what anthropologists call a joking relationship. In some parts of the world, membership in a joking relationship is determined by kinship connections, but in modern industrialized societies such relationships are elective and diverse, occurring between friends, spouses, and within other dyads, but also among small groups, especially in occupational settings. Since modern joking relations are elective rather than structural, the status of these relationships must be regularly affirmed. The joking relationship label describes rather than explains the centrality of jocular insults, humorous disrespect, practical jokes, and the like in the relationship, and it underestimates the extent to which humor support is an accomplishment. In fact, the parties in a joking relationship jointly sustain the play realm by offering and supporting each other's jokes, cooperatively building their relationship in the process. Humorousness and friendship are linked cooperative accomplishments.

Joking reciprocity is not necessarily a part of joking relationships. Structural and kin-based versions often mandate that only one party has the license to joke with the other, who is similarly mandated to accept this treatment with good grace (Radcliffe-Brown 1940). In Keith Basso's account of satirical Whiteman performances among the Western Apache, there is no sign that those who are enlisted as foils in the performances "get even" by returning the favor some other time (1979). In contrast, white Americans and New Zealanders commonly describe jocular give-and-take as the preferred norm in friendships between peers. Thus Rod assumes that his friend would have done the same to him, implicitly stating that his friend would be permitted to do so. Whether or not there was any actual exchange of practical jokes or other jocular play between them, the fact of their friendship means this reciprocity is assumed.

The targets of practical jokes must ask themselves whether or not the jokes are "all in fun" as the jokers claim. The joke is a transgression against the target wrapped in a mantle of play; to support it requires one to discount the transgression, and to withhold support is to discount the playful frame. The question usually comes down to the joker's intent, and since intentionality is always opaque, targets fall back on their knowledge of the individual and of the relationship. If the joker is a friend, there is more reason to believe that the playful claim is genuine. The mechanism by which targets may choose to support practical jokes is the same as the one that applies in the reception of jocular insults. "The knowledge of the relationship they bring to their interaction frames all messages," according to Elliott Oring, and "this frame transforms—inverts—their messages so that literal insults emerge as signs of affection" (1992,142). Within the frame provided by the relationship, the humorous mode reigns. It reverses meaning, turning insult into amity, aggression into affection (Basso 1979; La Fave, Haddad, and Maesen 1976, 82; Pilcher 1972, 102–113). The rules and meanings that hold sway in the outside world may be turned topsy-turvy.

The meaning and significance of practical jokes are inextricably tied to their social context, which is why they may be highly valued *within* a particular relationship or small group but readily disparaged in the abstract. The same joke that is viewed as hilarious by those involved often leaves outsiders cold. Considered in the abstract, practical jokes are much more likely to appear simply cruel or puerile and not at all funny because outsiders have little or no knowledge of the people involved or their prior relationships. They also have no stake in avoiding the threats to solidarity that such criticism would cause if it came from within a group. The external social context promotes a chorus of disapproval from social critics and scholars, whereas the insider's social context encourages the creation of the playful frame that turns insult into humor.

When the person supporting a practical joke or jocular insult is the target him- or herself, this support paradoxically transforms a transgression into a dual compliment. Whether practical joke victims laugh or retaliate within the play frame, they effectively applaud the joker and show themselves as having what people call "a good sense of humor," the ability take a playful attitude toward oneself, a capacity widely considered the epitome of psychological health (Wickberg 1998). By the same token, to play a practical joke on a friend, confident that he or she can "take it," is a way of praising the target (Basso 1979; La Fave, Haddad, and Maesen 1976, 82). It demonstrates faith that the person possesses a healthy psychological outlook and excellent social skills. Thus, successful practical joking reflects well on all parties.

Successful jokes enhance sociability and build solidarity between tricksters, targets, and anyone else who offers humor support (Buckley 2003, 178–190). To laugh at a joke "implies a community; a fellowship of laughers with whom the humor is shared" (Oring 2003, 56–57). This fellowship is "a tiny conspiracy of humour" (Kuipers 2006, 194), the conspiracy being an agreement to countenance transgression. Humor support suggests that joker and audience share the same norms and values, as against the hypothetical others who would disagree with the joking violation. Those who laugh together share a guilty pleasure, and their laughter announces this togetherness in a small but shared moral universe.

It is just as important for a group to claim a good sense of humor as it is for an individual. The paradoxical power of the joking relationship to reframe events becomes an esoteric measure for distinguishing not just a dyad but an entire group from all others. When the in-group supports joking transgressions, it may be thought that outsiders are unable to muster the same attitude; thus, this shared tolerance may be claimed as something that sets the in-group apart from outsiders. Many small groups believe that their propensity for joking is unique—that they joke with each other more than others do. The existence of an in-group joking culture becomes a badge of pride that proves just how tight their solidarity is.

BORASSING

Put a group of unrelated people together in a camp, barracks, or dormitory, and practical joking is almost certain to break out. College students, summer campers, military recruits, seal hunters, and Antarctic researchers are all fertile groups for a certain style of practical joking (Bronner 1995, 117–120; Posen 1974; Scott 1974; Steinberg 1992, 190–197). American college students have generic terms for this type of practical joking, the verbs *borass* and *rat fuck* (or simply *RF*) and their derivatives being among the most common.[1] The existence of such generic terms betrays an emic understanding that the joking that goes on in dormitories is of a piece, despite its superficial variety (Long 1979). Since the style of practical joking found in college dorm settings is equally common in ships, camps, barracks, and other temporary living spaces of enforced intimacy, I extend the emic term *borassing* to refer to all of them. Whatever the location, borassing pranks are generic—including such well-known traditional tricks as the short-sheeted bed and the booby-trapped toilet. They run the gamut from attacks on

individual dorm rooms or beds to booby-trapped bathrooms to depredations on underwear and finally to pranks played on people when they are
asleep and vulnerable. All invade and disorder the private and intimate
spaces left to residents who must coexist in settings where privacy is relatively limited. Neither this generic nature nor the intimacy is coincidental.

College dorm rooms are regularly subjected to borassing. When the
room's owner is absent—and sometimes even when he or she is present—
floor mates find ways to gain access and wreak havoc. Filling the entire room
with crumpled newspaper was a favorite in my undergraduate hostel at the
Victoria University of Wellington in the later 1970s, and data found in U.S.
folklore archives yields other favorites: dumping the contents of drawers
and closets onto the floor; booby-trapping doors and furniture; filling a
room with messy and incongruous substances. Elaborate variations include
removing all the furniture and contents and reassembling them somewhere
else—the more incongruous, the better; thus some hapless resident might
come home to find his or her room has been relocated to the quadrangle.
Some variations pile one booby trap on another to considerable effect:

> At the men's dormitory at the University of California, Riverside, all the
> boys who had not gone out on one weekend night decided to play a trick
> on a boy who had gone out. They first replaced the bolts in the door hinges
> of his room with light wood. Then they removed the large window oppo-
> site the door, tied a rope to the inside door knob and dropped the rope out
> the window with a large weight attached to the end. The window was two
> stories up. An electrical engineering student then attached a bag of flour
> to the outlet so that the bag would explode when the light was turned on.
> When the boy came home that night, he started talking to the boys sit-
> ting around the drinking fountain, an informal gathering place, but was
> ignored. So he gave up and went to his room. When he opened the door,
> it was pulled out of his hands, bounced across the room and out the open
> window, falling to the ground below. To see what had happened, he turned
> on the light and was showered with flour. (Selvin 1965)

Borassing on this scale requires the collusion of several tricksters, and accounts
suggest that borassing pranks always involve the actual or implied collusion
of an entire group.

Any behavior deemed to flout the norms of the group may provide
an excuse for a borassing attack. One such misdemeanor, as a male college
student at the University of California at Berkeley in the 1970s explained,
is spending more time in solitary study or other private activities than the
group feels is proper:

An evening prank, useful to "loosen up" a friend, is to ball up a roll of masking tape, attach it to the friend's window on the outside, and light it on fire. The object is to make the friend run out of his room, calling "Fire!" Hopefully the person will be embarrassingly attired. The jokesters try to pull the prank just after the victim has gone to bed, hoping to catch him in the nude.

Sam hastened to assure me that a fire extinguisher is handy at all times when this trick is played. He practiced the joke only once, in 1971, at Barrington Hull Student Cooperative. It is not easily repeated, he says, because it attracts a lot of attention.

This is an example of a college prank which uses extreme methods to wake up a person who is not conforming to group standards. This prank, says Sam, would be played on someone who had "gotten too serious" about studying, a girl friend, or another aspect of his life. It would not be played on a girl—the prank is strictly an attempt by peers to reassert themselves when they feel neglected. (Caulfield 1976)

The trickery is intended to remind fellow residents of their social allegiances and encourage them to balance individual and social demands. In this respect generic communal pranks have much in common with other ludic, ritualized customs such as charivaris and mumming, in which male youth groups assert their claims on the loyalty of individuals drawn away by competing claims such as marriage (Davis 1971; Glassie 1975). Borassing targets can usually enlist the help of fellow residents to set things back to rights, conveying a lesson in the value of relying on the group and the priority of group needs over individual dignity. Although generic in form and content, these pranks target one person at a time, each instance reproducing in concrete form a model of the ideal relationship between the individual and the group. Since the tricks are generic, not tailored to the personality of any target, and since they may be repeated on virtually everyone in the group, they send the message that no resident has a right to consider him- or herself better than the rest.

Whatever form the jokes take, borass pranks invade and discombobulate one of the few private spaces available to a resident. Privacy is even scarcer in camps, ships, and barracks, where private space shrinks to nothing more than one's own bunk or berth. Pranksters routinely tamper even with these spaces, introducing messy substances or perhaps noxious critters. A favorite is the short-sheeted bed, also known as the "apple pie" bed, in which the prankster folds the bedsheet in half in such a way that it is impossible to get into bed. In the following example, the prankster was the target's sister:

Short sheeting his bed was one of the pranks that he best remembers her
playing on him because it was always so funny for both of them. When
Suzie knew that Lawrence was going to bed she would wait outside the
bedroom door and try to stifle her laughter until he began to struggle.
When grunts of frustration and noises of ruffling and snapping would
come from the bed, Suzie would break out laughing. My father would then
begin to understand what had happened and would eventually start laughing himself, if only out of relief.

The short-sheeted bed trick is a well-known tradition in summer camps and
similar places, but this report shows that it is also found within families—
another place where people share intimate space. Lawrence, the victim here,
took the trick that he had learned from his sister and went on to play it on
others: "He short sheeted several bunks in his Navy submarine, with great
success (sailors really loved the thing) in the 60s and more than once short
sheeted my mother's bed in the 70s and 80s" (Ross 1994).

Residents of camps and dormitories must also share bathrooms, another
routine site for generic practical jokes. Tricksters insert bouillon cubes into
shower heads, coat toilet seats with Vaseline, toothpaste, and other viscous
substances, or sabotage the toilet itself by adding jello to the water or cover-
ing it with an invisible layer of plastic wrap. The net result is to turn a space
devoted to hygiene into a place of scatological dirt and mess. Given the
stress placed on hygiene in Western industrialized societies, such scatological play probably speaks to deep-seated fears and anxieties of both the jokers
and the targets.

In settings of enforced or incongruous intimacy, nothing is so intimate
that it is safe from the depredations of fellow residents. Underwear is stolen,
hidden, stowed in odd places, or subjected to mess that makes it unusable.
At the slumber parties of prepubescent American girls, stealing another girl's
bra and putting in the freezer overnight is a very traditional prank. This
trick no doubt is related to the anxieties of girls of this age about their bud-
ding sexuality, but the trick also expresses another anxiety. It is the girl who
falls asleep first who lays herself open for this treatment. To be asleep while
others are awake is to be an anomaly—and as we have seen repeatedly, an
anomaly always calls for a joke (Douglas 1975, 98).[2]

To sleep in the company of others is to be especially vulnerable to harassment and also to worry about the embarrassing things we might do when
not fully in control of our actions. Accordingly, we find several varieties of
pranks on sleepers. One of the most popular is the trick in which the joker—
typically accompanied by a sizable party of observers—places the sleeping
target's hand in a bowl of warm water. According to folk legend, this action

will cause the sleeper to wet the bed, thus infantilizing the victim (or so the jokers hope; in almost all accounts in which this trick was attempted, it did not work). The evidence in folklore archives suggests that this trick is talked about at least as often as it is enacted, but for dealing with deep-seated anxieties, talking about it is just as effective (and safer) than doing it.

Why are pranks of this kind so rife in dormitories and barracks? Simon Bronner (1995, 117–120) argues that college dorm pranks ridicule students' fear of being alone and their fear of confusion while also urging reliance on the group. While I agree that the effect of these pranks is to assert the importance of group norms and communal demands over individual ones, I think the fear that is reflected here is the discomfort of living in close quarters with relative strangers. Consequently, borassing-style pranks will proliferate wherever people find themselves in situations of enforced intimacy, with all the incongruity and vulnerability that implies. These pastimes are not explained simply by the high spirits—or immaturity—of adolescents, because they are equally popular among adults—for example, submariners, Antarctic researchers, and sealers (Harrowfield 1995; Scott 1974). The common denominator is not age, but rather the fact that all of these people find themselves living in temporary situations of enforced intimacy. Although family members sometimes torment each other in this way, by far the most common site for ravages of this kind are summer camps, barracks, and dormitories. People who never get involved in practical joking in any other part of their lives will do so in these situations.

Although many American middle-class adults have had the experience of going to camp or living in a college dorm, these living arrangements are understood to be a departure from the norm. In cultures where people normally share bathrooms and sleeping spaces only with family members, the prospect of sleeping and washing in close proximity to nonrelatives, or even strangers, is likely to give rise to anxiety. A dormitory or bunkhouse is both an incongruous and a liminal place. The American cultural norm is that one shares intimate spaces only with close relatives or intimate friends, but here people find themselves obliged to share these spaces with people they barely know. It is for this reason that borassing pranks are concentrated in bathrooms, bedrooms, or beds. Dorm residents also share dining and general living spaces, but practical jokes in these areas, while not unknown, are less common. The dining areas and living rooms of private homes are often open to visitors, and so it is less incongruous to share them even with large numbers of relative strangers.

Incongruity can be uncomfortable, especially when it is not voluntary and touches on topics that are very close to us; but if one can find a way to live with it, perhaps by discounting it, it becomes enjoyable and also a source of humor (Morreall 1989). Joking proliferates in the expressive realm to reflect a joke—that is, an incongruity—in the social situation (Douglas 1975, 98). While we may appreciate and enjoy incongruity when it is safely confined to expressive forms, as a feature of everyday life we tend to find it uncomfortable and seek ways to remove or resolve it.

Borassing pranks do more than express the incongruity built into dormitory life; they also offer an effective means of eliminating it by quickly shaping a semblance of the solidarity and close relations that are expected to go along with living in such close quarters. The presence of tolerated and reciprocal joking is widely recognized as a sign of close social relations. Dorm and camp residents start out without such close connections, but they can create the appearance of the desired closeness by engaging in widespread reciprocal practical joking. If this joking is successful, that is, if it meets with humor support in the form of shared laughter and/or reciprocal joking, it will in turn work to build the solidarity that is desired.

Reciprocal practical joking, along with other forms of jocular assault, both builds and relies upon intimate knowledge of the worldview and personalities of friends and relations. Bunkmates start out without such close knowledge of their fellows; since camps and dorms are liminal places— occupied for temporary periods and understood to be apart from residents' normal living arrangements—residents do not have the luxury of time that goes into building regular joking relations.[3] It is for this reason that virtually all dormitory pranks are of the generic type. Surrounded by relative strangers, would-be tricksters do not have the close knowledge of their fellows' habits and personality that they need to craft tailored practical jokes. Instead, they turn to jokes that rely upon common cultural scripts that are familiar to all—scripts for how to get into bed, use a shower, and so on. If the showerheads in a communal bathroom have been booby-trapped, it is a safe bet that before long a fellow resident will attempt to use the shower in the usual way and so walk into the trap. By exploiting such generic behaviors, generic pranks are almost assured of being effective.

Things do not always work this smoothly, of course. The pressure on practical targets to agree with their joking discomfiture can be intense, and the social implications of their response are far from trivial. To a large degree, one's future status in the group depends upon how one reacts to victimization at the hands of the group—so the same prank, according to its aftermath, can either build solidarity or work to exclude. Nevertheless, peer pressure does not always work, and not all targets are so biddable. Further, reciprocity is not always the goal, as there are many accounts of individuals who are singled out as practical joke targets because they are disliked or do not fit into the rest of the group for one reason or another. Often the very same generic prank that leads to reciprocity and solidarity in one case may lead to exclusion in another.

NOTES

1. The connotations of homosexual assault in this terminology are not accidental; they speak to anxieties that are exacerbated in same-sex groups that are obliged to share close quarters.

2. Occasioned by a similar anomaly, traditional wakes also give rise to practical jokes, for "a person being waked is physically still part of the community and is present at the social gathering, yet is unable to participate" (Harlow 1997, 151).

3. I am grateful to Christie Davies for this observation.

9

Pranks, Rituals, and Hazing

Practical jokes are about relationships, whether between individuals or between individuals and the groups to which they belong. The vernacular rhetoric of the genre emphasizes the role of individual personality as the engine that makes a fabrication work, and in most cases the joking spotlight is trained on the target while the individual trickster is surrounded, and sometimes entirely hidden, by a crowd of supporters whom he or she represents. Jokes between individuals grow out of and help to grow their personal relationships, and are treated as reciprocal (even if the reciprocity is a fiction). However, many other practical jokes dramatize the relationship and police the boundaries between the individual and the collectivity, especially the ritualized pranks that accompany rites of passage such as weddings and workplace initiations.

SHIVAREES AND WEDDING PRANKS

Western industrialized societies are relatively lacking in public rites of passage (Myerhoff 1982), but such are not completely absent. Weddings are one of the most commonly experienced rites of passage in modern America, and they are common sites for pranks and practical jokes. Folklorists have long documented ritualized pranks, especially before the wedding, when friends and coworkers submit the bride or groom to various kinds of ritualized degradation (Dyer 1979; Monger 1971, 197; 1978; Nickerson 1974, 137). The shivaree, a ritual hazing that occurs after the wedding to welcome the newlyweds into the community, frequently includes generic pranks aimed at creating disorder and mess, or at inhibiting the sexual act (Greenhill 1989; 2010, 179–193; Morrison 1974). While shivarees and prewedding rituals are no longer widespread, middle-class American weddings are similarly accompanied by a wide variety of pranks whose

DOI: 10.7330/9780874219845.c009

techniques and themes closely resemble rural shivarees and older prewedding hazing rituals.

The Internet offers a forum for sharing stories and ideas for wedding
pranks as it does for other kinds of practical jokes. Inspired by a prank that
they played on a brother-in-law's wedding, for example, Mark and Cheryl
Miller created a website devoted to collecting prank recipes and stories
about wedding pranks. Between 1997 and 2002 the site drew dozens of stories and recipes, which the Millers arranged according to every stage of the
ritual complex: bachelor and bachelorette parties, the rehearsal dinner, the
ceremony itself, the honeymoon, decorating the car, and so on. While the
pranks display a fair amount of creativity and variation, several themes recur
in the material. First are prewedding pranks in which the groom (brides
are far less often targeted in this way) is temporarily abducted. "Jeremy"
recounts a typical scenario:

> Three days before the wedding of Sean, a friend of mine, four of us got
> together to play a trick on him. We showed up at his house driving a
> black rented Buick and wearing black suits with dark sunglasses. We car-
> ried high-powered water guns (painted black). We forced Sean out of the
> house, tied him up, stuck him in the car and drove him to the home town
> of the bride (Jen). *For five hours* Sean was begging to be let out, but we just
> jabbed him with our guns. Jen's family knew about this, and helped us with
> the planning. We drove to a hospital fund-raising carnival and put Sean up
> on the dunk tank (still tied—every time he went in, we fished him out).
> For several hours he was dunked by young women (many of them friends
> of Jen) who read a sign saying "This man has taken one from your midst."
> Then we drove him home.
> We never did take off the sunglasses. (Miller and Miller 1997)

The "trick" Jeremy recounts includes the physical humiliation of the groom
as he is tied up, kidnapped, and dunked in water multiple times, but it also
includes clear-cut signs of play in the "'gangster" costumes, toy guns, and
the carnival dunk tank. However, it is unilateral play, initiated and carried
out by Sean's friends with the collusion of the bride's family. Notably, however, this account, unlike most of the practical joke stories we have considered so far, makes no mention of whether or not the target supported the
joke; in fact he has no active role in the narrative at all.

The morality of practical joking may throw light on these ritual pranks:
we may ask, how have the targets transgressed to warrant such correction
by means of practical jokes? In the previous example, the groom is playfully
punished by the female friends of his bride-to-be because he has "taken" one

of them out of singlehood. Although older relatives helped in the planning, this trick is presented as being conceived and carried out by friends of the bride and groom. Indeed, virtually all wedding pranks are the responsibility of young people. Older relatives may assist with ideas and materials, but responsibility for the pranks is assumed and claimed by the age set of the bride and groom. In this respect, contemporary wedding pranks resemble the charivaris and other ludic activities in traditional rural villages in which youth groups asserted their rights to marriageable partners (Davis 1971; Glassie 1975, 115–118).

Speeches by the best man and the maid or matron of honor are popular occasions for embarrassing the bride or groom by introducing bawdy elements from their supposedly unchaste past. Some participants go beyond verbal references into miniature dramatic rituals:

> I've got a good prank for my sis's wedding. At the dance, I'm going to give a bunch of young ladies keys ahead of time. I'm going to [set] out a bucket in the middle of the dance floor and give this big speal [*sic*] that since my sister's husband is now married, all the ladies are going to have to give up their keys to his apartment. Then the ladies will come and put them in the bucket. After that, I'm going to give the same speech for my sis. Except this time, I'm going to ask that all the men who have keys to my sister's home please return them and one old man will walk out and put his in. She'll die of embarrassment . . . can't wait!!! (Miller and Miller 1997)

Other wedding pranks similarly introduce the subject of sex in a public way, for example, by having several co-conspirators present condoms to the bride and groom in the receiving line. Again, the bride and groom are subject to ritual humiliation, being embarrassed by revelations of a topic, sex, which is pervasive but implicit in wedding symbolism.

The wedding ceremony itself can also be the site of foolery—most often concerning the wedding ring. When the officiant asks, "Do you have the ring?" some groomsmen will pretend to have lost it and turn the act of desperately looking for it into a comic performance. A video of one such performance, posted online in 2009, shows a groom, best man, and groomsman clowning to an extraordinary degree: while ostensibly searching for the ring they produce from their pockets a series of improbable objects including a bicycle horn, clothes brush, light sabers, bananas, and handcuffs (which the groom pockets), until the ring is "found" and the ceremony proceeds (Bornagainmuelle 2009). This motif of "losing" the ring expresses real anxieties that members of the wedding party have about actually losing it, but it also draws attention to the sexual symbolism of the ring (Legman

1968, 474). A wedding ring is not a prerequisite for marrying the couple, but symbolically it is essential. Fears of losing the ring reflect unconscious fears about an inability to consummate the marriage. By clowning with this essential symbol, members of the wedding party playfully threaten to prevent the entire marriage.

The same idea of preventing the consummation of the marriage is expressed in the elaborate booby-trapping of the car intended to take newly-weds to their honeymoon. Again, the tricksters are the age mates of the couple. They fill the car with rice, birdseed, packing peanuts, paper chads, wads of newspaper, and the like. Some pranks make the car temporarily undrivable. The doors may be wired shut or the battery or wheels removed. The effect of all these shenanigans is to delay the newlyweds' getaway from the church:

> One time when a good friend was getting married, they said they were going to hide their car so that no one could find it. That way we couldn't paint signs all over it. But we fooled them instead. Someone found out where it was hidden and a few of us took a load of newspapers with us and stuffed their car completely full of wadded up newspapers. They couldn't get in the car to go on their honeymoon till they had pulled all the papers out of the car. It took them almost twenty minutes to get all those newspapers out. (Wilson 1978, 14–15)

Less often, tricksters booby-trap the couple's home or honeymoon accommodations:

> This is what happened to my cousin at his wedding. When they got home to their apartment at about 4 A.M., they found a couple of hundred cups filled with water on the floor. The line of cups reached from the entrance up the stairs to the bedroom. It took them some hours to remove them, since the cups have been glued to the floor. After they had successfully reached the bedroom, they had the next surprise: no furniture in there. (Miller and Miller 1997)

Both accounts stress the time that it took for the targets to undo the mess. In postwedding booby traps, effectiveness is measured by how long the pranksters are able to delay the consummation of the marriage. These contemporary wedding pranks resemble the traditional rural shivaree pranks of invading the newlyweds' bedroom and rendering it either unusable or embarrassingly public if it is used. Both contemporary and traditional play symbolically inhibit the sexual consummation of the marriage while also drawing public attention to private sexual acts, asserting the community's interest in these private matters (Greenhill 2010; Legman 1968, 480–481).

Wedding tricksters assume that their targets deserve this treatment as part of their rite of passage, and that if they cannot agree with it they should at least support it. Targets may take steps to avoid their ritual degradation by keeping their plans secret or by other means, effectively treating the situation as a playful competition with their would-be antagonists. However, humor support is no more guaranteed with wedding pranks than with any other kind:

> Dear Miss Manners—
>   What is it about weddings that turns normal people—one's friends—into vicious pranksters from whom the bridal couple, on top of all their other anxieties, must protect themselves?
>   All too often, the poor bride, who has had nearly all she can take anyway, becomes the victim of her husband's old buddies. Clothes and cars are ruined, rice is flung into eyes, and the bride's nerves are frayed by half-serious threats of what the groom's buddies are going to do to prevent him from being able to get to the wedding.
>   My very expensive silk "going away" suit was ruined by the lipstick used to "decorate" our car, and frankly I feel pretty unforgiving. How can the bride and groom protect themselves from friends suddenly turned malicious? (Martin 1987)

Wedding pranks disrupt the contemporary emphasis on executing the perfect wedding. Weddings are meticulously planned and scripted, and the bride and groom exercise considerable temporary power over the wedding guests and especially the wedding party, down to what they will wear and where they will sit. This overweening individualism is encouraged by the wedding industry but often deplored by cultural observers. Advice columns are full of complaints about the petty tyranny of couples planning "their" day, and there is even a reality television show designed around the premise that brides-to-be can act like monsters, or "Bridezillas." Practical jokes introduce elements of surprise and unplanned levity into these hypercontrolled proceedings. They offer wedding participants a way to resist control, to reassert the rights of the group as against those of the individual, and to partially restore the balance of power between equals. This ritual humor is a reminder that individualism must have limits. The ritual elevation of the bridal couple makes them due for ritual degradation or "cutting down to size" (a common expression used to explain and justify targeting someone with a practical joke) (Greenhill and Magnusson 2010, 326).

Wedding pranks are unilateral play, in which the support or active participation of the targets is optional. Devices such as traditionalization, hyperbole, and familiar play objects like water pistols and balloons cue the joking frame and invite humor support, but wedding pranks have a different feel from April Fooling or spontaneous joking among friends. The "prank" and "trick" labels put these activities in the realm of individualized fun and optional play, but their themes are the primordial ones of sex, reproduction, and the biological perpetuation of the community (Greenhill 2010, 25). In addition to the play frame, a ritual frame is also invoked, lending a layer of compulsion to the jokes' reception. The targets' support or acquiescence is not invited but demanded; playful degradation is treated as almost inevitable.

At the same time, the valence of the ritual frame is uncertain and may be contested. In a modern, industrialized society, compulsory rituals are rare; when they do occur they are wrapped up in a mantle of play. Victor Turner suggested that that modern complex societies have *liminoid* rituals rather than truly *liminal* ones—that is, rituals are not obligatory but treated as recreation or leisure instead. Thus, in tribal settings, the rule breaking that occurs during the liminal phase of ritual is obligatory; it would be unthinkable for anyone to object to it. In contrast, individuals in modern societies may exercise the option to opt out. However, the example of ritual pranks suggests that rather than an absolute distinction between liminoid and liminal, contemporary culture has room for degrees of liminality. Turner suggested that even in modern industrialized societies, some liminoid genres "have something of the stamp of the liminal upon them" (1974, 86). This dynamic is apparent in wedding pranks, which are explicitly framed as pranks or jokes—that is, as play, but simultaneously framed as ritual. This dual framing as ritual play and playful ritual creates a paradox, for play is that which means less than it says, whereas ritual means more than it says.

INITIATION PRANKS

As shivarees and wedding pranks dramatize the relationship between newlyweds and their communities, initiation pranks highlight the relations between individuals and their coworkers. Commonly, newcomers to the workplace are subjected to fool's errands, many of which display considerable verbal creativity and reflect the esoteric vocabulary and conditions of the salient job. Initiation pranks are usually generic and "traditional," and all assume the support or active collusion of the entire group in fooling an individual target. Spontaneous creativity on the part of colluding tricksters can create an extended ordeal for the rookie. For example, a traditional trick played on new U.S. Navy submariners, or "nonquals," sends them from one end of the submarine to another to fetch *water slugs* for testing the torpedo tubes. What the nonqual does not know is that a water slug is simply a torpedo tube filled with water; testing the tubes consists of filling them with water and then firing these slugs. After going from the torpedo room in the bow of the boat to the engine room in the stern, he receives something very heavy to carry back:

> When the nonqual arrives in the torpedo room after having carried the weights the full length of the boat, the torpedoman tells him that there is another ship close by and that for this reason the water slugs cannot be fired at that time. The nonqual is then instructed to carry the "water slugs" (weights) back to the engine room. When the nonqual arrives in the engine room after having carried the weights the length of the boat for the second time, he is told by the engine room watch that the torpedoman wants to talk to him on the telephone. The torpedoman then tells the nonqual that the other ship has passed and that they have decided to go ahead and shoot the water slugs. Thus the nonqual is forced to carry the weights forward again. This procedure may continue until the nonqual figures out that he is being tricked or until someone feels sorry for him and lets him in on the joke.
>
> I learned this nonexistent errand in 1968 aboard the U.S.S. Tecumseh SSBN 628, from a torpedoman named Tom Pardick. I learned the hard way by carrying a box of garbage weights twice the length of the boat. (Jenlink 1974)

Although this former submariner had personal experience of the water slug trick, he chose to give his account in generic terms, which underlines his recognition that his discomfiture was neither unique nor intended as a personal attack. His choice of narrative style implies that all nonquals are at risk of the same treatment. The fool's errand is a generic trick not simply because it would be difficult to tailor a fabrication to a newcomer's personal qualities but because the generic quality of the joke allows it to be presented as "traditional" rather than personal, as part of a ritual that predates the current context. The de-emphasizing of the personal is a significant part of the meaning of initiation pranks.

Dale Jenlink interpreted his nonqual experience as "learning the hard way," but he does not specify what he was learning. Initiation pranks are often justified with the suggestion that they teach newcomers about the arcana of the job (Haas 1972). The neophyte sent the length and breadth of the ship in a fruitless search for the golden rivet or the like learns to "read" the ship. Fool's errands for nonexistent tools teach newcomers the jargon of the trade. These lessons are reinforced by physical effort and discomfort, and by the humiliation the targets feel when they discover the truth—a discovery that usually takes place in front of their more experienced coworkers. Having been fooled into mistaking a bogus tool name for a genuine one, one is unlikely to make the same mistake again.

Yet the pedagogic value of fool's errands is slight. Given the plethora of jargon and technical knowledge required to master any trade, there are not enough fool's errands that could teach the proper use of them all. Moreover, as Archie Green has pointed out, some of these apprentice tasks are not at all plausible, even for the greenest newcomer. Even I know that it makes no sense to fetch spark plugs for a diesel engine, and that a spark plug gap is not something that can be fetched at all. "What is under scrutiny," Green suggests, "is not the victim's commonsense but his response to the implication that he, at any rate, might be that stupid." The initiation prank pits the esoteric knowledge of the veterans against the supposed ignorance of the neophyte, but the symbolic significance of this mini-drama depends less on the neophyte's literal ignorance than on his or her inferior status in the organization. Occupational jargon is a secondary matter; the significant lessons conveyed by initiation pranks concern what Green calls the "social meaning" of being a miner, submariner, or seminarian (Green 1981, 62).[1]

HAVE YOU SEEN A SEA BAT?

The salient lesson in some initiation pranks has less to do with learning the tools of the trade than with subjecting neophytes to humiliation, physical discomfort, and sometimes outright physical violence, conveying the message that their seniors find it appropriate to mistreat them that way. Midshipmen in the US. Navy, for instance, are traditionally introduced to the sea bat:

> I heard over the 1MC (public address phone) that a couple of men had caught a sea bat, and anyone who wanted could go back on the fantail and take a look before it was let loose. I hadn't heard of what a sea bat was so I ask around. A couple of the guys told me that a sea bat was a rare mammal which roamed over the seas. Once in a long while someone on a ship would catch one. They said that you couldn't keep one for long because it was very bad luck to keep a sea bat in captivity. I decided that I had better hurry up and get back to the fantail for a look. When I got back there I saw a small group of men standing around a bucket set upside-down on the deck. They told me to get on my hands and knees and take a very quick look. I was getting pretty excited by now. Well when I bent over to take a

look I felt this hard whack across my ass. I looked up to find all of those
[____] laughing! (Green and Yazman 1975)[2]

Sea bats are a species of starfish found in tidal pools, but this knowledge is
relevant only to marine biologists, not midshipmen; what is relevant is the
realization that not only have your shipmates physically assaulted you but
that their laughter signals they find this treatment appropriate. As in many
traditional greenhorn pranks, the presence of puns imposes a play frame on
a mild but demeaning physical assault.

Apprentice fool's errands depend not just on the relative ignorance of
the neophyte but also on the informal seniority system at work. The jokes
are effective because everyone assumes that it is appropriate for a senior
worker to ask the new guy to serve as a gofer. This assumption is found
even in occupations where there is no formal hierarchy such as there is in
the navy, and it continues today even though the technical rank of apprentices, who were explicitly required to follow the orders of their superiors,
hardly survives any longer. In the military, the new recruit is ordered on a
fool's errand. In civilian life, the command is more likely to be in the form
of a polite request ("Hey, would you do me a favor and go up to the parts
department?"), but it will be treated almost as an order by the neophyte
who knows his or her social status. The gofer status of the newcomer lies
outside any organizational chart or reporting lines. In terms of official organizational structure, the hand hired last week may be on the same level as
the one who has worked there for years, but among the workers themselves,
status hierarchies depend more on seniority and experience. In this informal
social system, the newcomer is at the bottom, and in this structural sense
senior workers know exactly who they are dealing with even though the
neophyte's personal qualities are unknown. Initiation jokes dramatize this
relationship and throw it into relief.

THE ARCHANGEL'S FEATHER

Although veterans are acutely aware of the informal hierarchy, not every neophyte recognizes it. In vernacular explanations, one goal of initiation pranks
is to "cut the newcomer down to size," meaning to teach the neophytes their
proper place in the informal social structure they have just entered. These
playful lessons are not confined to factories or quasi-military occupations,
as witness this example from an American Catholic seminary circa 1943:

> At the Catholic seminary in Ossining, New York, Michael the Archangel
> was the patron saint. When the new guys came every fall they were told

that there was a big, solemn Mass on the feast day of St. Michael. We told them that one of them would be asked to play a very important role in the Mass, but that they wouldn't be chosen until a few days before the feast day. Anyway, they were all just dying to be picked, especially the little A+ students who were always picked in High School. We'd usually pick one of them too. They'd be so excited that they got picked, they'd call home, and they'd walk around campus just glowing!

Anyway, on the feast day we'd tell this guy that he would be bringing up the rear of the procession in the church. We'd also tell him what he was supposed to do. He had this beautiful little satin pillow, and we'd put a big feather on it; this was supposed to represent Michael the Archangel.

When the Mass began we all sat down in our places and waited. All the instructors would come first wearing fancy robes, then some of the older guys who were going to be ordained that year. Finally this little freshman would walk up carrying this little pillow out in front of him, with Michael's feather on it.

Ohh he looked so out of place. All the guys would start to snicker and when the fellow realized how stupid he looked he'd get sooo embarrassed he didn't know what to do with himself. He didn't know if he should run out of the church, or keep going up to the altar with this feather. (Donahue 1980)

Father Jack Manning, who recalled this initiation trick from his days as a seminarian, did not know how long it had been the custom but said that it was repeated every year he was there. His use of the "would always" tense to narrate it emphasizes the traditionality of the prank. According to him, the seminary administrators frowned upon the tradition and tried to locate the students responsible, but whether they failed to win any cooperation from the student body or did not try very hard, the custom continued year after year. This was a student-initiated custom, not an official one, and the administration did not officially sanction it. Recalling the historical suppression of the Feast of Fools, we would not expect the church officially to condone anything that burlesques or threatens the seriousness of the Mass. However, seminary faculty and administrators are also former seminarians, and so identify with the current crop of students. They may have different ranks in the hierarchy, but administrators and seminarians have a shared identity as members or future members of the priesthood. The initiation trick of Michael's feather is a shared, esoteric component of in-group culture. Indeed, the same or similar hazing pranks are known in other Catholic seminaries.[3]

It is not hard to imagine the freshman's embarrassment, realizing too late that he had been duped, that he was committing a very public error during a serious religious rite, and that he was the laughingstock of everyone present, including his fellow students and instructors. This public humiliation, reserved, according to Father Manning for "little A+ students," who had excelled in their former role in high school, highlighted their relative ignorance compared to the senior seminarians. More significant, it taught them in a visceral way that their status was no longer at the top. They had been riding on their achievements in a meritocratic system, but their ritual debasement at the hands of upperclassmen reasserted the claims of seniority over meritocracy.

Although most of the attention in initiation rites is directed at the initiates, the psychological functions are just as pertinent for the veterans who organize them. The hint of disdain in Manning's expression "little A+ students" expresses the feelings engendered in old hands by the influx of newcomers. In any organization, this influx arouses discomfort in veterans—fears that the newcomers will change familiar routines or disregard the privileges that veterans have earned through their hard work and contributions. Unconscious and possibly ill-founded though they may be, these feelings are real and explain the intensity of initiation rituals. Veterans respond to these concerns with initiation processes, sometimes tacit, sometimes explicit, to turn the threatening outsiders into insiders. The process of integrating newcomers into organizations is more than "socialization"; it arises out of significant feelings that both neophytes and veterans bring to the encounter, only some of which are conscious (Baum 1990, 59–63). Even in the absence of explicit rituals of initiation such as occupation-specific practical jokes, initiation processes go on tacitly, sometimes for years, before newcomers achieve subjective membership alongside their official membership.

HAZING RITES VERSUS INITIATION PRANKS

Initiation pranks are more than just jokes but less than hazing rituals. Practical jokes played on neophytes may be labeled *hazing* by outsiders, usually with a pejorative meaning (Mechling 2009), but they are not identical to full-blown hazing rituals, which involve more elaborate and extended ritual degradation and frequently are explicitly labeled as rituals. Today hazing rites are most often found in college fraternities (Dundes and Dundes 2002) or "Crossing the Line" rituals in the navy (Bronner 2006). At the same time, these practical jokes have a different dynamic than everyday pranks do. Accounts of initiation pranks are most often couched in generic, traditionalized terms and rarely describe the post-plays of the pranks. Few stories record the response of the targets unless the initiate reacts badly. It is as if the targets' submission to their joking discomfiture is simply assumed, and it is this assumption that pushes initiation pranks into the realm of playful ritual or ritual play.

The local joking culture specifies the preferred forms of response by initiates. Speaking of the initiation pranks played on greenhorn loggers in the American Northwest, for example, Barre Toelken comments that they "are not meant to engender fights, although it is assumed that the butt of any prank will properly become incensed" (1979, 62). In general, literal laughter is not essential, but submission to the fact of one's discomfiture and the group's right to mete it out is required. I have found no cases where initiates respond with reciprocal jokes, however. Initiation pranks are about establishing hierarchy, not reciprocity. Targets who respond appropriately will win the right to participate in the local joking culture, but they must earn that right by showing their willingness to submit to the unilateral play of the rest of the group.

Many contemporary hazing rituals are actually burlesques of ritual, but it is never entirely certain whether they are just rituals, play, or outright abuse (Houseman 2001; Mechling 2009). Like wedding pranks, initiation jokes are framed as optional, recreational, or fun activities, but these "liminoid" features do not erase the element of obligatory ritual. The mental and physical discomfiture of initiates in hazing rituals is real, but they are obliged to treat it as if it were "just" ritual—in other words, as if it were play. In short, they have to pretend to be playing. This paradoxical attitude has been labeled *metaplay*: people pretend to pretend, or play at playing (Houseman 2001). The outcomes of hazing rituals are tied to the ability of targets to adopt a metaplay attitude, or "play along" (43). The targets' submission may be a pretense, but it is no less effective for that.

The ritual function means that although initiation pranks are not strictly obligatory, refusal to play along can have lasting social consequences. Jokers commonly rationalize initiation pranks as tests to find out what kind of person the neophyte is, and whether he or she will "fit in." In risky occupations, the additional explanation is usually offered that workers need to find out whether the newcomer can be relied upon in an emergency (for example, Toelken 1996, 270). What is at stake is not humor but the proper way for an individual to relate to the group. Acceptance comes to those who react like good sports, meaning those who are "willing to give up something of their 'self-image' for the enjoyment of their fellow workers" (Fine 1988, 123). To be a good sport, a target must temporarily and playfully suspend attachment to personal dignity and support the joke at his or her expense.

Being a good sport means far more than being willing to sacrifice for the entertainment of others; it involves displaying a balance between self-regard and concern for the collectivity. Those who fail to play along are likely to be described as "self-important," "inflated egos," "better than they ought to be," and in need of being "cut down to size." The characteristic indexed by this language is the unwillingness (or inability) to see themselves as others see them and to balance self-regard with the altruism that the group demands (Green 1981, 62). "Joining with others in order to accomplish work requires submerging oneself in a collectivity, giving up some of one's freedom and specialness to create a disciplined group," according to Howard Baum. "Many people feel anxious or angry about making such a concession, especially if they don't know the other people involved" (1990, 63–64). Initiation pranks allow senior workers to observe whether the newcomers are willing to put group needs and desires ahead of their own, if only temporarily and in play.

Through childhood play, most people learn that "ordinary social objectivity is one obvious thing, their own personal subjective intentions and conclusions another," but "some blundering people . . . cannot easily synthesize their public and private dualities, which often reveals itself in their obsessive, single-minded egoism" (Sutton-Smith 2008, 118). Whether in a logging camp or in an office, egoism is not adaptive; it inhibits a worker's ability to get along with his or her coworkers. Contemporary industrialized culture favors the "simultaneous affirmation of an ever-deeper interior self—autonomous, natural, and of its own making—and an infinitely adaptable exterior self—supremely sensitive to social circumstance and the mitigation of conflict" (Wickberg 1998, 77–78). Play, including the playful attitude that is the basis of humor support, helps reconcile the duality between private and public selves, and playful victimization restores the proper balance between a person's subjective estimation of self and the objective one held by his or her fellows. This playful element is indexed by the vernacular expressions *good sport* and *playing along*, used to describe the desired response by targets to jokes at their expense.

The essence of a joke is that it combines both transgression and playful distancing and acceptance of that transgression. When the thing transgressed against is their own personal face, many people find playful distance difficult to achieve. What is often forgotten is that the targets' support of their discomfiture is itself framed as play. Jokers use this framing to mark distance between their real feelings and the attitudes expressed in the joke, and audiences similarly frame their support as a playful, temporary suspension of their everyday values. The distancing mechanism of play is available to both jokers and recipients.

JOKING AND HARASSMENT

Liz Fulton was a receptionist in the Auckland office of an advertising company. The office employed between twenty-five and forty people (Elliott 1992). When she interviewed for the job, she was advised—or warned—that the office had an "offbeat" joking culture. Sure enough, after working in the office almost a month, she became the target of a traditional practical joke. "Some time at the end of April a staff member requested Ms Fulton to page a Mike Hunt. She is said to have paged asking the question 'Has anybody seen Mike Hunt?' Only when she saw the reaction she got from fellow employees did Ms Fulton realize that she has been induced to utter a 'phonetic obscenity.'" She responded with a laugh, leading others to think she had accepted the joke. The outcome was different a week or so later, when "she was asked to page Ben Doon and Phil McCracken and did so. From the attitude of staff around her it became immediately obvious that she had again been induced to utter an obscene phrase over the paging system. This time she was very upset and made it plain to all that she did not find the matter amusing" (New Zealand Employment Tribunal, Auckland 1992, 40). The male joker apologized, but Fulton refused to accept it. She was so upset that she asked to be allowed to go home early, which her supervisor would not allow. That night, with the help of her father, she composed a letter of complaint to management in which she described the incident as "a sick joke." "Instead of any hint of sympathetic consideration at my obvious distress, the staff—including senior and supervising staff—scoffed at me, telling me not to be stupid and to take a joke," she wrote.

> I am acutely embarrassed and shocked over what is plain obscenity. It is
> not even bad taste. I am prepared to share in a joke or other fun even at
> my expense, but not of this denigratory character. For it to be passed off as
> frivolous is quite unacceptable to me.

Fulton made it plain that she considered these incidents to be harassment, that they hurt her job performance, and that she wanted senior management to prevent any repetition. "I do not want to be regarded as oversensitive or a troublemaker," she concluded, "but I have my dignity" (41). Management required the perpetrator to offer Fulton a written apology, but she refused to accept it.

Some weeks later, Fulton was given a written list of concerns about her job performance, including some issues that had been noted and discussed with her prior to the joking incidents. In a written response to these complaints, Fulton explained that the "recent harassment directed at me" was

continuing to affect her concentration and attitude to work. She felt that
the joke and her negative response to it had created a poor working relationship with the rest of the staff:

> My response to being acutely embarrassed and humiliated would seem to
> me to be met by even more ridicule which has been apparent in the atti-
> tudes of some of the staff. They have continued their taunts although in
> a different way. I know I lack respect for them, as they do for me. (New
> Zealand Employment Tribunal, Auckland 1992, 42)

Although there were no further practical jokes directed at Ms. Fulton, she
felt that her coworkers were finding other ways to "taunt" her, such as fabricating complaints about her work. Whatever the reason, it is clear that she
did not feel like a fully incorporated member of the work group and identified her complaint about the practical joke as a contributing factor. In this,
she may well have been correct. Since unlaughter is taken as reflecting badly
on both the joke recipient and its originator, it is very divisive.

This unhappy situation might yet have been repaired. At this point,
however, the chief executive met with Fulton, suggesting that she was over-
reacting to a joke and asking her why she continued in the job if she was
unhappy there. The next day she formally resigned, making it clear that she
felt she was being forced out and would be taking further action. She filed
a grievance with the New Zealand Employment Tribunal claiming that she
had been sexually harassed and "constructively dismissed," meaning that her
leaving, while voluntary, was tantamount to dismissal. The tribunal found
that "the fact that a young woman was induced to utter over the public
intercom system such 'phonetic obscenities' is not acceptable behavior in
the workplace":

> New workers, especially juniors, have been subjected to practical jokes
> from time immemorial. The young building apprentice sent out to pur-
> chase a "long weight" or "glass screws" springs to mind. Such actions can
> be termed harmless practical jokes which workers learn to cope with as they
> learn how to fit into a workforce. Needless to say the form of joke practiced
> on Ms Fulton steps far beyond these bounds. (New Zealand Employment
> Tribunal, Auckland 1992, 45, 46)

The question of whether or not the jokes in this case constitute harassment
turns on the context. When jokes are used with the purpose of exclusion
rather than ultimate inclusion, they may rightly be considered harassment
(Yoder and Aniakudo 1996). Since the joking frame lends role distance to

the joker, determining jokers' intentions is notoriously difficult when the jokes are considered in isolation. If the wider context includes other behaviors that are more unambiguously hostile, then the exclusionary and harassing intent can be imputed to the jokes as well.

In this case, the CEO's comments during his meeting with Fulton clearly show that he supported the jokers:

> I have heard that joke many times before and it is nothing to get alarmed about. It was only a joke Liz and nothing personal. Why are you taking it so seriously? . . . You have no right to tell my staff to change their attitudes. That is my job. They will not change their attitude for you Liz. You must accept that this is advertising. Your complaint is pointless and a petty concern. It was only a joke on their behalf to see if you would be the type of person they are. (New Zealand Employment Tribunal, Auckland 1992, 43, 44)

Initiation pranks are commonly rationalized by jokers as ritual, not personal; the targets are selected purely because of their position in the group's social structure, and the jokes are carried out on behalf of the entire group. The ritualized nature of the joking is underlined by its timing soon after the start of her employment, and by its generic and traditional content ("I have heard that joke many times before"). There is no evidence that any other exclusionary behaviors had been directed toward Fulton before the first joke (although she suspected that her unlaughter might have initiated some such behaviors afterward), and it seems reasonable on the face of it to accept the jokers' claim that the joke was, in fact, nothing personal. But the matter does not rest there.

I have argued that the humorousness of jokes lies not within their texts but in their reception. The decision of whether or not to support a joke is not purely an individual and subjective one; it is also strongly shaped by local joking cultures that cause topics and styles of joking to be accepted within high-context groups that would be anathema in others (Schmidt 2013, 103, 198). Like many small groups, the members of this advertising agency viewed their esoteric joking culture as unique. Part of this local joking culture is mirrored by the CEO. In New Zealand workplaces, social distance between management and workers tends to be less than in the United States, and informality and egalitarianism are highly prized (Plester and Sayers 2007, 178–181). The jokes, he suggested, were designed to see whether the newcomer "would be the type of person they are," that is, whether she would subscribe to the local joking aesthetic, which she had been advised of when she applied for the job.

What the CEO and the jokers he defended failed to realize is that joking cultures are also gendered. In this firm, it appears that sexually explicit jokes were considered within the limits of the humorous. The jokers might argue that the obscenity was mild; it was purely verbal, based only on a bad pun, and in any case was a very old joke. In his classic treatise on jokes, Freud argued that obscene jokes are aggressive because they force the listener to visualize explicit sexual scenes, contravening personal and social norms that brand such material as morally reprehensible (1960, 116). To support such jokes is to acknowledge that one has understood the sexually explicit content and also found it acceptable. For men, such an admission is usually understood as reprehensible but at the same time something to be proud of. However, sexually explicit humor impacts women differently than men. The sexual double standard that operates in New Zealand, as in the United States, grants women less license than men in thinking about or expressing sexual matters. If it is reprehensible for a man to think sexually explicit thoughts, it is doubly wrong for a woman to do so, especially a young, unmarried woman. Thus, even if the same tricks had been played on a man, the impact would not have been identical.

The main harm that women sustain from sexual humor lies not in the exposure to obscene content but in the exclusion from the local joking culture that follows when individuals are exposed to jokes that they cannot bring themselves to support. This exclusion impedes their full social inclusion and reasserts women's outsider status (Quinn 2000, 1176–1177). Similarly, if women are socialized to eschew the one-upmanship that characterizes a lot of male joking, then any kind of humiliating joking may serve to exclude them. In male friendship groups, being able to take playful humiliation in the right way and to give it back, including during hazing rituals, are tests of masculinity and belonging (Mechling 2009, 53). Whether female friendship groups have the same dynamic is uncertain and deserves further study.

The employment tribunal found that Fulton had indeed been unfairly dismissed. This outcome is an extreme version of a more common outcome that follows unlaughter by neophytes: exclusion from the informal joking culture. Such exclusion is even more likely when unlaughter takes the form of formal complaints to management or legal action, even though one may be in the right (Quinn 2000). Such complaints are read by the in-group as failures of the "test"—or the lesson—posed by initiation jokes. When Fulton insisted on her dignity in responding to a traditional joke, she appeared as someone who thought herself better than others. However, in a contest between "I have my dignity" versus "They won't change for you," the group will almost always win by ostracizing the proud.

It has been suggested that the modern diversified workplace no longer has the high-context folk group consensus needed for successful joking (Mechling and Mechling 1985). However, the social benefits of a vigorous local joking culture remain important; "to joke is to embrace the illusion—and the reality—of community" (Fine and Wood 2010, 299). The key to resolving the conundrum that women find themselves in when faced with a sexist joking culture is to forget the vernacular idea that the humorousness of jokes is an inherent quality and that unlaughter thus signals a flaw in the audience. Decisions about humorousness are as much social as individual. If Fulton had found others in the group who agreed with her that the jokes were beyond the limits, the situation might have had a different outcome, and the local joking culture might have been more successfully challenged. Local aesthetics are better modified from within than without; even though the senior staff in this case responded to the harassment charge as the law required (sanctioning the joker and securing both an apology and a promise that there would be no repetition), it seems that they privately agreed with the local joking culture. Mixed-gender workplace culture tends to be male dominated even if men are not numerically dominant, forcing women to play along if they wish to fit in (Fine 1987). Perhaps an explicit recognition that it is the local aesthetic that determines humorousness, plus an admission that such aesthetics are gendered, can lead to the evolution of joking cultures that are more equitable.

NOTES

1. Sometimes the same tricks are played on complete outsiders as well. Passengers onboard ships may be sent to watch for the nonexistent mail buoy just as raw midshipmen are; since there is no point in teaching a passenger how to be a sailor, the point of these pranks is simply to regulate social boundaries.

2. A similar traditional initiation ritual is to ask the apprentice printer if he has seen type lice; when he bends low over the movable type to look, the type is suddenly slammed together, splashing him with a mixture of water and ink (O'Connor 1981).

3. Msgr. Fred Easton, personal communication, April 2013, told me a variant of this joke on underclassmen, also involving "Michael's feather," from St. Mary's Seminary in Baltimore in the early 1960s.

10

Pranks in Public
Spoofs, Rags, and Stunts

PRACTICAL JOKES ARE ABOUT RELATIONSHIPS, even when they are anonymous and impersonal. Some of the most well-known examples of the genre are those that are set on the public stage—either on the streets or, in more recent times, in the mass media. These are communal tricks, pitting groups of usually anonymous jokers against collective targets and relying on the mass media to broadcast the results to mass audiences. Two groups in particular have adopted this style of practical joke as part of their expressive repertoires—journalists and university students.

JOURNALISTS' SPOOFS

The camera pans over a bird's-eye view of Antarctic ice floes, then cuts to a flock of Adélie penguins. In their midst, a BBC naturalist presenter explains that these penguins are unlike any other; they have no need of huddling together for warmth because these little fellows can do something no other penguins can. The music swells as one penguin after another jumps up and starts flying before our eyes. "Isn't that amazing!" the presenter exclaims, as panoramic shots show an entire flock of penguins on the wing. "How do they use this incredible ability?" he asks. "Well, they fly thousands of miles to the rainforests of South America, where they spend the winter basking in the tropical sun." The trailer closes with penguins landing, heavily, in the branches of tropical trees (BBC 2008a).

The flying penguin documentary was screened by the BBC on the first of April 2008, accompanied by major news stories in the *Daily Telegraph* and the *Daily Mirror*, and a video trailer on the BBC's YouTube channel. On the same date, Google Australia unveiled G'Day, a revolutionary app that would search for web pages before they had been created. Nestlé declared

DOI: 10.7330/9780874219845.c010

that it was shortening the name of its popular candy "Butterfinger" to just "Finger"; and a Canadian airline announced that it would be converting overhead bins on its planes into individualized sleeping compartments. Meanwhile, in New Hampshire, the National Public Radio affiliate broadcast a story about a secret project that had developed completely square trees (Smith 2009a).

This sampling of media April Fools' Day spoofs from 2008 illustrates the widespread enthusiasm with which journalists, advertisers, corporations, nonprofits, and even local governments have embraced April Fooling. For one day a year, print, broadcast, and Internet media are full of spoofs and fabrications. The sheer volume of public media spoofs has come to obscure the interpersonal practical joking of April Fools' Day. The perpetrators represent journalists, information and public relations officers, advertising and marketing teams—indeed, anyone involved in creating and delivering nonfiction content via the mass media. These professions are responsible for the sea of mass-mediated information that constitutes the postmodern environment, whose ultimate purpose is, as Noam Chomsky famously said, to deliver audiences to advertisers (Herman and Chomsky 1988, 303, 337).

April Fools' spoofs are a risky form of play because they depart from normal ethical and professional standards, but if successful they carry some beneficial payoffs. Broadly speaking, success in the mass media world is measured by audience size—circulation, ratings, downloads, and page views. Similarly, a media prank that attracts little or no attention is a failure; what the spoofers hope for is widespread attention as measured by calls, comments, letters, and traffic on their website. Effective spoofs attract readers and viewers and these audiences grow exponentially as the most effective examples are shared, tweeted, and reposted on the Internet.

By publicly engaging in play and joking with their audiences, media spoofers increase their likeability by showing themselves as fun-loving folk with a well-developed sense of humor. A review of humor research shows little evidence that humorous messages are more persuasive (Martin 2007, 136–139), but they do appear to increase the likeability of the message source, which in turn may improve ratings and increase audience size. Certainly the power of humor to win audiences, and win them over, is almost an article of faith in the advertising and other mass media professions. Media spoofers are also driven by personal and psychological motives, however. The Western cultural valuation of a sense of humor as essential to a well-adjusted personality affects those with mass-mediated public personas as much as anyone else. Spoofing is an opportunity to step outside of corporate and professional roles and reveal the human being hidden behind.

I use *spoof* rather than *hoax* because the former term does not carry negative connotations of using a fabrication for illicit gain. April Fools' spoofs are a form of play; more specifically, they are playful aestheticizations of professional techniques and skills. Spoofs use the full armamentarium of media content deliverers: video and audio recordings, interviews, stock footage, press releases and websites, and computer-generated animation. Commonly, spoofers create materials that explain precisely how they did it, such as the BBC's "making of" video, which was posted on its YouTube channel at the same time as the flying penguin documentary (BBC 2008b). By making these explanations public, the spoofers show off the skills that ideally are hidden from view during their everyday professional activities. "Making of" explanations also remove any doubts that the spoofs might have illicit motivations, clearly framing the fabrications as play rather than exploitation. The opportunity to play and have fun, detached from the practical concerns of the spoofers' normal work, is one of the motivations behind the spoofs (Smith 2009a, 284).

When a news story or documentary is recognized as a fabrication, the means of its construction become available for scrutiny and aesthetic critique, allowing audiences to evaluate it for how well it was carried out. Many of the online comments to the BBC's "making of" video take an explicitly aesthetic stance:

> Some of the most impressive CGI work I've ever seen! All for an April Fool's day joke, no less! Yes, I too thought it was real at first. I mean, it's so well done, that just about anyone watching it for the first time would think that it was genuine footage as well! When it got to the rain forest scene it became more apparent that it was CGI, however. Still a Damn Good Clip! and an excellent April Fool's joke! Good Job, BBC!

> Absolutely brilliant, well done to you all for creating this April fool masterpiece!!!

> It was amazing, the animation was to an extremely high level however i felt the cinematic views . . . which the BBC designed were slightly too . . . perfect as it were. Overall very convincing but it wouldn't be a penguin if it could fly, which is why I never believed it.

> What a technique...........i m impressed.

> Right down to their reflection on the water, brilliant. (BBC 2008b)

These comments and others like them all evaluate the flying penguins documentary not in terms of its ornithological claims, which had been revealed as untrue, but in terms of the skill with which it was carried out. Those who were temporarily fooled by the spoof tended to use their discomfiture as evidence for its effective performance and skillful execution. Others critiqued the production for being a little too good to be believable, while several other comments discussed at length which video editing software had been used. All of these responses treated the spoof essentially as a work of art.

To *spoof* someone means to impersonate them, and it is worth asking who or what is being impersonated in media April Fooling. Spoofs are an occasion for media professionals to burlesque themselves and their relationship to their audiences. Compelling news, persuasive advertising, and effective public relations all require craft, but to be effective this craft must remain muted and confined to backstage domains. By drawing attention to the constructedness of documentary discourse, spoofs throw the factuality and trustworthiness of the media into question. "It's scary," said one commentator on the flying penguins spoof. "If we can make people believe penguins can fly with computers . . . what else can we make them believe?" Another found the spoof "shameful, creepy, and very reminiscent of Orwell." He continued, "And BBC also covers news . . ." (BBC 2008b). In vernacular epistemology, construction is perilously close to fabrication. Spoof documentaries are fabrications that are very close to real news.

Journalists sometimes wrestle with this problem in their own professional discourse. Thomas Cooper asks whether the news itself is not "a deception, a sustained and commonly held hoax," and journalism a process in which "delimiting, inaccurate, and relative reductions of reality somehow become miraculously converted to 'reliable sources,' 'official spokespersons,' and 'eye witness accounts' in the fictional construction of news" (1996, 77). Cooper's analysis expresses unease with the ontological status of news as factual discourse. Journalists know better than anyone that the news is not merely reported but constructed, and media spoofs bring this realization to the attention of their public. Media spoofers actually spoof themselves— that is, they step outside of their public, professional roles to *play at* their roles, thus examining their everyday practice as if from an outsider's perspective. They laugh at themselves while raising disquieting concerns about their professional practice that are normally ignored.

STUDENTS: SOCIETY'S UNOFFICIAL CLOWNS

Public pranks—large-scale displays intended for general audiences—are also particularly associated with university students, at least in the modern era. Youthful energy, intelligence, and creativity, along with large amounts of unstructured time, are all certainly involved in the close association between tertiary students and public practical jokes, many of which are widely known and celebrated far beyond their cultures of origin. The specific social status of university students means that they claim for themselves, and are granted, considerable license to play in this fashion. The details and limits of that license and the local meanings attributed to each prank tradition vary even though some of the pranks are similar. Each era and locale has its own local variant of student pranks, with different emic terminologies to label the traditions—in the United Kingdom, they are *rags* and in New Zealand universities, student pranks on a public scale are called *capping stunts*. In the United States, the public pranks of students at engineering schools—most famously, at the California Institute of Technology (Caltech) and the Massachusetts Institute of Technology (MIT)—have already been thoroughly documented, not least by the institutions themselves (Leibowitz 1990; Peterson 2003; Steinberg 1992), and so I will be focusing on the lesser-known traditions of rags and capping stunts. However, the American student traditions share all the qualities of the other student public pranks discussed here.

Cambridge Rags

As media spoofs are a burlesque of the media, so the public pranks of university students are burlesques of antiauthoritarianism. A widespread form of this burlesque is to flout regulations and scale prominent campus buildings, leaving behind banners, flags, balloons, or more incongruous objects such as cars and telephone boxes (Leibowitz 1990, 5–21). Cambridge University historian F. A. Reeve reports that these activities were so popular among undergraduates there that three guidebooks were published between 1899 and 1970 describing the best routes (1977, 39). The climbs were rendered more challenging by devices that college authorities installed to try to prevent them. In Reeve's accounts, the aftermath of these pranks turned into contests between the anonymous student climbers who got the objects up there and the authorities who endeavored to fetch them down again. Take, for example, what he called "the best undergraduate prank of all time," in which students placed an Austin van on the roof of the university Senate House. The anonymous pranksters claimed they had hauled the vehicle up in one piece over three and a half hours. Even though closer examination revealed that the van had actually been raised in parts and bolted together on the roof, local officials insisted that the workmen who came to take it down do so by lowering it in one piece. After ten men had worked for two hours, they admitted defeat and removed the vehicle in pieces. Since it had taken much longer to get the van down than to put it up, "the undergraduates had clearly won the greater prestige" (48). In this contest responsible adult-hood was clearly and publicly defeated by the forces of ludic irresponsibility, sport, and play represented by the undergraduates.

The balloons, umbrellas, surplices, chamber pots, and other whimsical objects that anonymous climbers have left behind effectively placed a play frame around their rule breaking. The climbers endeavored to stay anony-mous, largely because the sanction for their activities was to be "sent down," or expelled from the university, but their flouting of the rules was public and inescapable. Night-climbing stunts were antiauthoritarian thrusts blunted by a frame of play.

A rag can also be an elaborate public hoax or piece of street theater, in which undergraduates carry their playful transgressive displays into the streets of the town. Most rags of this type are used a means of collecting funds for charity. Success in fund-raising depends upon attracting attention, and some rags focus on publicity while lacking the fund-raising component completely. The 1921 Pavement Club rag, for example, appears to have had no other purpose besides annoying the authorities, the latter being rep-resented by the Cambridge police and by the proctor and his "bulldogs," university officials whose job it was to enforce discipline. Reeve's account of the club's inaugural "meeting" stresses its playful character:

> A distinguished don said that it was the most surprising sight that he had ever seen. Hundreds of undergraduates sitting on the pavements and in the road of King's Parade. It happened at midday on a Saturday in 1921, and the occasion was the inaugural meeting of the Cambridge Pavement Club . . .
>
> The barrel organ arrived at 11:50 a.m. and departed a few minutes later, escorted by the police. The members of the Club arrived in hundreds and sat down. Some had wisely brought cushions. They played cards, marbles, shove ha'penny and tiddly-winks.
>
> The proceedings were interrupted by the arrival of the proctor and his bulldogs. Those nearest to him scrambled to their feet. Names were taken, the proctor passed on, and men sat down again. Then the proctor returned and the previous scenes were re-enacted . . .
>
> A man appeared at a window and addressed the crowd which now numbered about two thousand . . . The proctor came back again, took more names and departed. Someone suggested that the club ought to elect a president. There were many cries of "The Proctor" and he was elected with acclamation. (1977, 34–35)

Had it taken place today, the meeting of the Pavement Club would prob-ably have been a flash mob (Simon 2011; Wasik 2006). Reeve's sympathetic account presents the rag as a dance between the undergraduates and the authorities. As the proctor returns repeatedly, and ineffectually, to take the names of the offenders, and as the undergraduates not only insouciantly resume their rag but elect him club president, the forces of authority find themselves subsumed into the game. They and the local police (whom the undergraduates called "the Cambridge Roberts" in a high-register version of the more usual term *bobby*) cope with bizarre activity by the undergraduates who are in on the joke, but their responses are appropriated as another part of the show.

On other occasions, the antiauthoritarian thrust of Cambridge rags was more overt. Between 1918 and 1939, rags included boisterous celebrations of university athletic events, Guy Fawkes Day, and Armistice Day, with significant property damage and confrontations with police. Yet the discourse about these rags framed the violence as a kind of game, a competition between students and those over them. Reeve's book, for example, is illustrated with a series of humorous sketches from the turn of the twentieth century that depict the violent altercations between undergraduates and the authorities, complete with black eyes, torn robes, and smashed streetlights. The humorous style of the sketches supported the undergraduate view, treating the violence as a game.

This public and exaggerated disregard of authority continued despite the risks of sanctions up to and including expulsion from the university. The play expressed the social class of the players. As undergraduates, the raggers were technically subject to the authority of the Cambridge police and the university dons, represented by the proctor and his bulldogs, but many, perhaps most, Cambridge students came from the ranks of the British aristocracy and upper middle classes. In class terms, they outranked those who technically had authority over them. There was a symbolic contradiction between two social systems pertinent to the undergraduate experience, one based on seniority and occupational role, and another based on an ancient class system. Student rags were a symbolic way to express and work out these contradictions within a frame of play and humor.

The contemporary sketches in Reeve's book on Cambridge rags express this symbolic contradiction. The cover bears a sketch called "Safely Home!" which depicts a young man wearing the academic gown required of undergraduates and seated in a comfortable armchair in front of the fireplace in his rooms, with tea set out on the table beside him. He wears a satisfied smile and a black eye, and in pride of place on the mantle is his trophy— a policeman's helmet. Symbolically, superior class has won over superior force. Another sketch, "The Rag—The Police Make an Arrest!" shows a

Figure 10.1. "The Rag—The Police Make an Arrest!"

hapless young man in an academic gown being manhandled by two burly policemen who tower over him, truncheons in hand. The background shows the silhouette of a riot in progress, with streetlamps being smashed and more truncheons raised. The message is clear that the undergraduate is no threat, and the application of police force to respond to student rags is an overreaction.

Since the perpetrators of the rags were merely undergraduates, the rags could be framed as play and therefore of no consequence. Social rank as well as age played a part in the way these activities were framed (Saltzman 2012, 59–60); certainly a Cambridge rag would have been considered simply hooliganism if the perpetrators had been working-class youth. The relatively high social status of the students and their families helped to persuade observers that their violence was just youthful high spirits with no malicious or revolutionary intent. Rags were violations that were benign and therefore tolerable (at least to some). The result was a paradox: the violence and damage were real, but the play frame created the affective incongruity that is characteristic of humor. If this ludic framing did not win license for student rags from all quarters, it only heightened the symbolic distinctions between the undergraduates and everyone else.

Registering Cats and Inundating the Post Office

In 1978 I was an undergraduate student at Victoria University in Wellington, New Zealand, sharing a large house near the campus with several other students, a trainee chef, and a tabby cat. One morning we found a "Notice to Householders" in our mailbox that caused a bit of a commotion:

> By The Cats Act 1977, Section 13(b).
> The Wellington City Council hereby gives notice that all domestic, pedigree or mongrel cats must be registered on or before the 3rd day of May, 1978. Registration shall be $1.00 per cat, per household. Failure to comply with this Regulation by 3rd May will result in a penalty registration fee of $2.00. All registration forms are available from the Post Office.
> dated this 5th day of April, 1978.

The notice was signed by the secretary for the town clerk. Although it was dated in early April, we had received it at the beginning of May, which meant we had only two days to comply before our Tigger became a contraband animal. We were concerned, right up to the point when someone remarked that it was probably a hoax. "This is Capping Week," they observed. "Some students probably delivered these all over town as a capping stunt."

New Zealand university students have a tradition of public pranks during student celebrations of graduation, or *capping*, as it is known locally. *Capping stunts* resemble many of the rags of British students, including

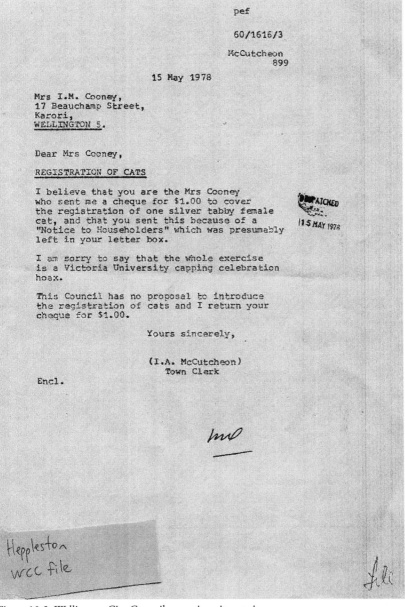

pef

60/1616/3

McCutcheon
899

15 May 1978

Mrs I.M. Cooney,
17 Beauchamp Street,
Karori,
WELLINGTON 5.

Dear Mrs Cooney,

REGISTRATION OF CATS

I believe that you are the Mrs Cooney
who sent me a cheque for $1.00 to cover
the registration of one silver tabby female
cat, and that you sent this because of a
"Notice to Householders" which was presumably
left in your letter box.

DISPATCHED
15 MAY 1978

I am sorry to say that the whole exercise
is a Victoria University capping celebration
hoax.

This Council has no proposal to introduce
the registration of cats and I return your
cheque for $1.00.

Yours sincerely,

(I.A. McCutcheon)
Town Clerk

Encl.

Heppleston
WCC file

Figure 10.2. Wellington City Council cat registration notice

street theater, ludic processions, and the like, but since the late 1950s the term has most often referred to large-scale practical jokes that target members of the public. The object of a capping stunt is to fool as many members of the public as possible, as publicly as possible, and the usual technique is for students to masquerade as bureaucrats or authority figures, using the authority of these bogus roles to convince their targets to take some action in a public setting. The heyday of capping stunts seems to have been during the 1950s through the early 1980s, although sporadic stunts have occurred more recently (Smith 2006).

Stunts lived longest in narrative form—as reports in the student newspaper and the city dailies, and as oral narratives. As capping returns each year, student newspapers rehash the classic stunts of the past as an inducement to plan more and better stunts, and the city papers do the same—ostensibly to warn residents to be on the alert for hoaxes but also to take vicarious pleasure in the jokes themselves. The annual rehearsals of capping stunts of the past resemble the journalistic treatments of April Fools' Day spoofs that are now almost obligatory in every medium. Prospectively, the stories provide students with templates of what an effective and successful capping stunt should look like.

Oral stunt stories are also retold chiefly among students, former students, and their families, even years after the original events and, following the dynamics of oral tradition, the narrated events tend to get mixed up with each other in the telling. Ten years after the cat registration stunt, I recorded the following version of what happened from another former Victoria University of Wellington student, Gordon Tait:

> Another one was the putting the cats down one. That was good, because people were really upset over that one. They wrote up a very official—this was all done on the right paper, you understand; it was written on Health Department paper and typed up neatly—and it takes a bit of organizing to get people to distribute about five thousand of these. On Wellington City Council paper you wrote a letter saying that feline flu was really rampant in a certain area, and that the city council had determined that all cats in this area had to be disposed of. Put down. And they gave you a little voucher; if you took your cat to the vet, the vet would do it for nothing [*laughs*]. Or you could put your cat in a box and drop it off at the city council and they would humanely dispose of the mog.
>
> Well, of course, people got this thing here and they went berserk; they weren't putting their favorite cat down, and they were ringing up to see if there were any vaccinations, or what the story was.
>
> So that was another one. (Tait 1988)

This account shows how capping stunt narratives are conflated. The original stunt concerned a regulation to register pets, in which failure to comply would result only in a $2 penalty. In Tait's version the scheme is a public health measure to eliminate an epidemic of "feline flu" through compulsory euthanasia mandated and paid for by the local government. He stresses the effectiveness of the fabrication in that the letter looked and sounded official, "all done on the right paper," and he also praises the organizational skill of the student hoaxers ("it takes a bit of organizing").

Notably, to this former student the stunt was exemplary precisely because it upset people ("That was good, because people were really upset over that one"), although he leaves it unclear whether they were upset while they were still contained in the fabrication or in the post-play. If they were distressed about the threat to their pets, the stunt was an effective one. However, if they were upset about being fooled by a capping stunt, or angry at students for causing needless alarm, the hoaxers and their fellow student apologists would count the stunt a success as well. A certain degree of negative response in the aftermath of a capping stunt was desirable; above all, what the students wished was that "people" would go "berserk," a measure of both effectiveness and success.

Gordon's story conflates the cat registration stunt with another one that is almost apocryphal in local tradition. It is known variously as the great swine flu stunt or urine sample stunt:

> The swine fever samples. Little circulars in the letter boxes around Kelburn, Karori, all round this area. Back in the '70s, early '80s. "Owing to the outbreak of swine fever in the greater Wellington district, would you mind taking a urine sample to your nearest post office, within the next twenty-four hours." All the post offices inundated with people coming in with big jam jars, or little Marmite jars, or forty-four-gallon drums or whatever they had [*laughs*]; and quietly getting up to the counter and bringing them out of their handbag . . . [*laughs*]. That one I think is fairly true. (Stewart 1988)

This version of the story comes from Gordon Stewart, a law professor at Victoria University who was a student there when the stunt took place in 1976. Different versions of the story place the stunt at various universities around New Zealand, but according to the archives of the Victoria University Students' Association, whose job it was to register all proposed capping stunts each year, this hoax seems definitely to have happened in Wellington. Nevertheless, the number of different versions of the story has led some people, like Gordon, to wonder whether it might not be a contemporary legend. True or not, the popularity of this stunt suggests that it has qualities that make it emblematic of the genre, and that speak to widespread interests and concerns of students and former students.

DEPARTMENT OF HEALTH

Wellington Office,
Education House,
178 - 182 Willis Street.
Ph 858 769.

Dear Householder,
Of much concern to the Department of Health over the past six months has been the abnormally high rate of 'swine' influenza in the city of Wellington. The reported incidence of 'swine' influenza in Wellington at present is estimated to be more than twice the rate for that of the rest of New Zealand. The graph below amply illustrates this:

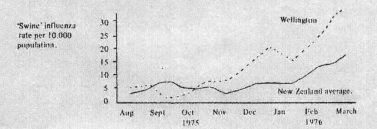

The Department of Health, therefore, in conjunction with the Wellington Hospital Board and the National Health Institute, is conducting a series of random surveys to calculate more accurately the incidence of 'swine' influenza in Wellington. The success of this survey will, however, depend entirely on the degree of public participation.

You, and each member of your family over the age of five years, are asked to take separate urine specimens on the morning of . Wed 28 April Each urine specimen should be placed in a clean, preferably sterile, bottle. On each bottle a label bearing the person's name, age and sex should be attached.

Each sample should then be taken that same morning to one of the following centres:
Reception desk, Wellington Hospital, Riddiford Street.
Enquiries desk, National Health Institute, 52 -62 Riddiford Street.
Wellington Hospital Board, Dalmuir House, 114 The Terrace.
District Health Office, Education House, Willis Street.
OR   The postal counter of your nearest Post Office.

If you have difficulty in delivering your urine specimen please contact the Wellington Medical Research Foundation by telephoning 859 844 during normal business hours, or 726 857 before 9.00 am.

Thank you for your cooperation,

K.B. Fraser,
Assistant Regional Director,
Department of Health.

Figure 10.3. Swine flu letter

The urine samples story was familiar to virtually every student and former student that I talked to in Wellington. It is not hard to see the appeal of this compound practical joke. Gordon's narrative is typical in its focus on the climactic scene, described in loving detail, as householders shamefacedly bring their samples to the unsuspecting clerks at the post office. He depicts the targets in an embarrassing situation, not in the privacy of a doctor's office but incongruously in a public setting that has nothing to do with medicine. Many variants of this story also use the metaphor of saying that the post office (or the reserve bank) was "inundated" with urine samples—a device that stresses not only the incongruity of the scene but also the imagined effectiveness of the fabrication.

Every storyteller assumes that many, many people were fooled by the swine flu letter and that the secondary target—the post office—was significantly impacted in its daily operations. There is no direct evidence for these claims, but it is the imagined and narrated outcomes of the stunt that matter. Most capping stunt narratives include similarly unverifiable claims. Some students incorporated devices such as a phone number that targets could call with questions that connected them to a student residence, designed to demonstrate the stunt's effectiveness, but most stunts had no mechanism for recording the outcomes.

By their public and impersonal nature, stunts usually unfolded out of sight of their creators. Of the hundreds of letters distributed, at least some could be relied on to be effective—but it would be impossible to predict which ones. No version of the swine flu stunt story includes direct witness of the dupes showing up in a post office, samples in hand. Stewart's account sounds like such firsthand observation, but he does not claim to have been present himself and the scene he describes is most likely entirely imaginary. Instead, students waited for coverage of their stunts, whether sympathetic or negative, in the local media. Effectiveness could be measured by the amount of publicity received.

The cat registration and swine flu stunts are typical of the corpus of capping stunts that were popular in the 1960s through the early 1980s. Table 10.1 lists twenty capping stunts that Victoria University students played between 1962 and 1986. Although the targets in this corpus are ill defined, all were understood to be members of "the public," that, is, nonstudents. One set of stunts involved transportation: bogus free passes for public transport or a fabricated plan for a one-way pedestrian system. According to student legend, traffic lights were turned off and motorway traffic was rerouted. The targets of this group of stunts were commuters and old-age pensioners. Another set exploited the anxieties of property owners, pet owners, and heads of families. A third group exploited the civic roles of the citizenry such as jury duty and government identity cards.

In the stunt discourse, these fabrications target specific groups, variously called "householders," "citizens," or "commuters," all of whom share

Table 10.1. Capping stunts

Year	Stunt	Entity impersonated
1962	Outsize trash collection: residents invited to leave "cumbersome" refuse on lawns for pickup	City council
1963	Official secrets leak: leaflet purported to reveal secret government defense plans in the event of nuclear attack	"Spies for Peace"; national government
1964	New university hall of residence: signs outside houses invited potential tenants to apply within	Ministry of Education
1966	10 p.m. closing starts today: bars no longer required to close at 6 p.m.[1]	National government
1971	Free tickets to screening of Waterloo	French embassy
1971	Free bonus savings bonds	Post office
1972	Kelburn airport: city announces plans to buy up properties to build airport in an affluent suburb; residents asked to direct complaints to minister of transport	Town clerk
1974	Free bus, train passes	National Railways; city transport department
1976	Save Pigeon Park: city announces plans to remove a popular local park	City council
1976	Swine fever survey: please bring urine samples to the post office for testing	Department of Health
1976	Water supply to be cut off next weekend: since water would be dirty when supply resumed, residents received vouchers that they could exchange for free detergent	Regional water board
1978	Registration of cats	City council
1978	Summons for jury duty	Sheriff
1978	VD scare: office workers receive letters, signed "Dr. S. I. Phyllis," advising them to get tested for VD	Hospital board
1979	Pigeon control: notices in Pigeon Park warn that poison will be laid on April 28	City council

continued on next page

Table 10.1—*continued*

Year	Stunt	Entity impersonated
1981	Corgi mating project: bogus fund-raising events, including film A Day at the Royal Kennels, to raise funds for a corgi mating project as a gift to Prince Charles and Princess Diana	NZ Kennel Club; British High Commission
1981	One-way pedestrian system test: arrows on city street show which direction to walk	City council
1981	No more fare discounts for pensioners	City transport
1984	Subsoil-sampling machine: residents advised to place metal objects on their lawns to keep the machine from accidentally digging through them	"NZ Seismic Activity Monitoring Bureau"
1986	Personal identity cards: residents asked to return forms with personal information or risk $10,000 fine for noncompliance	Inland Revenue

the significant characteristic of not being students. The nonstudent identity of the targets is significant, even though in practice many stunts would have reached targets who happened to be students, just like my flatmates and I, who were briefly taken in by the cat registration letter. Because the usual means of distributing capping fabrications was by public signs and posters, classified advertisements, and mass distribution of letters or fliers, the actual targets could not be controlled precisely, blurring distinctions between audiences and targets. Nevertheless, in the symbolism of the stunt discourse these groupings are mutually distinct and incommensurate. The stunt discourse emphasizes difference, not commonality.

The corpus also shows clear patterns as to who the students impersonated. In a word, they were authority figures—sometimes police officers but most often bureaucrats, including the local city council, the Ministry of Education, the post office, the French embassy, the British High Commission, the New Zealand Railways Department, and the regional Water Board. In short, this corpus consists of burlesques of bureaucracy and authority. The stunts show bureaucracy out of control and make fun of the arbitrary nature of official actions. At the same time, they construct a laughable image of "the public's" credulity and blind obedience to authority, putting the blame for the excesses of bureaucracy not on the governors but on the governed.

Like other practical jokes, capping stunts dramatize a persistent incongruity in their social setting. One such incongruity is between New Zealanders' aggressive egalitarian ethos and the considerable power held by government bureaucracies, both local and national. In addition, when capping stunts flourished, New Zealand university students were an educational elite—at the time, only 10 percent of the population had any tertiary education—and most could expect to graduate to elite positions as professionals and lawmakers. The tertiary education system resolved these incongruities by running on meritocratic principles—for example, most students matriculated by passing rigorous national examinations, which entitled them to free tuition and living expenses at government expense. The stunt stories repeatedly emphasize, and exaggerate, the specialized skills that went into producing the bogus letters and other media, and this emphasis reaffirms the meritocratic principles of the higher education system. The stunts burlesqued the students' current elite status and their future roles, making a humorous commentary on the incongruity of having elite status in a culture that was uncomfortable with the existence of elites.

PUBLIC PRANKS AS EXOTERIC DISPLAY EVENTS

Media spoofs, varsity rags, and capping stunts are all public pranks, but not random ones. They are public in that they are intended to attract wide attention. Unlike interpersonal practical jokes, they put the spotlight on the jokers' constructions as much or even more than on the targets, providing a stage for the display of skills that help to define in-group identity. "The public," defined as the salient out-group to the in-group represented by the jokers, constitutes both audience and target. Targets are selected en masse but not at random. So long as they are kept to a manageable level, negative reactions from the out-group only serve to accentuate the differences that the in-group believes lies between them.

As display events (Abrahams 1981), media spoofs and the public pranks of students enact and display the characteristics that each in-group thinks make it distinctive. Public pranksters seek *attention* from external audiences but *humor support* from the in-group that they represent. The chief role played by the salient external publics is not as audience but as the target of the pranks and the foil against which in-group identity is discovered. Negative assessments by these external audiences are something to be managed but not necessarily avoided. Indeed, unlaughter from the external audience may be welcomed. Since the object of the exercise is to enact social distinctions, negative responses from targets are additional fodder for the in-group discourse of distinctiveness. Negative reactions from outsiders may even be encouraged or exaggerated in pursuit of heightening boundaries and building displays of social difference.

Practical jokes are effective devices for displaying identity because they actually enact the perceived differences between parties. As collective targets are contained, they follow scripts that are based on the jokers' beliefs about how people in the targeted group behave. In the course of the jokes these distinctions are enacted, exaggerated, and publicly displayed in a ludic and humorous context. Collective public fabrications enact the alleged character of entire groups of people, both the in-group represented by the jokers and their various publics or salient others. Since targets are unaware they are following a script, their actions are taken as being authentic and genuine—as displaying people as they really are.

Public pranks assert the superiority of play over and above those of work. In a world where work and seriousness are paramount, public pranks are a high-profile form of play that temporarily disrupts work. The journalists and others who create media spoofs turn serious professional skills into displays for aesthetic critique and appreciation and in so doing subvert the media. Capping stunts stopped traffic, delayed people getting to work, and interrupted the normal operations of bureaucracy. Rags like the Cambridge Pavement Club literally occupied the road for brief periods, necessarily disrupting traffic. If traffic patterns signify business as usual, this prank, along with many others that I have not gone into here, symbolically brings work to a halt. In night climbing rags, skills that are a matter of livelihood for steeplejacks were outclassed by insouciant displays by upper-class climbers who had acquired their skills as alpine climbers—that is, as recreation rather than work.

If all the utilitarian and psychological benefits of public pranks and spoofs were to go away, we would still have pranks and spoofs because play is its own reward. Play has lasting effects, whether beneficial or harmful, although it does not exist to produce these effects, and it cannot be explained away by its supposed functions. Stepping outside social roles improves perspective, but it is also liberating and enjoyable for its own sake. Play is fun, and that is all the reason people need to do it.

NOTE

1. From 1917 through 1967, the mandatory closing time for bars in New Zealand was 6 p.m. In 1967 closing time was extended to 10 p.m. (New Zealand Ministry for Culture and Heritage 2014).

11

Some Practical Jokers

PROFILE 1: JOHN AND DON (OR, THE ETHNOGRAPHER HOAXED)

Soon after I arrived in Wellington to conduct research on this project, I had my fifteen minutes of fame. As a way of reaching people who have practical joke stories to share, I sometimes get in touch with the local press. In Wellington the local daily, the *Dominion Post*, took the bait and sent a reporter and photographer to interview me. The next week it ran a story in the education section of the paper, including an address where people could write to me. Two days later, I received the following letter:

> I read about your book in *The Dominion*. I think I'd be an excellent case study. I seem to attract practical jokes. In fact I have been on the receiving end of some very good ones. I don't understand why it's always me. I try to laugh at my misfortune. I'd be happy to help you with your research.

Fantastic! This note was the answer to a folklorist's prayer. Although I wanted to get the victim's point of view, I had found that not many people are anxious to talk to a researcher about being fooled by practical jokes. I e-mailed the author of the note immediately (I have used pseudonyms for everyone in this account):

> Dear Don,
> I received your letter this morning, and I would be delighted to talk to you. What I usually do is tape-record an informal interview . . . Would you be willing to have me interview you at a mutually convenient time and place?

This was the swift reply:

DOI: 10.7330/9780874219845.c011

Hi Moira

I must admit I'm a little confused. What's this all about?

Thanks

Don

At first I thought this guy was jerking me around—encouraging me to get in touch, then pretending to know nothing about it. A few minutes' reflection modified that thought. I e-mailed back, explaining further and adding, "Perhaps someone else has been playing a joke on both of us."

Don answered:

> Yes, we were both duped, the gentleman in question is a grumpy old fuddy duddy by the name of John A——, whom I have been a victim of on a few occasions, however after payback (see attached photo) he did stop. It seems he's back up to mischief!
>
> Mr A——has just handed me your article, and a copy of his letter. Having read the article, I'd actually be quite happy to participate. Maybe we should both be interviewed.
>
> P.S. Please let me apologise for Mr A——'s childish behavior and wasting your time. Payback will be arranged.

Attached was a photograph of an office cubicle in which the desk and everything on it was neatly wrapped in aluminum foil—an oft-repeated practical joke among the denizens of cubicleland.

The answer to a folklorist's prayer turned out to be a compound practical joke, and I had fallen for it hook, line, and sinker. The original letter had seemed a little odd, to be sure, but I simply put that down to the writer's personality, and it only made me more eager to meet him. Not even the confused e-mail that asked, "What's going on?" clued me into the joke; instead, I stuck to my theory that the name at the foot of the letter belonged to the writer, and thought his ignorance was feigned in order to mess with me. I was so sure of that interpretation that I was ready to be irritated with him for treating me this way. Only some minutes later, after I'd almost completed my e-mail in reply, did the alternative explanation come to mind: some third party was playing a joke on both of us.

John and Don were coworkers at a small start-up telecommunications company. Both were creative individuals, but their personalities and their personal practical joke styles were a study in contrasts. Don, the younger man, was an outsize personality by New Zealand standards. Physically big and tall, he had an ebullient personality to match. He was of Italian descent and proud of it. After the two of us had sorted out what was going on, he readily agreed to come up to campus for an interview. John, on the other hand, was not only older but also a quieter and more retiring personality. In fact, I never did meet him, and it was only after some intervention by his wife and another coworker that he agreed to let me interview him on the phone.

For the previous year, John and Don had been engaged in an ongoing sequence of reciprocal practical jokes at work. John had been with the company since soon after it started, whereas Don joined a few years later. After they had occupied adjoining cubicles for some time, the younger man began "having John on," directing jocular verbal abuse at him:

> He comes across and I'll have him on: "Have you had your grumpy pill?" "Why aren't you smiling?" "What's wrong, did you not get enough sleep last night?" "Did you not get your monthly dose of Viagra?" It's just for a bit of a laugh, to alleviate what is more or less a fairly serious office. There's not many people in the company you can do it with. So the simple target was this old bugger [*laughs*]. (Anonymous 2005a)

After taking this jocular abuse for some time, John eventually responded with the first practical joke. Using his computer graphics software, he created a "specimen jar" with a fake label for a nonexistent STD clinic, added Don's name, and left it in the fridge where all the employees would see it. At least, that's what Don thought. In fact, John told me, the jar "was never in the fridge, although he thinks it was. I put it on Don's desk and told him it had been in the fridge. To have actually put it there would have been going too far—too many people would have seen it" (Anonymous 2005b).

This indirect approach was typical of John's joking style. On another occasion, John fabricated a realistic-looking personal ad in Don's name for the local paper that read "Classic Italian Playboy. Big. Best of the best," and included his phone number. Again, John used a graphics program to fabricate something that looked like it had actually run in the paper, although it never had; instead, he showed Don the mock-up and led him to think that it had. Both of these tricks are meta–practical jokes; rather than publicly embarrassing the victim or causing him any direct inconvenience, they were designed to trick him into *thinking* he had been so treated. The chief outrage for Don was that, as Erving Goffman put it, he had to cope with "the fact that those who played him the fool thought it allowable and even appropriate to do so" (1974, 89).

After suffering several of these elaborate practical jokes, Don took advantage of John's absence on an overseas trip to get even. This was the occasion of the careful tin-foiling of John's desk that I described in detail in chapter 1. According to Don, this prank took hours of work, $100 worth of aluminum foil, and involved most of the rest of the employees as witnesses.

By the time I innocently entered the scene in September 2005, the pattern of joking between the two was well established. John simply used me to play another joke on his rival, sending me a carefully crafted letter guaranteed to elicit my unwitting cooperation. In turn, Don tried to use his interview with me to sow seeds of worry in his tormentor. When he left work to visit me on campus, he deliberately misled his coworkers as to where he was going and refused to answer questions about when he would meet with me or what he would say, and he swore me to silence on the topic as well.

John was not yet finished with the game either, as it turned out. The day that I was expecting Don to arrive for an interview, I received another e-mail from John:

Dear Ms Smith,

I am Don I——'s caregiver.

I know he is looking forward to meeting you on Wednesday. He was very disappointed to miss last week's appointment, but I thought it best he didn't come when he wasn't feeling himself.

I'm sure you will find him very entertaining. He has a lovely personality, and he really does enjoy a practical joke when he can comprehend it.

He is up to date with his medication, but can be inclined to spin when he meets someone outside his circle. Just suggest he has some "time out" if he becomes a little overwhelming.

Keep some tissues handy too as he does tend to "spray" saliva when over-excited. And don't be concerned if he quite suddenly bursts into tears—it happens all the time and he (usually) quickly recovers.

I'm sure you won't have any trouble. Keep your door open, and have someone nearby to assist if need be.

Regrettably Don's disability means he has a limited memory span, and sometimes little recall. I'll attach a couple of documents for you to prompt his recollections if need be. You might like to ask him what he remembers about the "Newlands Clinic," or about his dress and shoes for the "3rd Wellington Cross-Dressers' Ball" in 2004.

I hope it goes well.

Kind Regards,

John A——.

Unlike the first, this letter fooled nobody, but it didn't matter. By this stage the three of us were embroiled in a creative game. For the two principals, it was competitive play, but once I had been drawn in as an interested party, John used the occasion to display his considerable verbal skills and proudly showed some of the results of his graphic design expertise. For his part, Don paraded the photograph of John's desk after the tin-foil treatment and made dark promises about the next big "payback" joke that he was cooking up for the following summer. "All I'll say is that this summer's one involves a teenage actress," he told me. "Should be a bit of a laugh, this one. Won't be for him, but it will for everyone else!"

John and Don were both practical jokers outside of their relationship as well. Both played jokes on others—but their personal joking styles were very different. For Don, a good practical joke was one that made an impact and drew a lot of attention—not just from the victim but preferably from a large audience of onlookers too. In high school, he was the ringleader of a group of his mates who were known as the class clowns and made a name for themselves with outrageous, attention-drawing pranks which, he told me, were still being talked about at the school some years later. "We'll do it once, do it right, do it big, so it's memorable, and people talk about it," he said. In contrast, he described John's jokes as "these very subtle things. I don't even remember them." For John—a graphic designer—creativity and originality were what make an outstanding joke. "Don's tin-foiling joke was sort of funny," he said, "but it was not exciting, because it was not original. That joke is all over the Internet. It was not very clever." Yet John did have a grudging admiration for the trouble and effort that Don had gone to: "What was amazing about it was that my desk is very cluttered, and he individually wrapped everything and put everything back in its original place; it must have taken him *hours and hours*."

John and Don also differed in the way they managed the post-play of their jokes. John was the more hesitant; he took care not to go too far. "I always involve someone else as a safety measure, a check to see I am not going too far," he told me on the phone. "It adds to the satisfaction if others are observing. It's my safety net—to make sure I'm not overstepping the mark." His personal rule for practical joking was "no risk and no hurt." In contrast, Don professed not to care about what his victims thought about his treatment of them. "If you wanna play, you gotta play hard," he told me. But although he expressed scorn for his rival's timid approach, there was also a note of grudging admiration, for example, when he told me about the company-wide e-mail that John had sent out in Don's name, offering to give away two tickets to the "Third Wellington Cross-Dressers' Ball." Don admired the risk taking involved in this prank because it violated company rules about the use of e-mail. "He took a big punt," he told me. "Because if I'd decided to go the other way, and just say, '*No*, this is not on'" and laid a complaint, that's it. That's a sackable offense."

For John, practical joking was an outlet for creativity. Asked why he liked to play jokes, he answered, "It's enjoyable creating them, linking ideas together. I see something and get an idea. I never search the web looking for new practical jokes." Most often, what triggered an idea was noticing "an exaggerated behavior or personality" in another person:

> Certain people make me do things. I look for a vulnerability. Don shakes the floor when he walks; he's so Italian; he's completely harmless but assertive and dominant. I was looking for redress.

John's comments made it clear that for him, practical joking offers an outlet for his creativity that is almost impossible to suppress, despite his trepidation about jokes going too far or backfiring. "I get an idea and then design it in about a day," he explained. "I can't wait longer than that—I can't stand it; it's too exciting. Once you get an idea you have to act on it."

Don's motivation was different. Two themes emerged in his talk with me: ambivalence about the appropriateness of practical joking for an adult and a conflicted attitude concerning his relations with the older generation. He described his parents as "straitlaced. Very, very serious people." "My mother missed her calling in life; she should have been a nun." As for his father, he said, "When Dad first came out to New Zealand as a single guy, he would play the odd joke. You can sit down and talk with my father, and he'd deny it. Because he's a serious kind of guy." For Don, practical joking was a part of a youthful rebellion against authority and the demands of respectability. He said of himself that compared to the rest of the Italian community in Wellington, "you couldn't be more polar opposite to what the other guys did. I was just a bit different right from the beginning." This difference took the form of a propensity for clowning and joking around, for practical jokes, and for generally "winding people up"—that is, saying and doing things calculated to get a rise out of others, especially older males and other authority figures like teachers, who were the usual targets of his joking.

Don professed not to care what other people thought about him, but he also admitted that at age thirty-two, now that he was himself a father, his attitude had started to change. He had played jokes in his youth, but "when you're a father with a mortgage it's a different kettle of fish":

I used to have an attitude where I'd be serious from nine to five, but in my own time I did what the hell I like and I didn't care what anyone thought. Now I've got a child, it's like, she notices. She sees and understands everything you do. The influence that you can have; you may as well get it right now, and tone it down a little. But before that, after five, there was nothing serious about me. I was always getting a rise out of someone. A client or parents or family, whoever. And I didn't give a toss what they thought of me either.

This attitude about the age-appropriateness of joking matches the pattern he saw in his father, who had played jokes with his friends as a young man but was now very serious and would deny ever doing such things. Similarly, when he talked about his younger brother, who still behaved like a teenager, he said, "He's always been a bit of a kid." Making the transition from youth to fatherhood, Don was beginning to adopt the same attitude that he ascribed to the serious Italian community that he also enjoyed "winding up": "They don't like that sort of stuff over there. 'You gotta be serious; you've got a kid.'" The cultural expectation that Don had grown up with tolerated practical joking and similar forms of clowning from the young, but when a man acquired a family he was expected to grow up, get serious, and give up such youthful foolishness.

The curious thing is that Don talked about clowning around as if it belonged to his youthful past at the same time that he was gleefully telling me he was planning to play "something big" on his coworker. This apparent contradiction can be explained by considering the reasons he gave for playing jokes on his senior colleague. One was "payback—not just for making fools of other people but also for wasting people's time." From the outset, Don criticized John's practical jokes as a waste of time that should have been spent working. "He has nothing better to do with his time," he said. "While the rest of us work, John plays. He's an older gentleman, so you just go with the flow." John's seniority and age meant that he could not be criticized directly for this mildly bad behavior, but practical jokes offered an indirect form of critique and retribution:

But when it comes back, payback's always a bitch, as they say. I've never done anything to be polite or funny; it's always meant to get you worried, get you scared, or cost you money. That's [*laughs*] the way it has to work. If I'm going to invest some money in it, it's going to cost *him* some money.

I am not aware that the tin-foiling of John's desk cost him any money (although Don invested $100 in supplies), but it probably cost him in time and effort required to undo the trickster's work.

This trickster was able to rationalize his practical jokes, even though he professed disapproval of the genre, because they served as appropriate punishment for his rival's minor misdeeds. Paradoxically, he asserted the primacy of the work ethic by resorting to play—paradoxical, that is, if we accept the commonsense notion that play is the opposite of work. Practical jokes are indeed a form of play, as are all humorous genres (Mannell and McMahon 1982), but that does not mean that they are inherently antithetical to the work ethic. On the contrary, humor can be used, as it is here, to send a message about the importance of work and to criticize frivolity that seems inappropriate.

Practical joking also offered Don a solution to a conundrum: how to respond to a coworker whose actions cried out for payback but whose status as the older man demanded respect. Several times in our conversation, Don referred to the fact that John was older—a theme that began in his first e-mail to me, where he called him "a grumpy old fuddy duddy." John had left his own graphic design business to join the start-up company, which Don joined a few years later. Working in adjoining cubicles, the two of them reported to the same supervisor and occupied the same rung in the company hierarchy. After some time, Don reported, he began to develop a friendly relationship with John:

> I started to get comfortable with the guy, go out to lunch with him, could talk openly with him, and then the grumpy pill thing started . . . he moans a lot, so I started off, "Have you had your grumpy pill this morning? You're in a real bad mood." It's grown from that. Gotten comfortable with calling someone who's older—as an Italian you're always taught to respect your elders. Got comfortable with him to the point where you could start making jokes about his age—he's not that old; he's late forties, early fifties. I don't know exactly how old he is. You should respect the guy for his age, but you get to that comfort layer with him, and it's grown from there.

Respect for elders was a theme that recurred more than once in Don's talk. As he mentioned, in the Italian community where he was raised, "you're always taught to respect your elders." But in Pakeha (Anglo) New Zealand, there is not the same stress on respect for elders or for authority. An easy, friendly egalitarianism is the cultural ideal for everyday relationships, especially at work (Plester and Sayers 2007, 178–181). As Don described it, this is exactly the kind of relationship that he had at his previous place of employment. There he and another recent hire regularly joked with their senior coworkers, many of whom had been with the company for thirty years:

The beauty of it was, there was these relationships formed with these old guys where we'd walk up to them and go, "You crazy old bugger." It was me and a pup engineer, with all these *very*, very intelligent men who'd been at Telecom all this time. I felt comfortable having a laugh with these older guys, I felt a comfortable with calling them "you crazy old bugger" and go for Friday drinks with them. And when I went to [my present company], that was not there. All these serious guys. So the easy target was John, who was the old guy.

According to Mary Douglas, "The experience of a joke form in the social structure calls imperatively for an explicit joke to express it (1975, 100). Don's joking relationships with his older colleagues are classic examples of the way that humor in the expressive realm reflects and grows out of an incongruity in the social situation. Jocular abuse grew out of and managed the conflict between the competing demands for respect and for egalitarianism, and payback in the form of practical jokes was an indirect way of subverting the imperious demands of the work ethic in order to defend it.

PROFILE 2: MATT ELLIOTT: THE PROFESSIONAL

Many people would never play practical jokes at all. For others, practical joking is an intermittent entertainment, an occasional outbreak of play to leaven relationships and add spice to everyday life. For a small minority of people, however, practical joking is such a big part of their lives that it defines them. The names of a few of these jokers are well known, in part because these individuals are not only jokers but also tireless self-promoters. The pantheon of tricksters includes the Englishmen Theodore Hook (Hook and Barham 1849, 47–77; Smith 1953, 110–112) and William Horace De Vere Cole (Reeve 1977, 19–23; Smith 1953, 101–107; Stephen 1983), and the Americans Hugh Troy (Smith 1953, 134–151; Troy 1983) and Leon Varjian (Steinberg 1992, 169–189), all of whom achieved such reputations that they became figures of contemporary legend. Some well-known apocryphal hoaxes are attributed to them. Since their ludic careers have been well documented elsewhere (for example, Boston 1982, 28–44), there is no need to rehearse them here; instead I wish to draw attention to the existence of other practitioners of the art who may not be famous but who nevertheless qualify as semiprofessional practical jokers.

I met Matt Elliott in Wellington in 2005 when he got in touch after seeing a newspaper story about my research. Matt is a professional joker, literally—since 1989 he has performed as a stand-up comic on the stage, and he is also the author of the first book-length history of New Zealand comedy, *Kiwi Jokers* (Elliott 1997). In his day job he is a researcher in a law firm, where he is also the in-house comedian. He is the one who will disconnect the mouse on someone's computer, put confetti on the blades of a ceiling fan, or attach a colleague's shoes to the ceiling with Velcro.

Because of Matt's second career as a professional comedian, people at work expect him to play the same role for them, and he obliges by periodically enacting one of an array of comic fictitious characters, going around the office to entertain his coworkers:

> I think there's a little bit of an expectation there for me to be funny or to entertain them, which becomes a little bit of a chore at times. My league has actually said, "Matt's not a toy." Because there have been people just wanted me to entertain them. I established a couple of characters in the office. One very effeminate guy who would go around dusting people's offices. Quentin . . . [*in effeminate voice*] "Hi, how are you; do you want any dusting done today? Is your room dusty?" With a pink feather duster.
>
> Then there was another guy who was a builder. So I took my tool belt into work—it's at my desk at work now—but every now and then I put that on and I wander round and see if people have any maintenance that they needed doing. Different voice for that; it's a lot deeper, good sort of Kiwi bloke builder. People loved it. So much so that it became a bit of a chore because people wanted me to keep doing it. So it would take some of the spontaneity out of it. (Elliott 2005)

It is not uncommon for one or two individuals to become the star humor performers in the workplace—the company clowns. One of Matt's colleagues told me that his clowning and practical joking is usually well received and improves the quality of life at work. "It puts a bit of light in the day," she said. However, this acceptance can come at a cost for the clown—while successful joking makes him or her popular, the clown persona can hurt his or her chances for advancement (Plester and Orams 2008). Further, Matt himself found that his colleagues expected this role from him so much that it sometimes became less fun for him and more of a job.

Spontaneity is an important characteristic of a good practical joke for Matt. He draws a line between good-natured jokes and others that are a bit "darker" or crueler:

> In my practical joking, the thing for me is that it stays good-natured, so that it's a fun thing, and it's based around an element of surprise, which is in some ways a pure form of comedy. Set something up and the person gets a surprise and then you have a laugh, and that's it. You hear about people *plotting* to get each other back, and it becomes a bit darker than it should.

The point is to have fun and not go too far. Matt feels that his experience as a professional comedian helps him quickly ascertain if someone has a sense of humor or not, and he is careful to avoid those he knows will be offended. If someone does not respond well to one of his jokes, he will not aim at that person again. If people get unhappy because they suspect they are being specially targeted, he can defend himself by pointing out that he does it to everyone: "I'm just including you in the fun."

Matt got an early training in practical joking and in acting. Growing up, practical joking was the order of the day in his family—Christmas or birthday presents might be wrapped in excessively large boxes, or the present under the tree would be a pair of old socks. His parents actively encouraged the kids to play jokes on adults—for example, on their grandfather:

> *The* running joke was to go to Pop's and either push the doorbell or knock on the door and just step away to the side where he wouldn't see you, and he'd open the door, and he would play up with the whole thing—he'd be, "Oh! No one there! I could've sworn I heard a knock at the door." Then [he'd] shut the door and [we'd] wait a few seconds and knock again.

This is a traditional exoteric children's prank, most commonly known as "Knick-Knock" in New Zealand. As mentioned earlier, Iona and Peter Opie recorded over sixty different names for this game among children in Britain, and it is also widely reported among children in the United States (Opie and Opie 1959, 378–392; Sutton-Smith 1981, 81). Almost always, kids are the instigators of the joke, intending to harass and irritate adult neighbors, and they are neither surprised nor disappointed if their targets react with rage.

On the face of it, "Knick-Knock" and other children's pranks look like ritualized conflict between the generations, but Matt's experience reveals another side. In his family, the adults actively encouraged and helped their children to play these jokes, and the adult targets in the family supported the game by playing along—much to the delight of the kids. Matt said that his grandfather often played this role, for example, by feigning exaggerated surprise: "It became a bit of a semiperformance in itself the way he would carry on knowing that something wasn't right, and then act surprised," he said. "It was great merriment." This early training in comic acting has benefited Matt as an adult trickster.

When Matt went on a working holiday in Ireland, he met up with another inveterate practical joker who was a match for his skills as a trickster. Matt was working at a wildlife park where practical jokes among the workers were the order of the day, both among the old hands and in the form of fool's errands for the temporary summer employees. Tampering with each other's equipment was a regular occurrence:

> There were pranks going on there the whole time. Guys would climb up trees to cut browse for the giraffes, and the ladders would be taken away— the guys would be sitting up in the trees for a couple of hours. Health and safety wasn't an issue at all there. All sorts of things going on.
>
> Younger kids who would start at work just over the summer seasons, they were forever being told to fetch this, that, and the other, and caught out, much to the enjoyment of the senior staff. A couple of the older staff would enjoy the same tricks that they'd been using for years. Going to fetch a bucket of blue steam, or fetch me the skirting [baseboard] ladder, sky hook, left-handed hammer.

In the midst of this general hilarity, the head warden at the park, "a guy called Paddy," stood out as an exceptional joker. "He used to pride himself on catching people out," Matt explained. "And he was a target for a lot of people because he often caught people out."

When the young comic from New Zealand arrived for the summer, the stage was set for a battle between master practical jokers. As Matt tells this story, he and Paddy began "eyeing each other up as potential targets." They did not begin targeting each other with jokes at once, because "there were always other people that were a little bit easier to get." So the two bided their time, getting involved in the ongoing joking at the park but avoiding each other and "sounding each other out." In Matt's estimation, as is true of some other prolific practical jokers I have known, some jokers are pros and the rest mere amateurs. At the park, the joking with other workers was a warm-up while he and Paddy sized each other up for the main event, "just wondering how clever you had to be to catch the other person out." Nevertheless, each knew that at some point they would meet head-on. Matt took the plunge first and Paddy swiftly retaliated:

> A feud started between him and I when he was going to move a jeep which was stuck in some mud and I just put an egg, a chicken's egg under his seat. And he sat down on it and I said, "Oh, good *crack*, Paddy."
>
> And from there, later in the afternoon, I used to cycle home—he went and greased the brakes on my bike. And I checked my bike with great para- noia before I left—because I knew that he would have done something, he wouldn't just let me get away with him sitting on an egg—and found this grease and wiped it off and just cycled off towards home as though nothing had happened. And a few of the boyos from the park had passed me in the car. And stopped and said, "Oh, Paddy says have a nice ride home." I was

like, "Oh, okay, thanks," you know, pretending that I had no idea what he'd done.

Matt's "good crack" comment was a pun on *craic*, which in Irish English means "fun" or "entertainment" (see, for example, in Cashman 2008). Paddy's tampering with Matt's bike seems to be an extreme form of joking, but it was in line with the style of joking favored among the old hands at the park. Arguably, Paddy honored Matt by targeting him with an insider's style of prank rather than with one of the generic fool's errands usually meted out to summer workers.

The culmination of Matt's story is the joke that he said he was most proud of, in which he turned Paddy's prank back on him by pretending that it had gone seriously wrong:

> Got home, and I thought, "Oh, I'm not going to let this rest." So, went across the road to a nurse that worked over there and got a—just one of those foam neck braces and a sling. And we went across to this small town where Paddy lived, which was probably ten miles from where I was stay-ing, but I knew that he'd be in a particular pub playing cards that night. So went over and put the neck brace on and the sling around my arm, *stormed* into this pub, pushed the door open and walked in, and it was real saloon style thing.
>
> Everyone stopped and turned to see the entrance that I made . . . and I said to the woman at the bar, "Where's Paddy?" And, could see out of the corner of my eye this person slinking down in a chair. She said, "Oh, he's just over there." So I went over and stood in front of his table and said, "Did you do something to my bike, Paddy?" And he's blushing and he's like, "Ah, no, no, no, didn't do anything." He said, "What's happened?" I said, "Well, I've been up at the hospital for the last three hours. Came off my bike, I've done my shoulder in, have problems with my neck . . . I won't be able to come back and work in the park; and as you know I was saving, working there to go off on the next part of my trip to India. So that's not going to happen now either. I just wanna know who did some-thing to my bike."
>
> And he's like, "Um, oh, I've got no idea . . . Can I buy you a drink?" [*laughs*] And he stood up and took me across to the bar . . . and I said, "Oh, well, I shouldn't because I'm on all these painkillers but I will have a pint." So he called me a pint, and the woman put the pints on the bar [*laughs*]; he was just *very* flustered by the whole thing, and I said, "Oh, look, don't worry about it, Paddy," and with the arm that was in the sling lifted up the pint and drank it [*laughs loudly*].
>
> Which caused great mirth in the pub for other people who'd been watching this.

And he was so caught out by it, and enjoyed it so much, he actually was telling a lot of people about it. So I got to work the next day, and people were saying, "Oh, yeah, you caught Paddy out." Whereas previously, if he'd been caught he just wouldn't mention anything. Wouldn't say a word.

He enjoyed it.

Paddy's present of a drink was a peace offering, made under the false impression that he had inadvertently caused the younger man a serious injury with his prank. As Matt tells the story, Paddy appreciated and admired the way the younger man had "caught him out" in view of the entire clientele of the pub; in a departure from his usual practice, Paddy expressed his appreciation by telling everyone about it. So the exchange of jokes between these master practical jokers ended with mutual admiration.

It is not hard to see why this joke was the one Matt was most proud of. It included an element of risk—not only was he taking on an older man who was a more experienced trickster than he, he did so before a large crowd in a Republican pub, in a place where he was a recent arrival. Further, the trick involved one of the most difficult feats of fabrication: instead of setting things up behind the scenes or hiding behind a letter, e-mail, or telephone, he carried off the deception in person on the strength of his acting ability. "Everyone stopped and turned to see the entrance that I made," he said, and he played the role of injured and aggrieved victim well enough to draw the close sustained attention of not only his primary target but the entire establishment. He made his entrance not just into the pub but onto a stage, where in short order his intended victim unwittingly joined him. It was a bravura performance.

PROFILE 3: RUDOLPH AND PAULINE, LOVE AND LAUGHTER

Practical joking is often a family affair, and this was very much the case for Rudolph and Pauline Kotze. I attended services at St. Paul's Lutheran church in Wellington, where everyone told me the Kotzes were the ideal people to help me with my research on humor. They were active members of this small congregation, in which Rudolph served as an elder. Rudolph, forty-nine, a civil engineer, and Pauline, forty-eight, a high school French teacher, had recently immigrated to New Zealand from an Afrikaans area in South Africa. Fellow church members told me that this family was always joking.

As I became friends with the Kotzes, it was evident that people were right: this family was always joking. Interactions both within the family and with others were full of jokes and laughter. "We have a lot of laughs," said Pauline. "A lot of it, with the children as well" (Kotze and Kotze 2005). Moreover, the couple explicitly identified this shared humor style as a key element in their successful marriage. "I think Pauline and I have stayed together that long because we have a lot of laughter," Rudolph told me.

Laughter was a key element in this couple's "origin myth," their story of how they met. Rudolph had been invited to a party at Pauline's parents' house, and she was there. Balancing a plate of hors d'oeuvres, he accidentally dropped a cocktail sausage, which rolled under a chair. Dropping to the floor to retrieve it, he was asked what he was doing and replied, "I'm looking for my sausage." At that point, Pauline got the giggles, and he caught her eye. Rudolph concluded the story: "That was the point where I decided that to fall in love with you would be good, because you had a good sense of humor." A "good sense of humor" is a highly sought-after quality in contemporary courtship, and some scientists argue that it must be an adaptive trait in evolutionary terms (Martin 2007, 134–136; Weisfeld 2006, 10–12). However, research suggests that this concept means different things for men than for women—women value humor production and receptivity to humor equally, but men tend to look for partners who appreciate their jokes (Bressler and Balshine 2005).

Practical jokes were a part of the humor repertoire of the Kotze family, but husband and wife had different personal joke styles. Rudolph was an active practical joker, directing his trickery toward everyone in his circle: father, wife, children, friends at work, and even fellow parishioners. This predilection for joking came about even though he apparently did not come from a family of jokers. "We were a pretty serious family," he said. "Although that didn't stop me; I did play some pranks on my father which didn't go down too well. [He was a] very, very conscientious person."

Rudolph's personal style ran the gamut, from the simplest jokes—jumping out of corners or suddenly shouting to scare unsuspecting people—to elaborate and carefully planned fabrications that took a lot of thought and preparation. Appropriately for an engineer, his aesthetic of practical joking emphasized the importance of detail and control. "When it comes to practical jokes," he said, "my belief is that you have to really plan it well. And do it in such a way that you don't leave anything to chance." His practical joke stories are similarly detailed, describing every element of the background, preparation, and aftermath of his jokes at length, with Pauline contributing corrections of fact and detail.

In contrast, Pauline rarely played practical jokes. As she said, "I'm not good at doing it because I don't hold my pose; I get the giggles." She told me of only one time when she was the main player in instigating a practical joke; on that occasion, she played a trick on her high school students one April Fools' Day to get them back for fooling her. However, Pauline was a supporter of practical jokes and she came from a family where practical jokes were the tradition. Her father kept a booby-trapped mustard jar that sprang open with a loud whistle to startle unsuspecting dinner guests, for instance. Turning empty eggshells upside down was another common trick in her family, one that the adults would play up: "My grandfather would really make a big show of looking forward to eating this egg, knowing full well that it was just the egg[shell] that had been turned over. Playing along." With this upbringing, Pauline learned to support practical jokes and how to respond to them, qualities that come in handy when one is married to a practical joker.

Pauline's approach to practical joking is common among women, who in general do not indulge in this pursuit as much as men (Apte 1985, 69). Folklorists have described some women who enjoy playing practical jokes either at work (McEntire 2002) or within their families (Sawin 2004, 135–155), but there are far more documented cases of male pranksters. It is possible that women practical jokers get less attention simply because they are not *expected* to enjoy such a disreputable pastime, or that women's practical joking is less public than men's. Other women, like Pauline, enjoy and support practical jokes, sometimes thinking them up and encouraging the men in their lives to carry them out—thus leaving the limelight, and the risk, to their husbands, brothers, or male friends (Duenez and Duenez 1987). This pattern mirrors what we know about women's approach to verbal joke performance. Study after study shows that men tell more jokes than women (Ziv 1988). A Dutch study of attitudes toward joke performance found that women who did appreciate jokes were likely to leave the performance to their husbands, preferring instead to prompt them with whispered suggestions (Kuipers 2006, 44–47).

Rudolph and Pauline had different styles and histories when it came to practical joking, but these differences dovetailed in an effective way in their marriage. They formed a partnership: Rudolph was the chief instigator of jokes, while Pauline played the essential role of humor supporter. Their humor was a joint construction, and this dynamic is illustrated by the collaborative way in which they recounted practical joke stories. Sometimes the jokes themselves were very simple, but as the couple retold the events together the events became hilarious. This was the case with a story that I recorded as we sat in the living room of their Lower Hutt home after dinner one night:

R: And then one night, she was lying in bed reading the Bible. And I don't know why I did this, but she . . .

P: Oh! I was hiccupping.

R: You were hiccupping.

P: It was the same time.

R: And she was hiccupping and reading the Bible, and all of a sudden I turned around and said, "wah!"

P: Like loudly.

R: Really loud, unexpectedly. And I'm telling you, it was like a *millisecond*, she *slammed* the Bible shut—*bang!*—ripped open the drawer, put the Bible in, closed it, put off the light, turned around, and that was it. Okay. Must have been a *second*. She was *so* upset.

P: I was *furious* with him. Because I was reading, we were having a family devotion, I was reading the Bible out loud, but hiccupping all the while, and then he gave me a fright again but I didn't think it was appropriate. I *slammed* the book and I wasn't going to talk to him. At the end I could feel the bed next to me shaking, and he's giggling away. And he says, "You're not hiccupping anymore" [*laughs loudly*].

I laugh about it now but that night I was *furious*; I was really cross.

It was really funny, I remember; the more he laughed, the angrier I got! [*laughs*] I didn't see the humor at all [*laughs*]. But he does, he always says, it was a millisecond between closing the Bible to putting off the light, to turning around [*laughs*].

Husband and wife share equal responsibility for the performance of this story. Rudolph begins, but within a very short time Pauline joins in, supplying the details he omitted and giving him the opportunity to mirror what she said ("I was hiccupping."—"You were hiccupping"). When speakers "mirror" each other in conversation it indicates that they have a close, friendly relationship (Coates 2007).

Rudolph describes her reaction in dramatic style: "And I'm telling you, it was like a *millisecond*, she *slammed* the Bible shut—*bang!*—ripped open the drawer, put the Bible in, closed it, put off the light, turned around, and that was it. Okay. Must have been a *second*." He emphasizes the speed and dimensions of her reaction—both testaments to the success of his simple trick—a gratifying response apparently out of proportion to the minimalism of his action. As we reached this point of the story performance, all of us were laughing hard.

At this juncture Pauline takes over the narrative, reprising her reaction (again, mirroring his words— "I *slammed* the book.") Then she narrates the post-play of the joke, the evaluation phase in which she worked through the process of how to respond—not to the joke itself but to the fact that he had played a joke on her. The theme of this part of the narrative is her initial anger. Twice she says with emphasis, "I was *furious*," but she also mirrors Rudolph's description of her reaction, which implies that although she was angry with him at the time, she now supports his joke. This section of the story ends with a direct quote, "You're not hiccupping anymore," which serves as a punch line and elicits loud laughter.

Pauline's extended coda reiterates the contrast between her anger then and her amusement now. She emphasizes that she was not amused by the joke at the time because she thought it was inappropriate to play a practical joke during a religious devotion. Curiously, the more she expands on how she was not amused in this part of the performance, the more she laughs. One source for humor and laughter in this performance is the incongruity between Pauline's angry reaction then and her amusement now, which creates a feedback loop of amusement and laughter. However, Pauline's laughter does more than mark the presence of humor in this excerpt—it creates it. As the target of an in-group practical joke, she has the last word in deciding whether it is funny or not. Further, the fact that she is able to support Rudolph's prank in retrospect is further evidence of the solidarity between her and her husband.

Practical jokes are deeply embedded in relationships. The relationship between joker and target gives the idea for a joke in the first place and is also the single most important influence on the evaluation of the joke. Participants apply their knowledge of the relationship to frame the messages they exchange, and this frame has the power to invert meanings (Oring 1992, 142). Pauline was clearly not amused at the time, but she equally clearly chose to support the joke later. Her decision reflects more than the oft-made observation that distance makes events more amusing; it illustrates that the decision whether or not to support a practical joke is conscious and deliberate.

It is a truism that shared laughter builds solidarity and strengthens relationships, but the key element is that the laughter is shared. In the Kotzes' marriage, humor helps to cement their relationship not by its mere existence but because Rudolph and Pauline agree that it should be so. They agree that humor is important, and both support joking performances, including practical joking, when they occur in the family. In the case of this simple joke, its second life as a family story became for both partners an emblem of their strong and happy marriage.

Post-Play

THE POST-PLAY PERIOD IN PRACTICAL JOKE ENACTMENTS is for evaluation, critique, and sometimes argument. It also provides a space in which participants can transition from the play world back to what passes for the real world, sometimes taking lessons with them that can be applied in other contexts. So, too, books need a cool-down phase where author and reader may look back with a longer view and think about what has been learned that can be applied more broadly. My initial research question was, when is a practical joke just a joke? Put another way, when does a practical joke go too far? This issue of limits is pertinent to all jokes and to all humor. However, asking where the limits lie may be less significant than asking why that question inevitably comes up when we think about jokes, especially practical jokes.

Even in the abstract, practical jokes often elicit visceral reactions. When I tell people in conversation that I am studying this genre, the most frequent response is some variation on "How great! But some of them can be quite cruel." A close second is the earnest reply "I don't like practical jokes." These comments echo the more sophisticated assertion, made by popular and academic writers alike, that the practical joke is the lowest form of humor, if not excluded from the canon of humorous genres altogether. It seems to me that these almost reflex reactions are telling pointers to something important and essential about practical jokes.

To justify putting practical jokes at the bottom of the scale of humorous forms, one or more of the following reasons is usually offered. First, because they are primitive; second, because they are cruel; and third, because they can be dangerous. I will discuss each of these claims in turn.

Are practical jokes inevitably simple and crude? I submit that the preceding pages show that the "primitive" charge cannot stick. The practical joke in its various forms allows plenty of room for skill, creativity, elaboration, and personal style. Some fabrications are simply inspired. I am convinced that the practical joke is best understood as a widespread vernacular art form.

Artistry is all very well, but what if it is cruel or immoral? As anyone can see, any activity in which one of the actors is referred to as the "victim" must

DOI: 10.7330/9780874219845.c012

be aggressive, if not downright cruel. Humor scholars argue about whether jokes are essentially or even necessarily cruel or aggressive, and these debates show no signs of being put to rest. When jokes are purely verbal fictions or riddling questions, there is room for ambiguity about whether their targets are intended to be real or merely symbolizations created on which to hang elaborate verbal and semantic play. But the targets of practical jokes are unambiguously real, specific people. Even worse, the majority of practical jokes are structured so that targets become aware that they are targets—and public targets at that. How then to explain the jokes' fun and popularity, not to mention their power to cement social relationships?

The benign violation theory of humor, articulated by several scholars, suggests that amusement occurs when observers note a norm violation and simultaneously find a way to countenance it. This model describes very well the attitude that onlookers, collaborators, and targets take toward practical jokes. In this model, transgression and amusement are equally and simultaneously present. The aggressive treatment of the targets of practical jokes, often combined with violations of norms of taste and appropriateness, constitutes deliberate, aestheticized transgression that various audiences are invited to countenance after the fact. This model of joke reception challenges essentialist vernacular assumptions about what is funny and what is not. Instead, there is nothing inherently jocular or cruel in any joke. For this reason, I draw a distinction between effective and successful practical jokes. An effective joke is one in which the jokers can plausibly claim that events unfolded according to their script. Success, on the other hand, applies only to situations in which jokers can manage the post-play of a joke so that salient audiences react with support or with unlaughter, as the jokers wish.

Practical jokes highlight social boundaries rather than bridging them. The social setting is the key influence on whether or not a particular audience supports a practical joke—especially when the audience whose support is sought is also the target of the joke. A context of social inclusiveness, such as between good friends, tends to blunt the force of the aggression or cruelty in the joke, allowing targets to interpret aggression as love. When they show support for outrageous jokes, audiences create a state of shared benign wrongdoing that enhances social solidarity. In contrast, a context of social exclusion tends to accentuate the perception of cruelty and transgression, making humor support difficult to maintain. Unlaughter, the term that describes the withholding of humor support, tends to create division. Jokers who fail to secure support—that is, retroactive permission for their joke transgressions—risk censure, but it is even lonelier to be the only person not laughing when salient others are. This symbolic exclusion can lead to exclusion in fact.

We are left with a genre that combines aggressive and benign elements in equal measure. Different observers will notice or emphasize one of these aspects over the other, concluding either that practical jokes are just in fun (with the possible exception of a few bad eggs) or that the sunny joking frame that surrounds them is nothing but a thin disguise for naked cruelty. So long as essentialist conceptions of jokes are in play, then arguments over where a particular joke falls will never end. The benign violation model suggests a third way, one that recognizes that jokes are both transgressive, aggressive, and even cruel but also benign and even loving. To recognize this essential characteristic of jokes, we must become comfortable with ambiguity. We must also acknowledge the possibility that it is fun to be bad—within limits. Tricksters are entertaining and even admirable when seen at a distance; but they are much more likeable when safely raised to mythic status than when they pop up next door and start messing with daily life.

Tricksters and trickery are also seen as dangerous. Even boosters of practical jokes urge caution. They warn of the potential of jokes to "backfire," meaning either that the practical joker runs the risk of being made a joking target himself or herself or that jokes can cause actual material or physical harm to their targets. The first of these risks is realistic but trivial; the second is not at all trivial but much more unlikely.

The first kind of backfire risk includes the chance that intended targets will get wind of the joker's plans and scuttle them by turning the joke on the joker. It also includes the likelihood that one joke will be answered with another. Reciprocal joking exchanges are fueled by the inherent morality of the genre: every effective practical joke creates a moral imbalance that calls for redress. All targets of practical jokes are considered deserving of their jocular mistreatment, either because of petty social infractions of their own or simply because they allow themselves to be taken in. Among the minor infractions worthy of punishment with a practical joke are practical jokes themselves.

Finally, what of the chance that a practical joke could backfire by going too far and actually causing material harm? The press and contemporary legend both are full of accounts of practical jokes that unintentionally caused serious injury or even death, but verified instances of such tragic outcomes are rare compared to the vast number of practical jokes that are enacted. The attention to these isolated cases and to purely legendary instances is out of proportion to the real risks. Practical jokes are "dangerous," but not in the way that people think. I believe that the danger indexed in these warning tales is metaphor for another kind of danger, one that is felt but rarely acknowledged. It is the danger and the fearsomeness of play.

Practical jokes are unilateral play. This is the only definition I have found that can encompass the full range of activities that are commonly called practical jokes or pranks (the two terms are virtually indistinguishable synonyms). Unilateral play is simply play that is initiated and involves people without their permission. The unilateral move is accomplished sometimes through trickery and at other times by surprise. Either way, the individuals or groups who are the targets of practical jokes and pranks find that their everyday reality has been adulterated and transformed into a play world. Without warning they find that they are not acting but playing, or perhaps that walking down the mundane street has suddenly thrust them into some kind of theater. If we stick to an idealized image of play, full of swings and roundabouts and laughing children, we would be at a loss to understand why unilateral play should be so threatening. If play is a good thing, why would anyone object to being made a part of it?

By muddying the clear boundaries that usually surround the play realm, practical jokes provide a glimpse into chaos—and it is this brush with chaos that motivates the suspicion that practical jokes are somehow dangerous. William Fry argues that humor is a way for us to create, manipulate, and enjoy chaos, albeit within strict boundaries (Fry 1992, 230–31). I suggest that play, although normally even more carefully bounded than humor, is also a brush with chaos. The clear limits of time and space and the elaborate rules that surround play all exist to create the illusion that chaos is safely contained. Chaos is simply the universe as it exists outside of the social constructions that human beings impose upon it. "Social order, when it functions well, envelops the individual in a web of habits and meanings that are experienced as self-evidently real," according to Peter Berger (1997, 2). Unilateral play disrupts the constructed social order and so reveals that the social order is itself a construction—and that chaos lies beyond. Chaos is thrilling when it is safely bounded, but fearsome when it is on the loose. Practically joking pushes to the limit our reliance on boundaries and our simultaneous longing for chaos.

I have called this chapter "Post-Play" rather than "Conclusion" because conclusions are usually fake. They promise a wrapping up of loose ends, a display of QEDs and questions answered, all wrapped up in a tidy package with a flourish and a nice bow. In any genuine field of inquiry, of course, such promises are vain. Nothing is ever completely wrapped up—especially when it comes to the puzzle of humor. This chapter is not so much the conclusion of one book as the beginning of another—one that someone else might write. The post-plays of practical jokes can continue indefinitely, and so it is with books.

I find it interesting to speculate on how people will react to this book. I imagine that some readers will object because it challenges dearly held beliefs about joking and about humor generally. In my mind's eye, some readers are already thinking that the author should be taken down a peg or two, or at least have her wits and sense of humor tested by having some practical jokes played on her. One joke always deserves another, after all. To which I say: give it your best shot (aggressive metaphor intended). I will be watching.

References

Abrahams, Roger D. 1981. "Shouting Match at the Border: The Folklore of Display Events." In *"And Other Neighborly Names": Social Process and Cultural Image in Texas Folklore*, edited by Richard Bauman and Roger D. Abrahams, 303–321. Austin: University of Texas Press.

Abrams, David M., and Brian Sutton-Smith. 1977. "The Development of the Trickster in Children's Narrative." *Journal of American Folklore* 90(355): 29–47. http://dx.doi.org/10.2307/539019.

AmazingFX.net, and Kate Regan. 2008. *April Fool Zone: Fun & Harmless Pranks & Practical Jokes*. http://www.webcitation.org/6XnW3zI4I.

Anonymous. 1986. Interview by Moira Smith, Bloomington, IN, August 13.

Anonymous. 2005a. Interview by Moira Smith, Wellington, NZ, September 28.

Anonymous. 2005b. Interview by Moira Smith, Wellington, NZ, October 3.

Apte, Mahadev L. 1985. *Humor and Laughter: An Anthropological Approach*. Ithaca: Cornell University Press.

Aten, Ruth. 1986. Interview by Moira Smith, Bloomington, IN, June 27.

Audubon, John James. 1831. *Ornithological Biography; or, An Account of the Habits of the Birds of the United States of America; Accompanied by Descriptions of the Objects Represented in the Work Entitled the Birds of America, and Interspersed with Delineations of American Scenery and Manners*. 5 vols. Philadelphia: J. Dobson.

Babcock-Abrahams, Barbara. 1975. "A Tolerated Margin of Mess: The Trickster and His Tales Reconsidered." *Journal of the Folklore Institute* 11(3): 147–186. http://dx.doi.org/10.2307/3813932.

Bailey, F. G. 1991. *The Prevalence of Deceit*. Ithaca: Cornell University Press.

Bartos, Paul J. 1979. "The Royal Order of Siam: Troop 1198's Pseudo-Initiation Rite." *Indiana Folklore* A12:120–141.

Bass, Steve. 2007. *The Top 25 Web Hoaxes and Pranks*. http://www.pcworld.com/article/131340/article.html.

Basso, Keith H. 1979. *Portraits of "the Whiteman": Linguistic Play and Cultural Symbols among the Western Apache*. New York: Cambridge University Press.

Bateson, Gregory. 1972. *Steps to an Ecology of Mind*. New York: Ballantine Books.

Baum, Howell S. 1990. *Organizational Membership: Personal Development in the Workplace*. Albany: State University of New York Press.

Bauman, Richard. 1977. *Verbal Art as Performance*. Prospect Heights, IL: Waveland.

Bauman, Richard. 1986. *Story, Performance, and Event: Contextual Studies of Oral Narrative*. New York: Cambridge University Press. http://dx.doi.org/10.1017/CBO9780511620935.

Bauman, Richard. 2004. "'Bell, You Get the Spotted Pup': First Person Narratives of a Texas Storyteller." In *A World of Others' Words: Cross-Cultural Perspectives on Intertextuality*, 82–108. Malden, MA: Blackwell.

Bauman, Richard, and Charles L. Briggs. 1990. "Poetics and Performance as Critical Perspectives on Language and Social Life." *Annual Review of Anthropology* 19(1): 59–88. http://dx.doi.org/10.1146/annurev.an.19.100190.000423.

DOI: 10.7330/9780874219845.c013

BBC. 2008a. *Penguins.* http://www.webcitation.org/6WOnZXZUz.

BBC. 2008b. *Penguins April Fool—the Making of—BBC.* www.webcitation.org/6WO ngmjBg.

Benchmark Group. 2013. *Vous avez gagné une maison.* www.webcitation.org/6PcKe3UN4.

Berger, Peter L. 1997. *Redeeming Laughter: The Comic Dimension of Human Experience* New York: Walter de Gruyter. http://dx.doi.org/10.1515/9783110810660.

Bergson, Henri. (Original work published 1900) 1956. "Laughter." In *Comedy*, edited by Wylie Sypher, 61–190. Garden City, NY: Doubleday.

Bilefsky, Dan, and Maia de la Baum. 2015. "Terrorists Strike Charlie Hebdo Newspaper in Paris, Leaving 12 Dead." *New York Times*, January 7, A1.

Billig, Michael. 2005. *Laughter and Ridicule: Towards a Social Critique of Humor.* London: Sage.

Biotic Baking Brigade. 2004. *Pie Any Means Necessary: The Biotic Baking Brigade Cookbook.* Oakland, CA: AK Press in association with Rebel Folk Press.

Blank, Trevor J. 2013. *The Last Laugh: Folk Humor, Celebrity Culture, and Mass-Mediated Disasters in the Digital Age.* Madison: University of Wisconsin Press.

Boatright, Mody C. 1971. *Folk Laughter on the American Fronier.* Gloucester, MA: Peter Smith.

Boese, Alex. 2002. *The Museum of Hoaxes: A Collection of Pranks, Stunts, Deceptions, and Other Wonderful Stories Contrived for the Public from the Middle Ages to the New Millennium.* New York: Dutton.

Bornagainmuelle. 2009. Mueller Wedding Prank, 2009. www.webcitation. org/6WOoOtdI4.

Boston, Richard. 1982. *The C. O. Jones Compendium of Practical Jokes.* London: Enigma Books.

Bowman, John Robert. 1982. "On Getting Even: Notes on the Organization of Practical Jokes." In *The Paradoxes of Play: Proceedings of the Sixth Annual Meeting of the Association for the Anthropological Study of Play*, edited by John Loy, 65–75. West Point, NY: Leisure.

Brednich, Rolf. 2003. *Neuseeland Macht Spass: Eine kommentierte Anthologie Neuseeländischen Humors in Wort und Bild.* Berlin: Mana-Verlag.

Bressler, Eric R., and Sigal Balshine. 2005. "The Influence of Humor on Desirability." *Evolution and Human Behavior* 27(1): 29–39. http://dx.doi.org/10.1016/j.evolhumbehav.2005.06.002.

Bronner, Simon J. 1984. "'Let Me Tell It My Way': Joke Telling by a Father and Son." *Western Folklore* 43(1): 18–36. http://dx.doi.org/10.2307/1499427.

Bronner, Simon J. 1995. *Piled Higher and Deeper: The Folklore of Student Life.* Little Rock: August House.

Bronner, Simon J. 2006. *Crossing the Line: Violence, Play, and Drama in Naval Equator Traditions.* Meertens Ethnology Cahiers 2. Amsterdam: Amsterdam University Press. http://dx.doi.org/10.5117/9789053569146.

Brunvand, Jan H. 1963. "Classification for Shaggy Dog Stories." *Journal of American Folklore* 76(299): 42–68. http://dx.doi.org/10.2307/538078.

Buckley, F. H. 2003. *The Morality of Laughter.* Ann Arbor: University of Michigan Press.

Caillois, Roger. 1979. *Man, Play, and Games.* New York: Schocken Books.

Cashman, Ray. 2008. *Storytelling on the Northern Irish Border: Characters and Community.* Bloomington: Indiana University Press.

Cassell, Nancy. 1986. Interview by Moira Smith, Bloomington, IN, June 19.

Caulfield, Sharon. 1976. [Fire!] University of California–Berkeley Folklore Archives.

Chafe, Wallace. 2007. *The Importance of Not Being Earnest: The Feeling behind Laughter and Humor.* Amsterdam: John Benjamins. http://dx.doi.org/10.1075/ceb.3.

Chartois, Jo. 1945. "Hunting the Dahut: A French Folk Custom." Translated by Calvin Claudel. *Journal of American Folklore* 58(227): 21–24. http://dx.doi.org/10.2307/535332.

Coates, Jennifer. 2007. "Talk in a Play Frame: More on Laughter and Intimacy." *Journal of Pragmatics* 39(1): 29–49. http://dx.doi.org/10.1016/j.pragma.2006.05.003.

Cobra Patrol. 1982. Interview by Moira Smith, Bloomington, IN, October 24.

Cohen, Hennig. 1951. "Going to See the Widow." *Journal of American Folklore* 64(252): 223. http://dx.doi.org/10.2307/536643.

Comes, Michael L. 1978. [The Board Stretcher.] University of California–Berkeley Folklore Archives.

Cooper, Thomas W. 1996. "Racism, Hoaxes, Epistemology, and News as a Form of Knowledge: The Stuart Case as Fraud or Norm?" *Howard Journal of Communications* 7(1): 75–95. http://dx.doi.org/10.1080/10646179609361714.

Daniel, Tack. 2005. Interview by Moira Smith, Wellington, NZ, December 13.

Davies, Christie. 2011. *Jokes and Targets*. Bloomington: Indiana University Press.

Davis, Natalie Zemon. 1971. "The Reasons of Misrule: Youth Groups and Charivaris in Sixteenth-Century France." *Past & Present* 50(1): 41–75. http://dx.doi.org/10.1093/past/50.1.41.

Dégh, Linda. 2001. *Legend and Belief: Dialectics of a Folklore Genre*. Bloomington: Indiana University Press.

Dégh, Linda, and Andrew Vázsonyi. 1973. *The Dialectics of the Legend*. Folklore Preprint Series 6. Bloomington: Folklore Publications Group, Indiana University Folklore Institute.

Dégh, Linda, and Andrew Vázsonyi. 1976. "Legend and Belief." In *Folklore Genres*, edited by Dan Ben-Amos, 93–123. Austin: University of Texas Press.

Dégh, Linda, and Andrew Vázsonyi. 1983. "Does the Word 'Dog' Bite? Ostensive Action: A Means of Legend-Telling." *Journal of Folklore Research* 20(1): 5–34.

DeNatale, Douglas. 1990. "The Dissembling Line: Pranks in a North Carolina Textile Mill." In *Arts in Earnest: North Carolina Folklife*, edited by Daniel W. Patterson and Charles G. Zug III, 254–276. Durham, NC: Duke University Press.

Green, Johnny, and Pamela Yazman. 1975. Sea Bats. University of California–Berkeley Folklore Archives.

Donahue, Anne K. 1980. [Michael the Archangel's Feather.] University of California–Berkeley Folklore Archives.

Dornelles, Clara, and Pedro M. Garcez. 2001. "Making Sense of Nonsense: Fabrication, Ambiguity, Error, and Clarification in the Organization of Experience in Ordinary Conversation." *Journal of Pragmatics* 33(11): 1707–1730. http://dx.doi.org/10.1016/S0378-2166(00)00077-1.

Dorson, Richard M. 1982. *Man and Beast in American Comic Legend*. Bloomington: Indiana University Press.

Douglas, Brent. 1996. *How Big a Boy Are Ya?* Nashville: Capitol Nashville.

Douglas, Mary. (1968) 1975. "Jokes." In *Implicit Meanings: Essays in Anthropology*, 90–114. London: Routledge & Kegan Paul.

Duenez, John, and Susie Duenez. 1987. Interview by Moira Smith, Bloomington, IN, November 14.

Dundes, Alan. 1989. "April Fool and April Fish: Towards a Theory of Ritual Pranks." In *Folklore Matters*, 98–109. Knoxville: University of Tennessee Press.

Dundes, Alan, and Lauren Dundes. 2002. "The Elephant Walk and Other Amazing Hazing: Male Fraternity Initiation through Infantilization and Feminization." In *Bloody Mary in the Mirror: Essays in Psychoanalytic Folkloristics*, 95–121. Jackson: University Press of Mississippi.

Dyer, G. A. 1979. "Wedding Customs in the Office: A Note." *Lore and Language* 3(1): 73–74.

Eastman, Max. 1972. *The Sense of Humor*. New York: Octagon Books.

"Eat It: Anchovies." 2008. *Hospitality*, March 6.

Eliot, George. 1883. *The Essays of "George Eliot."* New York: Funk and Wagnalls.

Elliott, Matt. 1997. *Kiwi Jokers: The Rise and Rise of New Zealand Comedy*. Auckland: HarperCollins.

Elliott, Matt. 2005. Interview by Moira Smith, Wellington, NZ, December 9.

Elliott, Stuart. 1992. "Foote, Cone to Buy Mojo in South Pacific." *New York Times*, November 19.

Ellis, Bill. 1981. "The Camp Mock-Ordeal: Theater as Life." *Journal of American Folklore* 94(374): 486–505. http://dx.doi.org/10.2307/540502.

Emerson, Joan P. 1969. "Negotiating the Serious Import of Humor." *Sociometry* 32(2): 169–181. http://dx.doi.org/10.2307/2786261.

Emerson, Oliver Farrar. 1921. "Beguiling Words." *Dialect Notes* 5(4): 93–97.

Erard, Michael-Jean. 1991. "Novelties in Popular American Culture." *Journal of Popular Culture* 25(3): 1–16. http://dx.doi.org/10.1111/j.0022-3840.1991.684561.x.

Fine, Gary Alan. 1984. "Humorous Interaction and the Social Construction of Meaning: Making Sense in a Jocular Vein." *Studies in Symbolic Interaction* 5:83–101.

Fine, Gary Alan. 1987. "One of the Boys: Women in Male-Dominated Settings." In *Changing Men: New Directions in Research on Men and Masculinity*, edited by Michael S. Kimmel, 131–147. Newbury Park, CA: Sage.

Fine, Gary Alan. 1988. "Letting off Steam? Redefining a Restaurant's Work Environment." In *Inside Organizations: Understanding the Human Dimension*, edited by Michael Owen Jones, Michael Dane Moore, and Richard Christopher Snyder, 119–127. Newbury Park, CA: Sage.

Fine, Gary Alan, and Michaela De Soucey. 2005. "Joking Cultures: Humor Themes as Social Regulation in Group Life." *Humor: International Journal of Humor Research* 18(1): 1–22. http://dx.doi.org/10.1515/humr.2005.18.1.1.

Fine, Gary Alan, and Christine Wood. 2010. "Accounting for Jokes: Jocular Performance in a Critical Age." *Western Folklore* 69(3–4): 299–321.

Freud, Sigmund. (Original work published 1905) 1960. *Jokes and Their Relation to the Unconscious*. Translated by James Strachey. New York: Norton.

Fry, William F. (Original work published 1963) 1968. *Sweet Madness: A Study of Humor*. Palo Alto, CA: Pacific Books.

Fry, William F. 1992. "Humor and Chaos." *Humor: International Journal of Humor Research* 5(3): 219–232. http://dx.doi.org/10.1515/humr.1992.5.3.219.

Funt, Allen, and Philip Reed. 1994. *Candidly, Allen Funt: A Million Smiles Later*. New York: Barricade Books.

Glassie, Henry H. 1975. *All Silver and No Brass: An Irish Christmas Mumming*. Bloomington: Indiana University Press.

Goffman, Erving. 1961. "Fun in Games." In *Encounters: Two Studies in the Sociology of Interaction*, 17–81. Indianapolis: Bobbs-Merrill.

Goffman, Erving. 1974. *Frame Analysis: An Essay on the Organization of Experience*. New York: Harper & Row.

Grady, Don. 1997. "Maintenance Man Who Left a Big Imprint." *Nelson Mail*, August 12, 13.

Green, A. E. 1981. "Only Kidding: Joking among Coal-Miners." In *Language, Culture and Tradition: Papers on Language and Folklore Presented at the Annual Conference of the British Sociological Association, April 1978*, edited by A. E. Green and J. D. A Widdowson, 47–76. Sheffield: Centre for English Cultural Tradition and Language.

Greenhill, Pauline. 1989. "Welcome and Unwelcome Visitors: Shivarees and the Political Economy of Rural-Urban Interactions in Southern Ontario." *Journal of Rural Studies* 3:45–67.

Greenhill, Pauline. 2010. *Make the Night Hideous: Four English-Canadian Charivaris, 1881–1940.* Toronto: University of Toronto Press.

Greenhill, Pauline, and Kendra Magnusson. 2010. "'Your Presence at Our Wedding Is Present Enough': Lies, Coding, Maintaining Personal Face, and the Cash Gift." *Journal of Folklore Research* 47(3): 307–333. http://dx.doi.org/10.2979/jfolkrese.2010.47.3.307.

Grotegut, Eugene. 1955. "Going to See the O'Reilly Sisters." *Western Folklore* 14(1): 51–52. http://dx.doi.org/10.2307/1495954.

Grotjahn, Martin. 1957. *Beyond Laughter.* New York: McGraw-Hill.

Gruner, Charles R. 1978. *Understanding Laughter: The Workings of Wit and Humor.* Chicago: Nelson-Hall.

Haas, Jack. 1972. "Binging: Educational Control among High Steel Ironworkers." *American Behavioral Scientist* 16(1): 27–34. http://dx.doi.org/10.1177/000276427201600103.

Hall, Brian K. 1999. "The Paradoxical Platypus." *Bioscience* 49(3): 211–218. http://dx.doi.org/10.2307/1313511.

Hanlon, Mike. 2008. "How iFart iPhone Software Makes US$10,000 a Day." *Gizmag,* http://www.webcitation.org/6WP4TuHTL.

Harlow, Ilana. 1997. "Creating Situations: Practical Jokes and the Revival of the Dead in Irish Tradition." *Journal of American Folklore* 110(436): 140–168. http://dx.doi.org/10.2307/541810.

Harold, Christine. 2004. "Pranking Rhetoric: 'Culture Jamming' as Media Activism." *Critical Studies in Media Communication* 21(3): 189–211. http://dx.doi.org/10.1080/0739318042000212693.

Harrah-Conforth, Bruce. 1986. Interview by Moira Smith, Bloomington, IN, June 17.

Harrowfield, David L. 1995. *The Tip of the Iceberg: A Collection of Yarns and Ditties on New Zealanders in Antarctica.* Christchurch: South Latitude Research.

Hay, Jennifer. 2001. "The Pragmatics of Humor Support." *Humor: International Journal of Humor Research* 14(1): 55–82. http://dx.doi.org/10.1515/humr.14.1.55.

Henningsen, Gustav. 1965. "The Art of Perpendicular Lying: Concerning a Commercial Collecting of Norwegian Sailors' Tall Tales." Translated by Warren E. Roberts. *Journal of the Folklore Institute* 2(2): 180–219. http://dx.doi.org/10.2307/3813833.

Henricks, Thomas S. 2006. *Play Reconsidered: Sociological Perspectives on Human Expression.* Urbana: University of Illinois Press.

Herman, Edward S., and Noam Chomsky. 1988. *Manufacturing Consent: The Political Economy of the Mass Media.* New York: Pantheon Books.

Holmes, Janet, and Meredith Marra. 2002. "Having a Laugh at Work: How Humour Contributes to Workplace Culture." *Journal of Pragmatics* 34(12): 1683–1710. http://dx.doi.org/10.1016/S0378-2166(02)00032-2.

Honeyman, A. M. 1959. "Fools' Errands for Dundee Apprentices." *Folklore* 70(1): 334–336. http://dx.doi.org/10.1080/0015587X.1959.9717165.

Hook, Theodore Edward, and R. H. Dalton Barham. 1849. *The Life and Remains of Theodore Edward Hook.* 2 vols. London: R. Bentley.

Houseman, Michael. 2001. "Is This Play?: Hazing in French Prepatory Schools." *Focaal: European Journal of Anthropology* 37:39–47.

Hughes, Lee. 1999. *Shooting from the Lip: A Kiwi Soldier's Military Mischief.* Auckland: Random House.

Huizinga, Johan. 1950. *Homo Ludens: A Study of the Play-Element in Culture.* Boston: Beacon.

Hussey, Dana Kay. 1996. "Practical Jokes and Pranks." Brigham Young University William A. Wilson Folklore Archives, FA01 1538.

hyperbolic pants explosion. 2006. "The Pie Diary to End All Pie Diaries." http://www .webcitation.org/6WOqnQfOI.

IHTFP Hack Gallery. 1998. "Is Disney Buying MIT or Was the MIT Home Page Hacked?" http://www.webcitation.org/6WOrA2TSK.

Improv Everywhere. 2013. "The No Pants Subway Ride." http://www.webcitation. org/6WOsda7nL.

Jenlink, Dale. 1974. Sending a Nonqual for Water Slugs. University of California–Berkeley Folklore Archives.

Jerrold, Walter. 1912. *A Book of Famous Wits*. London: Methuen.

Jillette, Penn, and Teller. 1989. *Penn & Teller's Cruel Tricks for Dear Friends*. Red letter ed. New York: Villard Books.

Johnson, John. 1986. Interview by Moira Smith, Bloomington, IN, June 27.

Jones, Reginald Victor. 1957. "The Theory of Practical Joking: Its Relevance to Physics." *Bulletin of the Institute of Physics* 8:193–201.

Jorgensen, Marilyn. 1984. "A Social-Interactional Analysis of Phone Pranks." *Western Folklore* 43(2): 104–116. http://dx.doi.org/10.2307/1499863.

Jorgensen, Marilyn. 1995. "Teases and Pranks." In *Children's Folklore: A Source Book*, edited by Brian Sutton-Smith, Jay Mechling, Thomas W. Johnson, and Felicia McMahon, 213–224. New York: Garland.

King, David. 2003. "Fowl Play." *Christchurch Press*, June 11, 2.

Kotze, Rudolph, and Pauline Kotze. 2005. Interview by Moira Smith, Lower Hutt, NZ, October 13.

Kramer, Elise. 2011. "The Playful Is Political: The Metapragmatics of Internet Rape-Joke Arguments." *Language in Society* 40(2): 137–168. http://dx.doi.org/10.1017 /S0047404511000017.

Kuipers, Giselinde. 2006. *Good Humor, Bad Taste: A Sociology of the Joke*. Translated by Kate Simms. Berlin: Mouton de Gruyter. http://dx.doi.org/10.1515/9783110898996.

Labov, William, and Joshua Waletzky. 1967. "Narrative Analysis: Oral Versions of Personal Experience." In *Essays on the Verbal and Visual Arts*, edited by June Helm, 12–44. Seattle: University of Washington Press.

La Fave, Lawrence, Jay Haddad, and William A. Maesen. 1976. "Superiority, Enhanced Self-Esteem, and Perceived Incongruity Humour Theory." In *Humor and Laughter: Theory, Research and Applications*, edited by Anthony J. Chapman, and Hugh C. Foot, 63–91. New York: John Wiley & Sons.

Landers, Ann. 1988. "Women Work to Fuel the Home, not BMWs." *Chicago Tribune*, December 1, D3.

Landers, Ann. 1990. "High Blood Pressure in New York." *Herald-Times* (Bloomington, IN), August 7, D2.

Lasn, Kalle. 2000. *Culture Jam: How to Reverse America's Suicidal Consumer Binge—and Why We Must*. New York: Quill.

Leary, James P. 1979. "Adolescent Pranks in Bloomington, Indiana." *Indiana Folklore* 12(1): 55–64.

Leary, James P. 1982. "A Trickster in Everyday Life." In *The Paradoxes of Play: Proceedings of the 6th Annual Meeting of the Association for the Anthropological Study of Play*, edited by John Loy, 57–64. West Point, NY: Leisure.

Leary, James P. 1984a. "The Favorite Jokes of Max Trzebiatowski." *Western Folklore* 43(1): 1–17. http://dx.doi.org/10.2307/1499426.

Leary, James P. 1984b. "Style in Jocular Communication: From the Cultural to the Personal." *Journal of the Folklore Institute* 21:29–46.

Legman, G. 1968. *Rationale of the Dirty Joke: An Analysis of Sexual Humor*. New York: Grove.

Lehrburger, Egon. 1966. *The Deceivers: Lives of the Great Imposters*. London: John Baker.

Leibowitz, Brian M. 1990. *The Journal of the Institute for Hacks Tomfoolery and Pranks at MIT*. Cambridge, MA: MIT Museum.

Leonard, Mike. 1990. "Beware of Jokers Today or You Could Be an April Fool." *Herald-Telephone* (Bloomington, IN), April 1, C1.

Lewis, Paul. 2006a. *Cracking Up: American Humor in a Time of Conflict*. Chicago: University of Chicago Press.

Lewis, Paul. 2006b. "Islamic Rage: Sometimes, It Hurts to Laugh." *Hartford Courant*, February 6, A4.

Lockyer, Sharon, and Michael Pickering, eds. 2005. *Beyond a Joke: The Limits of Humour*. Basingstoke, UK: Palgrave Macmillan. http://dx.doi.org/10.1057/9780230236776.

Long, Rhonda. 1979. "'Boreas' Cult Has Large I. U. Following." *Indiana Daily Student*, September 13.

Looooooka. 2010. "Just Another Office Prank." http://www.webcitation.org/6VjAujMvi.

Mannell, Roger, and Lawrence La Fave. 1976. "Humor Judgments and the 'Playful Attitude.'" In *The Anthropological Study of Play: Problems and Prospects*, edited by David F. Lancey and B. Allan Tindall, 230–238. Cornwall, NY: Leisure.

Mannell, Roger, and L. McMahon. 1982. "Humor as Play: Its Relationship to Psychological Well-Being during the Course of a Day." *Leisure Sciences* 5(2): 143–155. http://dx.doi.org/10.1080/01490408209512998.

Marsh, Moira. 2012. "Foiled Again: The Playful Ethics and Aesthetics of Jokes." *Western Folklore* 71(3–4): 291–306.

Martin, Judith. 1987. "Dressed in Black? Are They Bridesmaids or Pallbearers?" *Chicago Tribune*, April 8, 7: 4.

Martin, Rod A. 2007. *The Psychology of Humor: An Integrative Approach*. Amsterdam: Elsevier Academic.

Maxwell, Thomas. 1994. Interview with Bernie Silveria. University of California–Berkeley Folklore Archives.

McEntire, Nancy Cassell. 2002. "Purposeful Deceptions of the April Fool." *Western Folklore* 61(2): 133–151. http://dx.doi.org/10.2307/1500334.

McFedries, Paul. 2003. "Mobs R Us." *IEEE Spectrum* 40(10): 56.

McGraw, A. Peter, and Caleb Warren. 2010. "Benign Violations: Making Immoral Behavior Funny." *Psychological Science* 20(10): 1–9.

McGraw, A. Peter, Caleb Warren, Lawrence E. Williams, and Bridget Leonard. 2012. "Too Close for Comfort, or Too Far to Care? Finding Humor in Distant Tragedies and Close Mishaps." *Psychological Science* 23(10): 1215–1223. http://dx.doi.org/10.1177/0956797612443831.

McLeod, Rosemary. 2003. "Kiwi Jokers Who Are Bully Boys." *Waikato (NZ) Times*. June 11, 6.

McNeish, James. 1984. *Tavern in the Town*. Rev. ed. Wellington: Reed.

Mechling, Elizabeth Walker, and Jay Mechling. 1985. "Shock Talk: From Consensual to Contractual Joking Relationships in the Workplace." *Human Organization* 44(4): 339–343.

Mechling, Jay. 2009. "Is Hazing Play?" In *Transactions at Play: Play & Culture Studies*, edited by Cindy Dell Clark, 45–62. Lanham, MD: University Press of America.

Miller, Cheryl, and Mark Miller. 1997. "Wedding Pranks: Pranks 4 the Memories." www.webcitation.org/6WOtl1BsH.

Mills, Rob. 1987. Interview by Moira Smith, Bloomington, IN, April 26.

MIT Museum. 2012. "IHTFP Hack Gallery." http://www.webcitation.org/6ViKt3hBG.

Monger, George. 1971. "A Note on Wedding Customs in Industry Today." *Folklore* 82(4): 314–16. http://dx.doi.org/10.1080/0015587X.1971.9716744.

Monger, George. 1978. "Pre-wedding Customs in Industry." *English Dance and Song* 40:112–113.

Morreall, John. 1983. *Taking Laughter Seriously*. Albany: State University of New York Press.

Morreall, John, ed. 1987. *The Philosophy of Laughter and Humor*. Albany: State University of New York Press.

Morreall, John. 1989. "Enjoying Incongruity." *Humor: International Journal of Humor Research* 2(1): 1–18. http://dx.doi.org/10.1515/humr.1989.2.1.1.

Morrison, Monica. 1974. "Wedding Night Pranks in Western New Brunswick." *Southern Folklore Quarterly* 38(4): 285–297.

Mulkay, Michael. 1988. *On Humour: Its Nature and Its Place in Modern Society*. Oxford: Polity.

Myerhoff, Barbara. 1982. "Rites of Passage: Process and Paradox." In *Celebration: Studies in Festivity and Ritual*, edited by Victor Turner, 109–135. Washington, DC: Smithsonian Institution Press.

Neat-O-Fun. 2012. Fartdroid Fart Machine. www.webcitation.org/6WOuhE6mS.

Neber, Nicholas. 1996. Sobriety Test. University of California–Berkeley Folklore Archives.

New Zealand Employment Tribunal, Auckland. 1992. "Fulton V Chiat Day Mojo Ltd." *Employment Reports of New Zealand* 2:38–48.

New Zealand Ministry for Culture and Heritage. 2014. "The End of the 'Six O'clock Swill.'" http://www.webcitation.org/6WOmpPQJR.

Nickerson, Bruce E. 1974. "Is There a Folk in the Factory?" *Journal of American Folklore* 87(344): 133–139. http://dx.doi.org/10.2307/539473.

O'Connor, Alan. 1981. "The Real Live Type: Research Technique in an Industrial Folklore Project." *Canadian Folklore Canadien* 3(2): 149–152.

Opie, Iona, and Peter Opie. 1959. *The Lore and Language of Schoolchildren*. London: Oxford University Press.

Oring, Elliott. 1990. "Legend, Truth, and News." *Southern Folklore* 47(2): 163–177.

Oring, Elliott. 1992. *Jokes and Their Relations*. Lexington: University Press of Kentucky.

Oring, Elliott. 2003. *Engaging Humor*. Urbana: University of Illinois Press.

Oring, Elliott. 2008. "Legendry and the Rhetoric of Truth." *Journal of American Folklore* 121(480): 127–166. http://dx.doi.org/10.1353/jaf.0.0008.

Oring, Elliott. 2011. "The Joke as Art." Paper presented at the International Society for Humor Studies Annual Meeting, Boston, July 6.

Paterson, Caroline, and Satinder Bindra. 2004. "Bhopal Hoax Sends Dow Stock Down." CNN.com. www.webcitation.org/6WOvJdYuG.

Peterson, T. F. 2003. *Nightwork: A History of Hacks and Pranks at MIT*. Cambridge, MA: MIT Press, in association with the MIT Museum.

Pilcher, William W. 1972. *The Portland Longshoremen: A Dispersed Urban Community*. New York: Holt, Rinehart & Winston.

Piotrowski, Dorothy. 1996. "Amazing Tin Foil Ball." http://www.webcitation.org/6WOvraDqj.

Plester, Barbara, and Mark Orams. 2008. "Send in the Clowns: The Role of the Joker in Three New Zealand IT Companies." *Humor: International Journal of Humor Research* 21(3): 253–281. http://dx.doi.org/10.1515/HUMOR.2008.013.

Plester, Barbara, and Janet Sayers. 2007. "'Taking the Piss:' Functions of Banter in the IT Industry." *Humor: International Journal of Humor Research* 20(2): 157–187. http://dx.doi.org/10.1515/HUMOR.2007.008.

Posen, I. S. 1974. "Pranks and Practical Jokes at Children's Summer Camps." *Southern Folklore Quarterly* 38(4): 299–309.

Provine, Robert R. 2000. *Laughter: A Scientific Investigation.* New York: Viking.

Quinn, Beth A. 2000. "The Paradox of Complaining: Law, Humor, and Harassment in the Everyday Work World." *Law & Social Inquiry* 25(4): 1151–1185. http://dx.doi.org /10.1111/j.1747-4469.2000.tb00319.x.

Radcliffe-Brown, A. R. 1940. "On Joking Relationships." *Africa* 13(3): 195–210. http://dx .doi.org/10.2307/1156093.

Rafinesque, C. S. (1820) 1899. *Ichthyologia ohiensis,* or, Natural History of the Fishes Inhabiting the River Ohio and Its Tributary Streams. Cleveland: Burrows Bros. https://archive .org/details/cu31924002863367.

Raskin, Victor. 1985. *Semantic Mechanisms of Humor.* Boston: D. Reidel.

Reeve, F. A. 1977. *Varsity Rags and Hoaxes.* Cambridge: Oleander.

Richardson, Willie P. 1998. *Christmas Pranks.* Nacogdoches, TX: Landmark Productions.

Ritvo, Harriet. 1997. *The Platypus and the Mermaid and Other Figments of the Classifying Imagination.* Cambridge, MA: Harvard University Press.

Roemer, Danielle Marie. 1977. "A Social Interactional Analysis of Anglo Children's Folklore: Catches and Narratives." PhD diss., University of Texas, Austin.

Roper, Jonathan. 2012. "Folk Belief and Folk Scepticism." Paper presented at the American Folklore Society Annual Meeting, New Orleans, Oct. 25.

Ross, Ezra. 1994. Short Sheeting the Bed. University of California–Berkeley Folklore Archives.

Salter, Matthew. 1998. Snipe Hunt. University of California–Berkeley Folklore Archives.

Saltzman, Rachelle Hope. 2012. *A Lark for the Sake of Their Country: The 1926 General Strike Volunteers in Folklore and Memory.* Manchester: Manchester University Press. http://dx .doi.org/10.7228/manchester/9780719079771.001.0001.

Santino, Jack. 1986. "A Servant and a Man, a Hostess or a Woman: A Study of Expressive Culture in Two Transportation Occupations." *Journal of American Folklore* 99(393): 304–319. http://dx.doi.org/10.2307/540807.

Santino, Jack, ed. 1994. *Halloween and Other Festivals of Death and Life.* Knoxville: University of Tennessee Press.

Santino, Jack. 1998. *The Hallowed Eve: Dimensions of Culture in a Calendar Festival in Northern Ireland.* Lexington: University Press of Kentucky.

Santino, John Francis. 1978. "The Outlaw Emotions: Workers' Narratives from Three Contemporary Occupations." PhD diss., University of Pennsylvania.

Sawin, Patricia. 2004. *Listening for a Life: A Dialogic Ethnography of Bessie Eldreth through Her Songs and Stories.* Logan: Utah State University Press.

Schmidt, Claire. 2013. "'If You Don't Laugh You'll Cry': The Occupational Humor of White American Prison Workers and Social Workers." PhD diss., University of Missouri, Columbia.

Scott, John R. 1974. "Practical Jokes of the Newfoundland Seal Fishery." *Southern Folklore Quarterly* 38(4): 275–283.

Selvin, Steve. 1965. [Dorm Prank]. University of California–Berkeley Folklore Archives.

Simon, Lizzie. 2011. "Riding Footloose and Pants-Free." *Wall Street Journal,* January 8. http://www.webcitation.org/6WP3SqWRn.

Small, Contessa. 1999. "Occupational Narratives of Pulp and Paper Mill Workers in Corner Brook, Newfoundland: A Study in Occupational Folklife." MA thesis, Memorial University of Newfoundland.

Smith, H. Allen. 1953. *The Compleat Practical Joker.* Garden City, NY: Doubleday.

Smith, Johana H. 1957. "In the Bag: A History of Snipe Hunting." *Western Folklore* 16(2): 107–110. http://dx.doi.org/10.2307/1497027.

Smith, Moira. 1990. "Jokes and Practical Jokes." In *The Emergence of Folklore in Everyday Life: A Fieldguide and Sourcebook,* edited by George F. Shoemaker, 73–82. Bloomington, IL: Folklore Publications Group.

Smith, Moira. 2006. "Soiling the Post Office: The Capping Stunts of New Zealand University Students." *Culture and Tradition* 26: 38–55

Smith, Moira. 2008. "Laughter: Nature or Culture?" Paper presented at the International Society for Humor Studies meeting, Alcala de Henares, Spain, July 9. https://scholarworks.iu.edu/dspace/handle/2022/3162.

Smith, Moira. 2009a. "Arbiters of Truth at Play: Media April Fools' Day Hoaxes." *Folklore* 120(3): 274–290. http://dx.doi.org/10.1080/00155870903219714.

Smith, Moira. 2009b. "Humor, Unlaughter, and Boundary Maintenance." *Journal of American Folklore* 122(484): 148–171. http://dx.doi.org/10.1353/jaf.0.0080.

Smyly, Virginia. 1970. [Whiffenpoofs]. University of California–Berkeley Folklore Archives.

Southland Times. 1998. "Victim Thought Robbery Was a Prank." *Southland (NZ) Times*, June 23, 1.

Stahl, Karl, and Douglas B. Kirby. 1958. "Going to See the Widow." *Western Folklore* 17(4): 275–276. http://dx.doi.org/10.2307/1496193.

Stahl, Sandra K. D. 1977. "The Oral Personal Narrative in Its Generic Context." *Fabula* 18: 18–39. http://dx.doi.org/10.1515/fabl.1977.18.1.18.

Steinberg, Neil. 1992. *If at All Possible, Involve a Cow: The Book of College Pranks*. New York: St Martin's.

Stephen, Adrian. (Original work published 1936) 1983. *The "Dreadnought" Hoax*. London: Chatto & Windus.

Stewart, Gordon. 1988. Interview by Moira Smith, Wellington, NZ, February 25.

Stewart, Susan. 1978. *Nonsense: Aspects of Intertextuality in Folklore and Literature*. Baltimore: Johns Hopkins University Press.

Stewart, Susan. 1991. *Crimes of Writing: Problems in the Containment of Representation*. New York: Oxford University Press.

Story, G. M., W. J. Kirwin, and J. D. A. Widdowson. 1990. *Dictionary of Newfoundland English*. 2nd ed. Toronto: University of Toronto Press.

Sullivan, Jim, ed. 1999. *As I Remember: Stories from 'Sounds Historical'*. Auckland: Tandem.

Sutton-Smith, Brian. 1981. *A History of Children's Play: New Zealand, 1840–1950*. Philadelphia: University of Pennsylvania Press.

Sutton-Smith, Brian. 2008. "Play Theory: A Personal Journey and New Thoughts." *American Journal of Play* 1(1): 80–123.

Taft, Michael. 1983. *Tall Tales of British Columbia*. Victoria, BC: Sound and Moving Image Division, Province of British Columbia Provincial Archives.

Tait, Gordon. 1988. Interview by Moira Smith, Wellington, NZ, March 16.

Tallman, Richard. 1974. "A Generic Approach to the Practical Joke." *Southern Folklore Quarterly* 38(4): 259–274.

Thomson, Ainsley. 2002. "Death of a DIY Sunday as Painting Proves Too Noisy." *New Zealand Herald*, April 24, A1.

Todd, Charlie Scordelis Alex. 2009. *Causing a Scene: Extraordinary Pranks in Ordinary Places with Improv Everywhere*. New York: William Morrow.

Toelken, Barre. 1979. *The Dynamics of Folklore*. Boston: Houghton Mifflin.

Toelken, Barre. 1996. *The Dynamics of Folklore*. Rev. ed. Logan: Utah State University Press.

Trask, Boyd. 1967. Mischief Nights. Memorial University of Newfoundland Folklore Archive, MUNFLA 68-024E.

Troy, Con. 1983. *Laugh with Hugh Troy, World's Greatest Practical Joker: A Happy Memoir*. Wyomissing, PA: Trojan Books.

Tuleja, Tad. 1994. "Trick or Treat: Pre-Texts and Contexts." In *Halloween and Other Festivals of Death and Life*, edited by Jack Santino, 82–102. Knoxville: University of Tennessee Press.

Turnbull, Colin M. 1962. *The Forest People*. New York: Simon & Schuster.

Turner, Victor W. 1974. "Liminal to Liminoid in Play, Flow, and Ritual: An Essay in Comparative Symbology." In *The Anthropological Study of Human Play*, edited by Edward Norbeck, 53–92. Houston: William Marsh Rice University.

Tyler, Vicky. 1996. "Bitter $3.7m Pill." *Sunday News*, December 29, 2.

Utley, Francis Lee, and Dudley Flamm. 1969. "The Urban and Rural Jest (with an Excursus on the Shaggy Dog)." *Journal of Popular Culture* 2(4): 563–577. http://dx.doi.org /10.1111/j.0022-3840.1969.0204_563.x.

Vale, Vivian, and Andrea Juno. 1987. *Pranks! Re/Search*. San Francisco: V/Search.

Van der Dussen, Kurt. 1987. Interview by Moira Smith, Bloomington, IN, November 9.

Van Rensselaer, Alexander. 1941. *Try This One! A Hundred and Two Stunts and Practical Jokes*. New York: D. Appleton-Century.

Veatch, Thomas C. 1998. "A Theory of Humor." *Humor: International Journal of Humor Research* 11(2): 161–215. http://dx.doi.org/10.1515/humr.1998.11.2.161.

Wasik, Bill. 2006. "My Crowd; or, Phase 5: A Report from the Inventor of the Flash Mob." *Harper's Magazine*, March, 56–66.

Weisfeld, Glenn E. 2006. "Humor Appreciation as an Adaptive Esthetic Emotion." *Humor: International Journal of Humor Research* 19(1): 1–26. http://dx.doi.org/10.1515 /HUMOR.2006.001.

Werth, Brian. 1980. "Reporter Becomes an April Fool." *Herald-Telephone* (Bloomington, IN), April 2, 2.

Werth, Brian. 1987. Interview by Moira Smith, Bloomington, IN, April 28.

Wettergren, A. 2009. "Fun and Laughter: Culture Jamming and the Emotional Regime of Late Capitalism." *Social Movement Studies* 8(1): 1–15. http://dx.doi.org/10.1080 /14742830802591119.

Wickberg, Daniel. 1998. *The Senses of Humor: Self and Laughter in Modern America*. Ithaca: Cornell University Press.

Wight, John. 1927. "April Fools' Day and Its Humours." *Word-Lore* 2:37–40.

Wiley, Lauren. 1999. "Hold the Anchovies." *Adweek*, New England edition, July 19.

Wilson, Janet A. 1978. [Wedding Pranks]. Indiana University–Bloomington Folklore Archives.

Wolf-Beranek, Hertha. 1968. "Zum Aprilscherz in Den Sudetenländern." *Zeitschrift für Volkskunde* 64:223–227.

Wolfenstein, Martha. (Original work published 1954) 1978. *Children's Humor: A Psychological Analysis*. Bloomington: Indiana University Press.

Yoder, Janice D, and Patricia Aniakudo. 1996. "When Pranks Become Harassment: The Case of African American Women Firefighters." *Sex Roles* 35(5–6): 253–270. http://dx.doi.org/10.1007/BF01664768.

Yount, Angela K. 1984. "The Memories of a Smokey Mountain Man: Bill Yount's Life Stories." *Collage* 4:15–39.

Zijderveld, Anton C. 1983. "The Sociology of Humour and Laughter." *Current Sociology* 31(3): 1–59. http://dx.doi.org/10.1177/001139283031003003.

Ziv, Avner. 1984. *Personality and Sense of Humor*. New York: Springer.

Ziv, Avner. 1988. "Humor's Role in Married Life." *Humor: International Journal of Humor Research* 1(3): 223–229. http://dx.doi.org/10.1515/humr.1988.1.3.223.

About the Author

MOIRA MARSH is a folklorist, former editor of the *Journal of Folklore Research,* and the curator of the Folklore Collection at the Indiana University–Bloomington Libraries. She is a member of the executive board of the International Society for Humor Studies and section editor for the *Encyclopedia of Humor Studies* (published by Sage). She bears an uncanny resemblance to Moira Smith, under which name her work has appeared in the *Journal of American Folklore*, the *Journal of Folklore Research*, *Culture and Tradition*, *Western Folklore*, and *Folklore*. This is her first book.

Index

Index of Practical Joke Examples

(in order of appearance)